Contemporary Debates in Education: An Historical Perspective

THE EFFECTIVE TEACHER SERIES

General editor: Elizabeth Perrott

EDUCATION AND CULTURAL DIVERSITY by Edward Hulmes

THE EFFECTIVE TEACHING OF ENGLISH by Robert Protherough, Judith Atkinson and John Fawcett

THE EFFECTIVE TEACHING OF MODERN LANGUAGES by Colin Wringe

THEORY OF EDUCATION by Margaret Sutherland

PUPIL WELFARE AND COUNSELLING: AN APPROACH TO PERSONAL AND SOCIAL EDUCATION ACROSS THE CURRICULUM by David Galloway

THE EDUCATION SYSTEM IN ENGLAND AND WALES by Paul Sharp and John Dunford.

PRIMARY SCHOOL TEACHING AND EDUCATIONAL PSYCHOLOGY by David Galloway and Anne Edwards

CONTEMPORARY DEBATES IN EDUCATION: AN HISTORICAL PERSPECTIVE by Ron Brooks

THE LEGAL CONTEXT OF TEACHING by Neville Harris with Penelope Pearce & Susan Johnstone

EFFECTIVE TEACHING: A PRACTICAL GUIDE TO IMPROVING YOUR TEACHING by Elizabeth Perrott

THE EFFECTIVE TEACHER SERIES

Contemporary Debates in Education: An Historical Perspective

Ron Brooks

LONGMAN
London and New York

Longman Group UK Limited,
Longman House, Burnt Mill, Harlow,
Essex CM20 2JE, England
and Associated Companies throughout the world.

Published in the United States of America
by Longman Inc., New York

First published 1991

British Library Cataloguing in Publication Data
Brooks, Ron
Contemporary debates in education: an historical perspective. — (Effective teacher series).
1. Great Britain. Education
I. Title II. Series
370.941

ISBN 0–582–05797–3

Library of Congress Cataloging-in-Publication Data
Brooks, Ron, 1939–
Contemporary debates in education: an historical perspective/
Ron Brooks.
p. cm. — (The Effective teacher series)
Includes bibliographical references (p.) and index.
ISBN 0–582–05797–3:
1. Education — Great Britain. 2. Education — Great Britain — History.
3. Education — Great Britain — Curricula — History.
I. Title. II. Series.
LA632.B76 1991
370'.941 — dc20

90–21351
CIP

Set in 10/11 Times Roman

Printed in Malaysia
by Percetakan Anda Sdn. Bhd., Sri Petaling, Kuala Lumpur

CONTENTS

EDITOR'S PREFACE

This new series was inspired by my book on the practice of teaching. (*Effective Teaching: a practical guide to improving your teaching*, Longman, 1982) written for trainee teachers wishing to improve their teaching skills as well as for inservice teachers, especially those engaged in the supervision of trainees. The books in this series have been written with the same readership in mind. However, the busy classroom teacher will find that these books also serve their needs as changes in the nature and pattern of education make the inservice training of experienced teachers more essential than in the past.

The rationale behind the series is that professional courses for teachers require the coverage of a wide variety of subjects in a relatively short time. So the aim of the series is the production of 'easy to read' practical guides to provide the necessary subject background, supported by references to guide and encourage further reading, together with questions and/or exercises devised to assist application and evaluation.

As specialists in their selected fields, the authors have been chosen for their ability to relate their subjects to the needs of teachers and to stimulate discussion of contemporary issues in education.

The series aims to cover subjects ranging from the theory of education to the teaching of mathematics and from primary school teaching and educational psychology to effective teaching with information technology. It will look at aspects of education as diverse as education and cultural diversity and pupil welfare and counselling. Although some subjects such as the legal context of teaching and the teaching of history are specific to England and Wales, the majority of subjects assessment in education, the effective teaching of statistics and comparative education are international in scope.

Elizabeth Perrott

AUTHOR'S PREFACE

This book is intended for all educationists. The 1980s brought about the redefinition of this term so that it now includes not only teachers and related professionals but all those who, through recent legislation and other means, have been called upon to help run Britain's education service. Though of great value to teachers, it is intended for a broader audience which includes parents and governors. To this end it has been made deliberately issue orientated to enable a progressive deepening of understanding of the bewildering number and range of issues facing educationists today.

It turns history on its head with the first rather than later chapters surveying recent developments. This was a deliberate strategy with two goals in mind. The first was to provide an informed basis for immediate discussion of those matters that are of most pressing interest. The second was the identification of the generic issues that have long since occupied the attention of educationists in a variety of forms. Today's issues appear new but they often have a long and distinguished (or, in some cases, not so distinguished) pedigree. The remaining chapters of the book trace their development during this century and earlier in order to help educationists gain an understanding not just of their present form but of their very nature. It is also a different kind of history of education in another way. It uses and quotes evidence from a wide variety of sources to further discussion. In the first chapter this is done in a more restricted way to achieve a more direct and succinct style to point up issues for consideration, particularly through concentration upon Callaghan's Ruskin College speech of October 1976.

I should like to thank Professor David Loades for giving me every encouragement to write this book, and Professor Iolo Williams and the staff of the School of Education, University College North Wales, Bangor, for advice and documentary material for use in each of its chapters.

Ron Brooks

LIST OF TABLES

LIST OF FIGURES

ACKNOWLEDGEMENTS

We are grateful to the following for permission to reproduce copyright material;

the Labour Party for extracts from *The Labour Party's Advisory Committee on Education Memorandum 6* by Percy Nunn et al (pub 1918); Ewan MacNaughton Associates for the article 'Call to scrap varsity teacher training' by Sarah Johnson from *The Sunday Telegraph* 10.6.90, © The Sunday Telegraph Ltd.; Ewan MacNaughton Associates for the Garland cartoon 'Because it's here!' from *The Daily Telegraph* April 19, 1979, © The Daily Telegraph plc, 1990; Tables 1.1, 1.2 and 1.3 from The Times Educational Supplements of 7 December 1984 and 7 October 1988 © The Times Supplements; The Controller of Her Majesty's Stationery Office for tables 2.2, 2.3, 3.1, 3.2, 3.3, 3.4, 3.5, 4.1, 4.2, 4.7 and the indented material on page 167; Tables 3.7 and 4.3 © A H Halsey, A F Heath and J. M. Ridge 1980. Reprinted by permission of Oxford University Press.

PART ONE

Contemporary Issues in Education

CHAPTER 1

A decade and more of debate

Teachers in post and students in training face a dilemma. The reforms of recent years, which have left no sector of education untouched, have made and will continue to make demands on the time and energies of teachers in training and in post which are far greater than at any other period in the history of the profession; yet, more than ever before, they need time to reflect on the nature of the changes and reforms in order to meet effectively the challenges which they pose. But time is in short supply whether it be on the overcrowded timetable of teacher training courses or in the increasingly busy schedules of the classroom. Such apparently simple questions as 'What are the aims of the national curriculum?', 'Does the concept of a state curriculum stand outside British tradition?' or 'Why has technical education been given such a high priority in recent years and do the values upon which this priority depend conflict with the traditional values of British education?' require careful thought in order to arrive at an informed response. Satisfactory answers to such questions can only be given by reference to historical developments. This book seeks to help students, teachers and the many lay people now involved in running the nation's schools to understand the historical nature of change by turning history on its head. This approach is used in order to maximise understanding in the short time available.

TURNING HISTORY ON ITS HEAD

The relevance of the history of education to an understanding of contemporary issues in education has sometimes been obscured by its treatment on training courses. On initial training courses it has taken the form of a historical chronology of developments in education from early times to the present day. This approach, from Bell to Baker or from Montessori to MacGregor in less than twenty lectures, is thankfully in decline. It was often too brief and sketchy to provide any satisfactory or immediate insights into the historical nature of present-day issues in education. At in-service meetings it tends to be replaced by a second approach, that usually subsumed under the programme heading 'historical background' or 'historical introduction'. This tends to marginalise the value of the history of education. It treats it akin to a booster rocket which can be discarded once the lecture is lifted into scintillating orbit. It ignores the vital point that today's issues in education are not simply historical in their background; they are historical in their very nature. To change the metaphor, it is not akin to a plug and socket, something which is detachable. The following chapters seek to avoid the chronological gallop and plug-and-socket history by adopting a third approach.

The third approach is to turn history on its head, to consider first not the most distant but the most recent history in order to identify within their historical context those issues which today confront the student, teacher, school governor, educational administrator or the many other groups involved in education. The term 'educationist' covers a much wider group of people than have been involved in education hitherto. Having identified these issues within their recent history, the book then traces their more distant but equally relevant historical development on an issue-by-issue basis rather than by a bland historical chronology. By doing this it aims to show that present-day concerns are historical in the sense that it is their history that gives them their meaning. Brief documentary extracts will be provided to point up key aspects of educational history and to provide a succinct basis for discussion of particular issues. By turning history on its head, by considering more recent historical developments first, it is hoped that discussion will be encouraged from the outset, with later chapters dealing with earlier developments this century progressively widening the scope and deepening the content of such discussion.

THE EDUCATIONAL AGENDA SINCE 1976

Where do we begin the identification of current issues within their recent historical context? For one main reason, 1976 makes a convenient starting point. That was the year in which the Labour Prime Minister, James Callaghan, made his Ruskin College speech – a sort of educational state-of-the-nation speech – which launched what his Education Secretary, Shirley Williams, termed the 'Great Debate' of February and March the following year. Rarely do prime ministers make public pronouncements about education, and thus his speech is of importance for several reasons. Firstly, it signifies the growing interest of central government in the various sectors of education. Coming as it did two years after the reorganisation of local government which seemed to leave education more firmly in the grip of the 104 enlarged local education authorities than ever before, it marked a stage in the assertion by central government of its stake in the nation's education system. This stage was followed by the rapid extension of the powers of central government in the 1980s. Secondly, it marks a stage in the transition of Britain from the expansionist, swinging sixties, through the sober seventies to the austere eighties. The sober tones of the Ruskin College speech marked the realisation that the public purse was not bottomless and that education should give value for money in the sense of contributing to what politicians believed was the national good. This was interpreted by Callaghan, his Labour Government and successive Conservative governments of the 1980s largely in economic terms. Thirdly, the Prime Minister's homely rhetoric, eminently quotable, spanned most of the items on the educational agenda. It crystallises much contemporary political opinion on a broad range of issues from primary to university education. There is, however, a fourth reason of particular relevance to the approach of this book: it provides a good basis not simply for identifying current issues in education but also for outlining some of the views on these issues. In his speech Callaghan acknowledged his indebtedness to one of the leading Labour educationists of the twentieth century, R. H. Tawney, from whom he claimed to have 'derived a great deal of (his) thinking years ago in the early days ... when he was one of the originators of the Labour Party programme on education'.[1] In fact, Tawney had very different views from Callaghan on most educational issues. Educated at Rugby and Balliol College, Oxford, he defended a traditional system of liberal values and practices in the years to 1950, so very different from that advocated by Callaghan and his immediate advisers in 1976.[2] Thus we have a bifocal perspective on the issues. The Ruskin College speech provides the structure for the present chapter and the framework for discussion in later chapters. Tawney provides the historical peg on which we can later hang these issues.

Daily Telegraph, April 19, 1979

Fig. 1.1 ***'Because it's there!'***

CENTRAL GOVERNMENT AND THE CURRICULUM

It is not my intention to become enmeshed in such problems as whether there should be a basic curriculum with universal standards – although I am inclined to think that there should be. (Callaghan, 1976)

Callaghan's Ruskin College speech testifies to the growing interest of central government in the school curriculum. While he was cautious not to make any explicit reference to government direction of the curriculum, it was difficult to believe – given his diagnosis of the problems confronting education and the general drift of his thinking about how they should be resolved – that he was not envisaging some kind of increased central government involvement. In the opening paragraph of his much-heralded speech, he argued that educational matters were of public concern, and deplored those who had advised him 'to keep off the grass'. His homely horticultural imagery was not too far removed from that of Sir David Eccles, the Conservative Minister of Education in 1960, who argued that the school curriculum should no longer be regarded as a 'secret garden'.[3] Callaghan was insistent that there should be no 'holy cows' in education, that there should be no areas that 'profane hands' were not 'allowed to touch'. He did not say precisely whose 'profane hands' these should be, but the purpose of the 'Great Debate' to which his speech was a prelude was intended, in part at least, to justify increased government involvement in the running of education. He had to be mindful as a Labour prime minister not to antagonise the teachers' unions, especially the NUT, but was anxious to do something about the fact that government had little direct leverage on the curriculum.

Tawney belonged to a different age and had fought long and hard to remove central government's stranglehold on the curriculum in the years to 1926.[4] His fear was that government had, and could in the future, abuse its power over the curriculum to make it serve the interests of those other than pupils, such as industry or political ideologies. As a member of the Board of Education's Consultative Committee, and close friend of such educationists as Percy Nunn, he had come to respect the judgement of professionals and argued that, within the general framework of a balanced curriculum, the teachers were the people best able to decide its content. In *Secondary Education for All* (1922) and during the Consultative Committee's enquiry into adolescent education (1924–26) he argued for variety of curricular provision to meet the needs of the different abilities and interest of pupils. He thus saw the role of the state largely in terms of making provisions for raising the school leaving age and providing free secondary education for all to ensure that all pupils were able to benefit from a teacher–controlled curriculum up to the age of 16. The task of central government was to make such provision and to prod laggardly local education authorities into making sure that local resources were adequate and well directed.

This kind of thinking was very much in retreat half a century later. While Shirley Williams, Callaghan's Education Secretary, was noted for her willingness to enter into prolonged discussions about educational issues with teachers and other interested parties, the Conservative governments of the 1980s reduced the length of consultation to effect legislation in a manner which was totally alien to that in which earlier legislation, especially the 1944 Education Act, had been effected. The more forthright ministerial style of Conservative education secretaries was characteristic of most Ministers in the Thatcher era. Shortly after coming to power in 1979 the Conservative Government published a document on the curriculum, signalling its intention to strengthen the centralist grip over this area. While '*A Framework for the School Curriculum*' was intended as a discussion document it indicated clearly the avenues along which discussion should proceed, advocating a subject-based core curriculum. Circulars were issued to LEAs calling for urgent curriculum planning and in 1985 a White Paper *Better Schools* was issued to assist this process. Increasing political concern about courses such as 'peace studies' and the stress upon value for money led to a strengthening of government influence. The abolition of the Schools Council, announced in 1982, and its replacement in 1984 by two government-controlled bodies, the Secondary Examinations Council (SEC) and the Schools Curriculum Development Committee, marked the virtual end of teacher control over the curriculum. The close supervision which the SEC exercised over the GCSE examination[5] heralded the government's wider and more detailed control over the school curriculum in the 1988 Education Act. Callaghan's personal inclination for 'a basic curriculum with universal standards' had been translated into effective legislation in little over a decade. Though Kenneth Baker, the author of the Act, argued that his reforms were 'not about enhancing state control', but were 'educational' and not concerned with 'the distribution of power',[6] many teachers in the 1980s and 1990s believed that they represented a significant shift of power in curricular matters away from them to the Secretary of State for Education. Their duties as laid down by the 1988 Act seem to provide conclusive evidence in favour of the latter view.[7]

It shall be the duty:

(a) of the Secretary of State . . .;
(b) of every local education authority . . .; and
(c) of every governing body or head teacher of a maintained school, to exercise their functions (including, in particular . . . functions . . . with respect to religious education, religious worship and the national curriculum) . . . with a view to securing that the curriculum for the school satisfies the requirements of this section.

The curriculum for a maintained school satisfies the requirements of this section. If it is a balanced and broadly-based curriculum which:

(a) promotes the spiritual, moral, cultural, mental and physical development of pupils at the school and of society.

(b) prepares such pupils for the opportunities, responsibilities and experiences of adult life.

[This clause is to implement] for every maintained school ... a basic curriculum which includes ... religious education ... and a curriculum for all registered pupils at the school of compulsory school age (to be known as the national curriculum) [comprising] the core and other foundation subjects and [specifying] in relation to each of them:

(a) the knowledge, skills and understanding which pupils of different abilities and maturities are expected to have by the end of each key stage (... 'attainment targets').
(b) the matters, skills and processes which are required to be taught to pupils of different abilities and maturities during each key stage (... 'programmes of study').
(c) the arrangements for assessing pupils at or near the end of each key stage for the purpose of ascertaining what they have achieved in relation to the attainment targets for that stage (... 'assessment arrangements').

The core subjects are:

(a) mathematics, English and science.
(b) in relation to schools in Wales which are Welsh-speaking schools, Welsh.

The other foundations subjects are:

(a) history, geography, technology, music, art and physical education.
(b) in relation to the third and fourth key stages, a modern foreign language specified in an order of the Secretary of State.
(c) in relation to schools in Wales which are not Welsh-speaking schools, Welsh.

It shall be the duty of the Secretary, of State so to exercise the powers conferred by subsection (2) below as:

(a) to establish a complete national curriculum as soon as is reasonably practicable (taking first the core subjects and then the other foundation subjects).
(b) to revise that curriculum whenever he considers it necessary or expedient to do so.

(2) The Secretary of State may by order specify in relation to each of the foundation subjects:

(a) such attainment targets.
(b) such programmes of study.
(c) such assessment arrangements, as he considers appropriate for that subject.

An order made under subsection (2) above may not require:

(a) that any particular period or periods of time should be allocated during any key stage to the teaching of any programme of study or any matter, skill or process forming part of it; or
(b) that provision of any particular kind should be made in school timetables for the periods to be allocated to such teaching during any such stage.

No course of study leading to a qualification authenticated by an outside person shall be provided for pupils of compulsory school age by or on behalf of any maintained school unless the qualification is for the time being approved by the Secretary of State or by a designated body.

In relation to any maintained school and any school year, it shall be the duty of the local education authority and the governing body to exercise their functions with a view to securing and the duty to the headteacher to secure:

(a) that the national curriculum as subsisting at the beginning of that year is implemented.

For the purpose of enabling development work or experiments to be carried out, the Secretary of State may direct as respects a particular maintained school that for such period as may be specified in the direction, the provisions of the national curriculum:

(a) shall not apply.

(b) shall apply with such modifications as may be so specified.

During its implementation in the 1990s the national curriculum was made less prescriptive. However this did not necessarily 'signal a retreat' from central control of the curriculum.

SCHOOLS AND THE BASIC SKILLS OF LITERACY AND NUMERACY

But I am concerned on my journeys to find complaints from industry that new recruits from the schools sometimes do not have the basic tools to do the job that is required ... there is concern about the standards of numeracy of school leavers ... There is little wrong with the range and diversity of our courses. But is there sufficient thoroughness and depth in these required in the after life to make a living? ... the basic purposes of education require the same essential tools. These are to be basically literate, to be basically numerate. (Callaghan, 1976)

The above quotation reflects the general thrust of the Ruskin College speech in that it was concerned directly and indirectly with the views and needs of industry and measured the success of schools primarily in terms of the extent to which they were able to supply industry with literate and numerate recruits. Such a view was in marked contrast to Callaghan's mentor, who, while acknowledging the importance of pupils becoming literate and numerate, constantly argued that the influence of industry upon education was both restrictive and narrowing. Tawney's advocacy of a liberal, humane education for all of the nation's children and not just for those who attended the independent sector led to his being deeply suspicious of the intentions of industry in education. Secondary education for all implied a move away from elementary education which had been based largely on the three Rs. To Tawney, Callaghan's speech would have been seen as an attempt to put the clock back (see pp. 52–54), to give to primary and secondary education the priorities of elementary education.

Callaghan had accepted uncritically two views that many educationists of the 1970s hotly contested. The first was that standards of literacy and numeracy were low and were falling; the second was that education was largely about providing students with the skills to fit them for employment. The evidence upon which the former view was based was, to say the very least, tenuous; though he claimed that his speech should not be seen as 'a clarion call to Black Paper[8] prejudice' Callaghan seemed to have accepted much of the Black Paper propaganda about declining standards which had emanated from their authors since 1969. By the mid-1970s, concern that the basic skills were not being taught effectively was no longer the monopoly of the political right. Tawney, an economist and statistician, would have pointed to the fact that there was no unanimous body of research evidence to show that standards were falling, rising or remaining steady. A life-long friend of teachers and the National Union of Teachers he would have preferred to have listened to professional opinion rather than 'complaints from industry'. Tawney would certainly not have accepted the priority given by Callaghan to the vocational needs of industry. He had vigorously attacked the influence of industry upon the educational policies of the Conservative governments of the inter-war years and had consistently argued for a broad, liberal, secondary education for all which went far beyond the overwhelming concentration on the basics. Callaghan's emphasis on the theme of back-to-basics seemed to be an attempt to turn secondary education back into some form of elementary education – a kind of education which Tawney had so vigorously attacked as limited and limiting.

The political parties were united in their concern for standards, and to this extent the Ruskin College speech echoed contemporary opinion. The Bullock enquiry into the teaching of English was set up by a Conservative government in 1972; it reported to a Labour government in 1975. It could find no convincing evidence for the decline in standards to which Callaghan referred. Formal work in English was not found to be decaying in 'a climate of undetected activity'; though many correspondents believed standards had fallen, expert witnesses could not find any convincing evidence for such a claim. The tests used since 1949 by the National Foundation for Educational Research (NFER) were regarded by the Committee as too narrow a basis upon which to make a judgement. But the Bullock Committee, Callaghan and leading Conservatives were in agreement that standards ought to be higher. This was as true in the case of Mathematics as of English. In 1978, the year before the Labour Government left office, a committee was set up under W. H. Cockcroft to examine the teaching of Mathematics. Its terms of reference reflected in part Callaghan's concern about the need for a fully numerate workforce: 'To consider the teaching of Mathematics in primary and secondary schools in England and Wales, with particular regard to the mathematics required in further and higher education, employment and adult life generally, and to make recommendations.'[9]

The Committee reported in 1982, in the third year of the first Conservative Government of the 1980s. The complaints from industry about lack of basic standards of numeracy, to which Callaghan referred in his speech, were met with the criticism by the members of the Cockcroft Committee that,

The kind of tests which are used and the level at which they are set vary widely. We are concerned that testing procedures are often in the hands of people who have neither training nor appropriate experience in testing procedures, including the setting and marking of papers. We have been surprised to find that this can be the case even within major companies.[10]

The Committee also pointed out that in many cases employers set tests at a higher level of mathematics than was required by the job and the tests themselves were often badly worded and set out. However, it recognised also that the path to improvements in the teaching of mathematics in schools lay in developing in-service work already in progress, especially in the production of differentiated curricula for different needs, in relating computational problems to real-life situations, in improved resources and in the need to ensure an 'adequate supply of suitably qualified mathematics teachers'.

This latter concern was reflected in the Conservative Government's scheme of giving additional grants to Science and Mathematics graduates embarking on initial training and in trying to attract into teaching suitably qualified people from industry and elsewhere under the licensed teacher scheme. One of Kenneth Baker's first acts as Secretary of State for Education was to publish 'Action on teacher supply in Mathematics, Physics and Technology', subjects which he deemed vital to the needs of an industrial nation. He also initiated the licensed teacher scheme which by-passed the one-year teacher training by enabling people over 26 who had successfully completed at least two years' higher education to go straight into schools to teach as licensed teachers, training largely in-post with day release to local training colleges. This scheme was not without its critics from within the teachers' unions and elsewhere.

The priority which both the Labour and Conservative parties attached to improving the teaching of the basics was reflected in the National Curriculum. Callaghan, in 1976, had indicated that he was favourably disposed towards the idea of a 'core curriculum' which gave priority to Mathematics and English. Baker's National Curriculum, brought into being by the 1988 Education Act, gave priority to Mathematics, Science and English. The original timetable (Table 1.1) for implementing the core curriculum indicates its priority.[11]

Though placing Mathematics and English at the core of the National Curriculum seemed like the restoration of the Revised Code of over a century earlier, there was strong resistance to a return to an age of rote learning and formal grammar. The traditionalists were victorious on neither of the working groups created to draw up attainment targets for the teaching of Mathematics and English. The group concerned with English was chaired by one of the editors of the Black Papers, Brian Cox; despite his Black Paper views, the traditionalists were unsuccessful in their bid to win a place for the formal teaching of English grammar. The group rejected Baker's demand for 'greater emphasis in writing on mastery of grammatical structure'. Clause analysis and

Table 1.1 ***Timetable for implementing National Assessment and Testing***†

	Maths Science	*Technology*	*English*
Autumn 1989	Attainment targets etc. for key stages 1 and 3		Attainment targets etc. for key stage 1 (probably)
Autumn 1990	Attainment targets etc. for key stage 2	Attainment targets etc for key stage 1–3 possibly (or 1 and 3)	Attainment targets etc. for key stages 2 and 3
Summer 1991	*Unreported assessment for key stage 1	–	Unreported assessment for key stage 1 (probably)
Autumn 1991	–	Attainment targets etc for key stage 2 (possibly)	–
Summer 1992	Reported assessment for key stage 1 Unreported assessment for key stage 3	Unreported assessment for key stage 1	Reported assessment for key stage 1 (probably)
Autumn 1992	Attainment targets etc. for key stage 4	–	Attainment targets etc. for key stage 4
Summer 1993	Reported assessment for key stage 3	Reported assessment for for key stage 1 Unreported assessment for key stage 3	Unreported assessment for key stage 3
Autumn 1993	–	Attainment targets for key stage 4	–
Summer 1994	GCSEs for key stage 4 Unreported assessment for key stage 2	Possibly, unreported assessment for key stage 2 Reported assessment for key stage 3	Unreported assessment for key stage 2 Reported assessment for key stage 3 GCSEs for key stage 4
Autumn 1994	–	–	–
Summer 1995	Reported assessment for key stage 2	Reported or unreported assessment for key stage 2	Reported assessment for key stage 2

Table 1.1 *Cont'd.*

	Maths Science	Technology	English
Summer 1996	–		GCSEs for key stage 4 Possibly reported assessment for key stage 2

Key stage 1 = 5–7 (Infant 1 and 2)
Key stage 2 = 7/8–11 (junior 3–6)
Key stage 3 = 11/12–14 (years 1–3 of secondary)
Key stage 4 = 14/15–16 (years 4 and 5 of secondary)
*Dummy run, results not published
†This was the original timetable

parsing were not to return. Also, whereas the Education Secretary wanted priority to be given to reading and writing, the group's report favoured an equal emphasis upon reading, writing, speaking and listening. The National Curriculum Council, intent on not becoming the Government's poodle, slipped its leash and supported its working group.

Public and political opinion were scarcely affected by the conclusions of research in the 1980s; the view that the basics were being neglected in schools rested on very little evidence. An NFER survey published in 1984 showed that, as in the results of many other surveys,

Table 1.2 ***Frequency of classroom activities***

Rank	*Name of activity*
1	Work in mathematical computation
2	Silent reading as a class
3	Practice in learning tables/number bonds
4	Vocabulary and dictionary work
5	Comprehension exercises
6	Descriptive writing
7.5	Learning lists of spellings
7.5	Creative writing
9	Spelling tests
10	Formal grammar
11	Science
12	Practical maths
13	Individual project or topic work
14	Cooperative group work
15	Maths tests
16	Free choice periods
17	Modern maths
18	Drama
19	Dictation
20	School visits/field trips
21	Homework

the primary school classroom was remarkably conventional in giving priority to Mathematics and English. Table 1.2[12] shows the rank order of frequency of classroom activities.

Teaching methods were found to be different from the 'progressive' model which public and politicians alike believed held sway in the primary school classroom (Table 1.3).

Table 1.3 ***Main methods of teaching Mathematics and English***

Main method	*Maths*		*English*	
	Large schools %	*Smaller schools %*	*Large schools %*	*Smaller schools %*
Class teaching	33	19	42	30
Ability group teaching	29	32	21	21
Individual teaching	20	26	11	20
Variety of methods	18	23	26	29
	100	100	100	100
Number of teachers giving information	1,844	490	1,816	488

A report on Newcastle primary schools published in August 1989 confirmed on a regional scale what the NFER survey had shown five years earlier on a national scale. It found that emphasis was still placed in the city's primary schools upon reading, writing and mathematics. More surprising were the findings concerning parental fears. There were fears that the National Curriculum would lead to more teaching of a 'progressive' kind, with emphasis upon topic work in English teaching and upon Modern Mathematics, even though in the case of the latter they recognised that the traditional methods of teaching had failed in their own school days.

In the early 1990s reports alleging a continuing decline in the standards of literacy and numeracy helped to keep education at the top of the political agenda.

PROGRESSIVE EDUCATION

The methods and aims of informal instruction . . . there is the unease felt by parents and teachers about the new informal methods of teaching which seem to produce excellent results when they are in well-qualified hands but are much more dubious in their effects when they are not. (Callaghan, 1976)

1976 was a bad year for the progressives. Callaghan's Ruskin College speech showed the extent to which Black Paper views on progressive education had gained widespread support. Black Paper Three of November 1970 had taken up the claim made by Professor Bantock in the first of the papers that, 'At primary school some teachers are taking to an extreme the belief children must not be told anything, but must find out for themselves' with the result that 'the traditional high standards of English education are being overthrown'.[13] The republication in 1971 of the three Black Papers on progressive education, *The Centrality of Reading, Freedom in Junior Schools* and *Discovery Methods* (in that order), helped to connect together in the public mind the issue of the falling standards of literacy and numeracy with progressive education in a simple causal relation. The stereotypical picture of the 'informal' primary school classroom as one of unstructured and random activity dominated by discovery methods was traced back by the Black Paper authors to the Plowden Report of 1967. Such an image had a ready appeal to politicians who wished to limit teacher autonomy and to extend central government influence over the curriculum. It was a concern that crossed party lines. Margaret Thatcher's appointment of the Bullock Committee in 1972 reflected her concern about the effects of informal styles of teaching in English; 1976 provided the Labour Prime Minister with further ammunition to attack progressive education. The Auld Report attacked the radical teaching methods employed at the William Tyndale Junior School in Islington; one of the teaching staff had complained how the school's 'educational programme has stultified into a late sixties style of informal progressive repression.'[14] Neville Bennett's initial conclusions about the relative effectiveness of formal and informal styles[15] seemed to add the voice of independent authority to the growing volume of criticism of progressive education. It had indeed been a year when informal methods of teaching had been constantly under attack. The activities of a small, extremist group of teachers in Islington had provided the popular press with ready-made anti-progressive headlines; the alleged faulty analysis of evidence by a prominent researcher (who was later to revise his conclusions) had been used to support the attack on progressive teaching; and the Prime Minister, briefed by education specialists in his Policy Unit, had made the issue a principal point of discussion for the Great Debate.

Had Callaghan traced the history of progressive education he would have found that official blessing to many of its basic ideas was given not just by the Plowden Committee in 1967 but also by the Board's Consultative Committee on Education in its reports on the primary school (1931) and the nursery school (1933) (See pp. 89–91). Tawney sat on both committees and was primarily responsible for establishing that on nursery education. He would have been most unlikely to have joined the Prime Minister's thinly veiled attack on progressive education. The Consultative Committee's report on the primary school gave its firm backing to the concept 'that the curriculum is to be thought of in terms of activity and experience rather than of knowledge to be acquired and facts to be stored ... to open out his (the pupil's) imagination'.[16] Tawney's concept of a humane education led him to support such an approach to the primary school curriculum. But it was this concept of the curriculum that was increasingly under attack from the 1970s onwards.

It was advantageous to both political parties to point the finger at the progressives. The bogey of the unruly classroom from which the effective teaching of the basics was absent was politically useful to those seeking to impose a national curriculum on schools. Thus, towards the end of the 1970s and throughout the 1980s the arguments about what Callaghan had called 'new informal methods of teaching' became part of the debate over the National Curriculum. This process was begun by Shirley Williams, Labour's Education Secretary in 1976, who saw the curricular debate as part of the discussion about monitoring and assessment. The first and second items on the 'agenda for the Great Debate' – the curriculum and monitoring and assessment – were not intended to be treated separately. Though the Green Paper, *Education in Schools: A Consultative Document* (1977) aimed to summarise the outcome of the debate and not to dwell upon teaching methods, its stress upon the need to investigate a 'protected' or 'core' part of the curriculum which 'can offer reassurances to employers, parents and the teachers themselves' was a veiled attack on the so-called informal methods of teaching. Thereafter the concept of the core curriculum with a series of assessments was seen as a means of countering the alleged excesses of the progressive movement in education and of reasserting traditional values. The research surveys of the 1970s into the relative merits of formal and informal teaching could never have resolved the political debate; the spectre of William Tyndale was a useful ally to those who wished to extend central control over the curriculum. The Labour Ministers of the 1970s could scarcely agree with such Black Paper authors as Angus Maude and Brian Cox that the move towards comprehensivisation was one of the causes of the declining standards of literacy and numeracy. They could, however, accept the Black Paper indictment of progressive teaching methods and use it for political ends. What is interesting is that within five years of Callaghan's speech the issue of formal versus informal teaching methods had disappeared as a separate issue on the educational agenda. Labour and Conservative Ministers alike used exaggerated descriptions of progressive education, supported by claims by industrialists that standards of English and Mathematics were declining, to argue a case for extending central authority over the curriculum.

It would have been inconceivable for a book on the central issues in education in the 1970s to have omitted a chapter on progressive education. Yet it is a measure of how speedily the grounds of the debate had shifted that none of the fourteen chapters of a survey of the central issues of *Education in the Eighties* completed in 1981 by a number of distinguished educationists was devoted solely to that subject. Where such references to it occurred, it was mainly in the contexts of accountability, evaluation and the common curriculum. The 1980s had opened with a veiled attack by the Conservative Government upon progressive education, as part of the discussion of the concept of a core curriculum. In *A Framework for the School Curriculum* Mark Carlisle, the Education Secretary, expressed a concern about the diversity of curricular practice in schools and urged consideration of the notion of a core curriculum. He raised the question whether such a curriculum should 'be expressed in terms of traditional school subjects ..., appropriately taught?'.[17] A further report in 1983 entitled 'Curriculum 11–16: A Statement of Entitlement' called for the acceptance of 'the need for assessment which monitors pupils' progress in learning and for explicit procedures, accessible to the public, which reflect and reinforce ... methods of teaching and learning which ensure the ... acquisition by pupils of the desired skills, attitudes, concepts and knowledge'. Testing, one of the symbols of traditional educational values, was thus seen as a vehicle for checking the excesses of progressive education. In the following year Sir Keith Joseph called for 'an explicit definition of the objectives of each phase and of each subject area of the curriculum'. This approach, which tightened the grip of central government, lay at the heart of Kenneth Baker's thinking in his Education Act of 1988. Published and prescribed syllabuses with defined objectives and stated attainment levels at 7, 11, 14 and 16 in the core and foundation subjects were seen as a means of raising standards and of providing pupils with the same opportunities wherever they attended school. This was a way of avoiding what was deemed to be the educational lottery in which the losers received the kind of informal education attacked twenty years earlier by the Black Papers and by Callaghan in his Ruskin College speech.

INDUSTRY AND EDUCATION

There seems to be a need for more technological biases in science teaching that will lead towards practical applications in industry rather than towards academic studies. (Callaghan, 1976)

Callaghan believed that the aims of education were 'clear enough'. Rejecting the aims of a liberal education to which his mentor, R. H. Tawney, had been so faithfully wedded, he side-stepped the debate by the simple assertion that the aims of education were two-fold, 'to equip children to the best of their ability for a lively, constructive place in society and also to fit them to do a good job of work'. The social and vocational aims were given priority in his speech over the claims of personality, and of the two he argued that vocational aims should be given pride of place. 'There is no virtue in producing socially well-adjusted members of society who are unemployed because they do not have the skills.' He went on to link competency in the basic skills with employability, especially in industry, though he argued that schools were not in the business of producing 'technically, efficient robots' but required people with 'lively, enquiring minds'.

One of the key themes of the Ruskin College speech was the need for closer links between industry and education. Britain's industrial decline and the role of the education systems (both state and private) in bringing about the decline increasingly occupied the attention of Ministers and educational historians, such as Correlli Barnett, in the 1970s. Shirley Williams expressed her concern about the academic-vocational split which was, in her view, as serious as the grammar school–secondary modern split and equally damaging to education and the national economy. The down-grading of vocational education, even by scientists who preferred 'pure' science to its more practical forms, was a feature not just of Britain's education system but of British society as a whole. Britain, it was said, was long on thinkers and short on doers. The educational aspect of the problem was, in fact, multi-faceted. Few girls chose to take up technological subjects; over-specialisation in the sixth form encouraged the neglect of science and technological subjects; the examination system at Ordinary and Advanced levels gave little attention to practical work; practical subjects were held in low esteem because of the emphasis upon liberal and academic values; resources necessary for the effective teaching of such subjects were short from the primary school to the university. Primary schools provided little or no foundation in science and technology and few primary school teachers were trained to teach the new technologies. Shirley Williams admitted her helplessness in dealing directly with these matters. There was no guarantee that money given by central government to local education authorities to boost the teaching of technological skills, especially the new information-based skills, was spent for that purpose.

One way forward mentioned in the Prime Minister's speech was through the reform of school government and management. The Taylor Committee was set up by the Labour Government to achieve this in the hope that it would bring together 'local authority, parents and pupils, teachers and industry more closely'. As a result of this he hoped that the school curriculum would reflect and respond to the nation's technological needs. A survey at the end of the eighties by the National Foundation for Educational Research revealed that 41.5 per cent of new governors, other than teacher governors, came from business, industry and the professions. The Conservative governments of the 1980s took on board the idea of reforming the governing bodies of schools in the 1986 Education Act, but this was only one of several ways by which they intended to promote the teaching of technology in schools. One of the main initiatives in this direction was the Technical and Vocational Education Initiative (TVEI) announced by the Conservative Prime Minister, Margaret Thatcher, in November 1982 and launched the following year. Callaghan would have had little to disagree with in the TVEI statement of aims.

(a) In conjunction with LEAs to explore and test ways of organising and managing the education of 14–18-year-old young people across the ability ranges so that:

(i) more of them are attracted to seek the qualifications/skills which will be of direct value to them at work and more of them achieve these qualifications and skills;

(ii) they are better equipped to enter the world of employment which will await them;

(iii) they acquire a more direct appreciation of the practical application of the qualifications for which they are working;

(iv) they become accustomed to using their skills and knowledge to solve the real world problems they will meet at work;

(v) more emphasis is placed on developing initiative, motivation and enterprise as well as problem-solving skills and other aspects of personal development;

(vi) the construction of the bridge from education to work is begun earlier by giving these young people the opportunity to have direct contact and training/planned work experience with a number of local employers in the relevant specialism;

(vii) there is close collaboration between local education authorities and industry/commerce/public services, etc., so that the curriculum has industry's confidence.

However the project was placed in the hands of the Manpower Services Commission (MSC); this was interpreted by teachers organisations as further evidence of a government-backed bid by the MSC to 'colonise' education following on two other MSC schemes, the Youth Opportunities Programme and the Youth Training Scheme. Teachers and their unions were placed on the defensive and relations between teachers and the Government deteriorated rapidly.

Yet another controversial Conservative initiative to promote the teaching of technology was the launching in 1986 of a new kind of college, inner-city science and technology colleges to be paid for by industrial sponsors. The first such college, Kingshurst City Technology College, was opened in 1988; a further twenty-five were to be opened by 1991. The CTC programme changed direction partly because large industrial sponsors were hard to find and partly because there was strong opposition in some areas from parents and local politicians. One major criticism of the high-profile government scheme was that it was of no benefit to the majority; however, the extension of the TVEI programme to all state schools, announced in a White Paper in 1986, coupled with a scheme to create a new framework to cover all existing vocational qualifications and the priority given to Science and Technology in the National Curriculum, were seen by the Conservative Government as moves to give pride of place to science and technology in the schools of the 1990s.

PUBLIC EXAMINATIONS

Another problem is the examination system – a contentious issue. The Schools Council has reached conclusions about its future ... Shirley Williams intends to look at the examination system again. (Callaghan, 1976)

To the Black Paper authors the 'problem' was one of defending the existing examination system, which they regarded as one of the last bastions of academic values and standards against the onslaughts of those whom they called the egalitarians. To Callaghan and his Education Secretary, Shirley Williams, the 'problem' was different. They did not regard the reform of examinations and the examination system as synonymous with the dilution of standards; they argued that reform of the examination system was necessary in order to bring it in line with developments in schools since the mid-sixties and early seventies and to meet the needs of modern society and the nation's economy. The emphasis which Callaghan placed upon the need to improve standards suggests that he did not accept that the broadening of the nature and clientele of public examinations meant lower standards, that is 'the-more-means-worse argument' of the Black Papers. Callaghan did not spell out in detail in his Ruskin College speech what he believed were the problems facing the examination system; his intention was to make more central the debate about examinations at 16+ and 18+ which had been going on since the 1960s and earlier.

The examination system at the time when Callaghan was speaking was dominated by the General Certificate of Education (GCE) Ordinary and Advanced levels, dating from the early 1950s. Ordinary level was intended for those pupils who had passed the 11+ examination and entered grammar schools, some 25 per cent of the school population. Though increasing numbers of pupils from other types of school, especially secondary modern schools, sat Ordinary level the examination ill served the majority of 16 year olds who, by the mid-1970s, were in comprehensive schools and who, from 1973, were legally obliged to stay on at school to that age. The alternative public examination, the Certificate of Secondary Education (CSE), was introduced in the mid-1960s for a further 40 per cent of the school population but it was held in much less public esteem than Ordinary level.

The problem was not simply that GCE catered for a very restricted percentage of the school population in an age which increasingly demanded paper qualifications. At Advanced level, designed for an even smaller percentage of 18 year olds, it encouraged over specialisation and at both Ordinary and Advanced levels it was said to overemphasise academic content at the expense of practical skills. Shirley Williams took up Callaghan's call for broader examinations and to this extent brought to the centre of the political debate two issues which were occupying the attention of the Schools Council, the merging of the GCE and CSE into a common examination at 16+ and alternatives to Advanced levels at 18+.

Reform at 16+

The idea of a GCE–CSE merger had been favoured by the political left for several years. As early as 1966 the Socialist Educational Association had argued that a two-tier examination merely shifted the increasingly anachronistic 11+ selection to the age of 14 when the decision about which examination to sit two years later would have to be made. This kind of division, the Association argued, ran contrary to one of the basic principles of comprehensivisation. The idea of a single examination quickly gained the support of the National Union of Teachers (NUT) and in 1971 the Schools Council, on which the NUT had a major influence, embarked on a series of feasibility studies into a common examination at 16+. It reported to the Labour Government just before Callaghan delivered his Ruskin College speech that a common system was both feasible and desirable. Neither Callaghan nor Shirley Williams wished to rush the matter and set up a further enquiry under Sir James Waddell. The Waddell Report of 1978 found a single system feasible and the Education Secretary began discussions over who should run a common system.

The Waddell Report helped to place the issue high on the educational agenda of both of the leading political parties, even though the Conservative Party came to power in 1979 with an ambiguous policy on the common examination but committed to maintaining 'O' level standards. Within a year the new Secretary of State for Education, Mark Carlisle, had pronounced in its favour, and the machinery for its introduction was to be the grouping of the GCE and CSE boards into five regional bodies; standards were to be maintained through the laying down of national criteria for each subject with which each syllabus had to comply and which were to be enforced nationally by the Secondary Examinations Council. The SEC published the proposals for grade-related criteria in 1985. With the new syllabuses due to be taught from September 1986 and the first examination, replacing 'O' levels, to take place in 1988, there were pleas from teachers, head teachers and local authorities for a year's delay in implementing them – pleas ignored by the Education Secretary, Kenneth Baker.

THE TIMETABLE OF REFORM

1951	GCE 'O' level introduced. A single subject examination replacing a grouped-certificate examination.
1965	First CSE exams taken 1966. Socialist Educational Association called for single exam at 16+.
1969	National Union of Teachers recommended a merger of GCE and CSE.
1970	Schools Council decided to look into feasibility of a common examination system at 16+.
1971–76	Schools Council recommended single system to Labour Government. The Secretary of State, Shirley Williams, said a common system could have considerable advantages but decided further enquiry was needed. Set up Waddell Committee.
1978	Waddell Committee found single system feasible.

1979	Conservative Government elected with ambiguous policy on 16+ but committed to maintain 'O' level standards.
1980	Secretary of State, Mark Carlisle, accepted common 16+ desirable. Asked exam boards to draw up national criteria in every subject.
1981	Composition of five new groups of exam boards finalised and first drafts of criteria published.
1982	Sir Keith Joseph, new Secretary of State, said single 16+ would only proceed if he was satisfied with national criteria and that the new system would maintain standards.
1983	Keith Joseph wrote to SEC – which, in part, replaced the Schools Council – asking its advice on feasibility of single system. SEC replied single system was feasible and desirable.
1984	Keith Joseph announced decision to merge 'O' level and CSE into single system. SEC working parties start work on grade-related criteria in first ten subjects: English, Mathematics, French, Welsh, History, Geography, CDT, Physics, Biology and Chemistry. Also revised versions of national criteria submitted to Secretaries of State.
1985	National and subject grade-related criteria published.
1986	May: last date for new syllabuses based on national criteria to be published. GCSE courses taught from September.
1987	Last 'O' level and CSE exams sat.
1988	First GCSE examinations sat.
1988	Future of GCSE clouded by National Curriculum.

The General Certificate of Secondary Education (GCSE) proposals were criticised for the undue haste with which they were introduced. Other criticisms were voiced in the first few years of their operation, several of which focused on the perennial issue of standards. The claim made by the joint council of the GCSE after the second year of the new examination that the results when compared with the last year of 'O' level and CSE (1987) showed a rise in standards was met with scepticism by Rhodes Boyson, a former Conservative Education Minister and Black Paper author, and by the Centre for Policy Studies, the Conservative Government 'think-tank'. Kenneth Baker, the Education Secretary, hailed the increase in the percentage of candidates gaining Grade A (10.3 per cent, 1989; 6.8 per cent 1987) and a pass grade (46 per cent 1989; 40 per cent 1987) as 'unusual and significant'; HM Inspectorate interpreted these figures as evidence of the 'greatest single leap forward in the history of education in England and Wales'. Rhodes Boyson and the Government's own 'think-tank' were less impressed, as was George Walden, former Minister of Higher Education. Their point was that the GCSE was so fundamentally different from the system which it replaced as to invalidate all claims about higher standards. This was particularly evident in the inclusion of coursework in GCSE assessment, and not widely used in the 'O' level examination. Boyson pointed in particular to Mathematics, the only GCSE subject not to include coursework, where the percentage increases were less marked, as evidence that the claim about higher standard was misleading. In his view, GCSE lacked the challenge to able students which 'O' level had offered. GCSE was intended to be different from 'O' level in placing greater emphasis upon practical skills and in testing a broader range of skills for up to 90 per cent of 16 year olds; thus there was some truth in the argument that it was difficult, if not impossible, to compare two very different types of examination. The examining groups had been given the impossible task of maintaining 'O' level standards. To many teachers, however, the fact that comparison was impossible was insufficient reason for altering what was a more appropriate examination for students in the 1980s and 1990s. The new system had scarcely got underway, however, when it was in danger of being overtaken by the development of a National Curriculum which set attainment targets for 16 year olds in each of the school subjects. While the National Curriculum Council wanted to keep the GCSE roughly in its existing form but extending the idea of modular assessment, the School Examination and Assessment Council advised the Education Secretary, Kenneth Baker, that GCSE should become part of the system of assessment at 7, 11, 14 and 16, and thus a modular system which examined at points between 14 and 16 was unacceptable. Senior head teachers also predicted that GCSE, as such, would be phased out after the National Curriculum and its associated testing arrangements were fully implemented in the mid-1990s. Students aged 16 would face externally supervised 'standard assessment tasks' and regular evaluation by their own teachers in all ten National Curriculum subjects, as well as having records of achievement which would provide employers with details of their academic and non-academic activities. In such a situation, it was claimed, GCSE would have little or no place.

Reform at 18+

One of the main 'problems' concerning the examination system which Callaghan had in mind in his Ruskin College speech was that of overspecialisation in the sixth form, both in the sense of the number of subject areas studied and in the overemphasis upon theory as opposed to what he termed 'practical applications'. At the time of his speech, the Schools Council, set up in 1964 as a forum for debate on curricula and examinations, was conducting a series of feasibility studies into a radical alternative to GCE Advanced level. In 1966, it had published a series of proposals for a system of major and minor courses which, by 1973, had taken on the more definite form of Normal and Further levels. It was this alternative to GCE Advanced levels which was being discussed around the time of Callaghan's speech. Its main features were as follows:

(N)ormal and (F)urther levels

- A two-level syllabus and examination structure – (N)ormal and (F)urther levels.

- A norm of five examination subjects, not more than two studied to 'F' level.
- A single-subject examination for both 'N' and 'F', i.e. no compulsion to study five subjects and no compulsory grouping of subjects.
- Both 'N' and 'F' to involve two-year courses beyond a standard equivalent to at least GCE Ordinary level Grade C.
- Total study time for each 'N' level course to be about half of that for an 'A' level and for 'F' about three-quarters.
- 'N' and 'F', if approved, to replace 'A' level.

These proposals had an appeal to those people who believed that over-specialisation in the sixth form had increased, was increasing and ought to be diminished. To the Labour Party they had a particular appeal because they appeared to cater better for the wider ability range and greater numbers found more in the sixth form of comprehensive schools than in the traditional grammar school. The Schools Council Report published in 1978 illustrated the inadequacies of 'A' level and argued that the alternative system of 'N' and 'F' levels was both feasible and desirable. The report showed how the traditional pattern of sixth-form study was changing. The traditional three-subject 'A' level course, though still dominant, was in retreat. The changing nature of sixth forms and sixth-form study (Figure 1.2) meant that the kind of provision that was suited to the needs of the 1950s when 'A' level was introduced was less suited to the needs of the last quarter of the century.

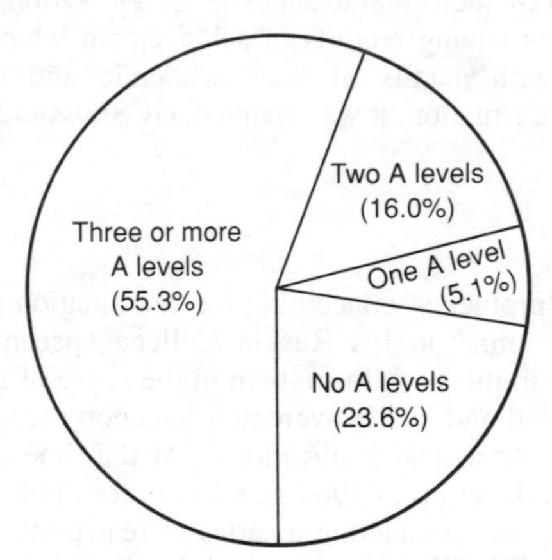

Fig. 1.2 ***Estimated proportions of first-year sixth-formers in schools studying different numbers of 'A' level subjects 1975***

It was argued that the five-subject system would help broaden the sixth-form curriculum enabling students to combine the study of sciences, humanities and languages, and that it would cater better for the needs of the new sixth form. It would also facilitate the introduction of new kinds of assessment, including those of a practical kind; opponents argued that two-year courses would not necessarily cater better for sixth formers who required shorter term goals and could lead to a heavy examination load at the end of the sixth form. But it was on the rock of standards that the proposals came to grief; 'N' and 'F' levels involved the disappearance of the traditional yardstick, Advanced level, by which sixth-form standards were measured and led to the objection from the university sector that their entrants would be far less well prepared with the possibility of three-year degree courses being extended to four years as a consequence.

> From the university point of view the foremost aim must be to continue to meet the national need for well-educated and highly trained graduates which in turn depends on the advanced level of education provided for the most able students at all stages of secondary education. The universities are therefore agreed that nothing should be done which might put the supply of graduates at risk.

Shortly after taking office in 1979 the Conservative Government announced that, owing to the overwhelming opposition, particularly of the universities, there would be no replacement of 'A' levels in the foreseeable future. This decision, and the reason given, came as a surprise to those who had for many years operated a five-subject sixth-form curriculum north of the English border.

The reform of the sixth-form curriculum in the 1980s to 1990s had to take three things into account: firstly, the generally accepted view that despite falling school roles and in part because of the increasing number of sixth-form and tertiary colleges, the diversity of the sixth form would continue; secondly, that maintenance of standards was interpreted as the need to preserve 'A' levels as the arbiter of standards; thirdly, the need to encourage a broader sixth-form curriculum. (See Figure 1.3.)

When Mark Carlisle, the Secretary of State, decided to retain GCE 'A' level he invited the Schools Council to suggest an alternative path forward to 'N' and 'F' levels. The Council suggested ways of improving the 'A' level and recommended the consideration of an intermediate ('I') examination alongside the 'A' level. Candidates could take some 'As' and some 'Is' enabling them, through judicious combinations, to study sciences and humanities or sciences and a modern language. Students could thus have a broader course. However, it did little to meet the needs of many of the 'new sixth' in that it was a two-year course for students taking 'A' levels; it failed to cater for those who wished only to spend one year in the sixth form. Its successor, Advanced Supplementary ('AS') level, suffered from the same inflexibility. The concept of a two-year course linked to 'A' level was seen by the Government as the chief means of maintaining standards while introducing some innovation. The first candidates sat 'AS' levels in 1989 having studied syllabuses equivalent to half the content and time of corresponding advanced level syllabuses over a two-year

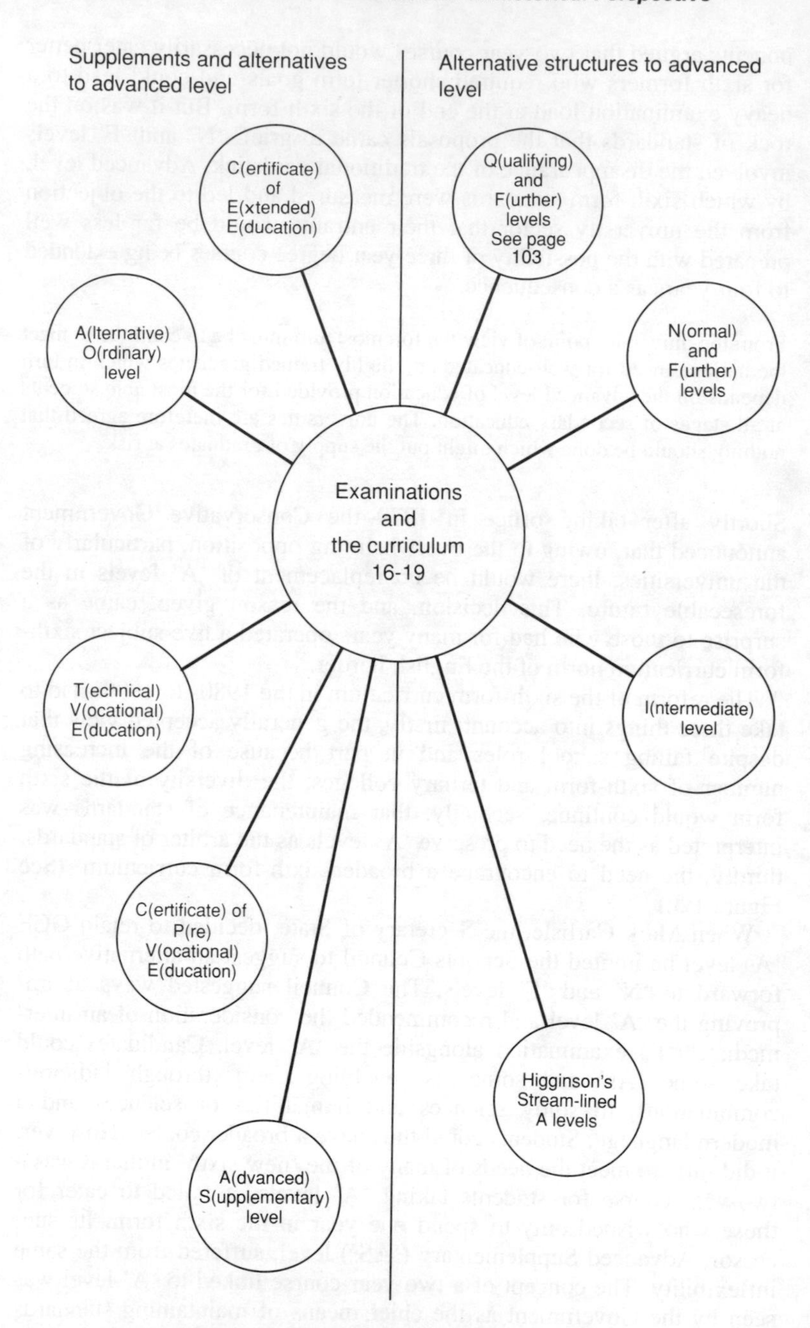

Fig. 1.3 ***Examinations and the curriculum 16–19***

period. However, the achievements of 'AS' candidates in the first year of the examination were disappointing.

There was growing concern in the late 1980s that the traditional 'A' levels were out of step with the GCSE which assessed a much broader range of skills. In February 1987, Kenneth Baker announced that the Higginson Committee had been set up to review 'A' levels. The Committee identified a general consensus that the system was rigid, narrow, encouraged passive learning and all too frequently failed to test higher level skills. It generally recommended the streamlining of 'A' level syllabuses to reduce time on them, and as a result to reduce factual content. The system, drawn up in 1951 for a clientele predominantly aiming at university entrance and almost entirely educated in selective and independent schools, was seen to be failing sixth formers and those in tertiary education. The Committee recommended a five-subject examination, using streamlined 'A' levels. The recommendations were attacking what many believed to be the very basis of standards in the sixth form and were swiftly rejected by Kenneth Baker in June 1988. 'AS' levels remained the main instrument by which the Government hoped to broaden the sixth-form curriculum, though take up was generally poor in their first year of operation.

There were, however, other developments which helped to broaden the choice for 16–19 year olds but whose very range led to the criticism that the governments of the 1980s had no coherent policy for this age group. Alternative Ordinary level, which was phased out when 'AS' levels were introduced, offered the opportunity for students to pursue a one-year ordinary level course designed for those who were older than the normal ordinary level candidate. The Certificate of Extended Education also fulfilled a similar function but was aimed primarily at the 'new' sixth former who wanted to stay on at school for another year, having already gained some CSEs with good grades. The Certificate of Pre-Vocational Education (CPVE) was another one-year course for 17+ students, but of a rather different kind. It, too, was aimed at the 'new sixth', comprising: core courses to teach skills which could be applied in a variety of situations through the integration of subject areas; vocational studies, which included placement experience; and additional studies, including community and leisure activities. Intended as a broad alternative to academic studies when it was fully launched in 1985, it rapidly became aligned to the vocational qualifications system and found a more secure home in colleges than in schools. TVEI launched a little earlier was aimed at the 14–18 age group but faced similar pressures as CPVE.

Public examinations were confined largely to GCE Advanced and Ordinary levels and CSE when Callaghan initiated the 'Great Debate' in 1976; a decade or so later they had changed considerably though Advanced level still dominated sixth-form studies. His call for more practical and technical studies had been taken up vigorously by the ensuing Conservative governments; and Labour's concern about the narrowness of the sixth-form curriculum was shared by the Conservatives, though attempts to provide a broader system to the traditional three Advanced level (or less) model had made little headway by the close of the 1980s. 'AS' levels, which in several ways provided more of the same, seemed to do little to broaden the nature of study or the mode of enquiry. Two decades and more of debate had not resulted in any coherent or flexible policy for broadening sixth-form study. One alternative model which was discussed in the educational press in the 1980s was that of the International Baccalaureate. Though it had the disadvantage of being based upon a two-year programme of study, it had a structure that would enable a broader sixth-form curriculum.

THE EDUCATION SYSTEMS

... the endowment of our children is the most precious of the natural resources of the community. So I do not hesitate to discuss how those endowments should be nurtured. (Callaghan, 1976)

These words from the introduction to the Ruskin College speech suggest that Callaghan was about to embark on a bold and broad-ranging critical survey from which no areas of education would be excluded. However, in his next paragraph he linked his analysis to the issue of public expenditure on education and settled into a diatribe against particular practices in the state sector which he believed meant that the annual sum of £6 million was not well spent. This approach set severe limits to the scope of his discussion and to the Great Debate itself. It excluded consideration of the private sector of education which some educational historians believed was more responsible for Britain's economic decline than the state sector, especially in supplying the model for the curricular development of the latter. As with the Conservative governments of the 1980s there was no suggestion that the reforms thought so necessary to raise standards and promote technical education in the state sector should also be applied to the independent sector. Also, as in the case of his Conservative successors, there was no consideration of the comprehensive system *per se*, which the Black Paper authors[18] blamed for Britain's educational problems.

> It is one of the more grotesque ironies of our times that a Labour Government claiming a particular interest in the needs of the poor and lowly as well as a special concern for high national standards in work and living should have determined a policy for secondary education which will beyond a doubt lead to a decline in standards and a reduction in the opportunities open to able children – from whatever social background they come. I am particularly concerned here with this able minority for it is on the talented that national welfare ultimately depends.

Callaghan was not even willing to go as far as R.H. Tawney, and suggest that the origins of many of the problems which he claimed to identify were to be found in the survival of class values within the comprehensive system. For Callaghan their origins lay in particular teaching methods, unbalanced curricula, an outmoded examination system and unrepresentative governing bodies – things that could be rectified without any root-and-branch reform of the system itself. Thus neither the independent schools nor the comprehensive school system appeared on the agenda of the Great Debate. The former were ignored and reform was to be within and not of the latter, a position which Shirley Williams accepted at that time.

The Conservative governments of the 1980s were equally unwilling to advocate the unscrambling of the comprehensive school system though they were willing to see a more diversified education system; this sometimes resulted in some incongruities. Grammar schools, which generally felt more secure in the eighties, existed alongside comprehensive schools. Parental choice was likely to strengthen the former and reduce the 'comprehensive' nature of the latter. Much needed money was diverted from the state to the independent sector through the Assisted Places Scheme which aimed at helping children of low-income families to attend independent schools and so not be subjected to the National Curriculum which was deemed so important for the nation's children. The scheme was introduced in 1981 to enable academically able children from low-income families to attend such schools. Critics pointed to the fact that it benefited very few working-class children. Only 9 per cent of assisted pupils had fathers in working-class occupations; the Independent Schools Information Service in reply pointed out that class was a blunt instrument of analysis; 60 per cent of places in 1988 went to pupils whose parent(s) had an income of less than £8,000, many of whom were single-parent families of middle-class background. The City Technology Colleges were also introduced by the Conservative Government as a means of extending parental choice, of encouraging the involvement of industry in schools and of meeting Britain's technological needs. These schools, also exempted from the National Curriculum, were said by their critics to be failing in their bid to gain major industrial sponsorship and thus causing State money to be diverted from maintained secondary schools; this, in turn, reduced the resources and as a consequence the range of choice for students in such schools. Thus, for example, one of the campaigners for the advancement of state education argued that the Nottingham City Technology College planned to have 160 computer terminals; if this money were divided between Nottingham's comprehensive schools, the schools would be better equipped and parental choice would be increased. Labour maintained its 1970s position of increasing diversity within the comprehensive school system to the age of 16, and was against creating special schools of the CTC kind.

Another way in which Kenneth Baker, the Conservative Education Secretary from 1986 to 1989, sought to extend the variety of schools was through the creation of grant-maintained schools, which were similar in their financing to the direct grant schools which Labour had abolished in 1976. Baker argued that 'with grant-maintained schools we now seek to carry the concept of parental choice to the heart of our education system ... Governors and parents should be able to run schools themselves without being forced to finance the enterprise from fees'.[19] Thus grant-maintained schools would receive their finance not from local education authorities but direct from central government, thus opting out of local government control. He saw the advantage of this as forcing local education authorities to pay more heed to school governors and parents who could threaten to opt out of their control. Grant-maintained schools could become centres of excellence. Critics saw this merely as a backdoor means of restoring grammar schools, of reinforcing and extending élitism in education.

One further way of increasing diversity for 16–18 year olds was the development of sixth-form colleges and tertiary education. In some ways this was the result of falling school rolls and small uneconomic sixth forms; it also resulted in some areas from an ideological commitment to education as a broad highway. Tertiary education in particular was seen by many of its proponents as a way of broadening the curriculum and student choice. They argued that the 1944 Education Act produced an institutional change (see pp. 60–63) but not a curricular change; DES Circular 10/65 had a similar result (see pp. 124–127). Both left the system dominated by advanced levels; only a radical reorganisation along tertiary lines could, in their view, allow real choices to be made and a broad curriculum to be offered. Richmond upon Thames was the first education authority to put all of its 16–19 eggs in one tertiary basket in 1983; many other authorities had a mixture of sixth-form colleges and colleges of further education. For supporters of tertiary colleges only this type of institution could really offer a broad highway open to all with a wide choice of lanes in an adult atmosphere. This kind of institution met Labour's commitment to broadening education and the Conservative's concern to extend choice. The latter, however, could only be achieved if other forms of provision such as the traditional sixth form and the sixth-form college were on offer at the same time, an uneconomic proposition for most local education authorities (LEAs).

TEACHER ACCOUNTABILITY AND PARENTAL RIGHTS

To the teachers I would say that you must satisfy the parents and industry that what you are doing meets their requirements and the needs of their children. For if the public is not convinced then the profession will be laying up trouble for itself in the future. (Callaghan, 1976)

In the opening paragraphs of his Ruskin College speech, Callaghan answered the question 'What do we want from the education of our children and our young people?' by reference to the words of R. H. Tawney, an eminent historian, who was a major influence upon Labour Party policy in the years 1918 to 1950. He quoted Tawney's answer, 'What a wise parent would wish for their children so the State must wish for all its children.' Callaghan, in the above quotation from his speech, seems to have taken this to mean some kind of teacher accountability to parents and industrialists. However, Tawney did not favour parental domination of the school curriculum, still less that of industry, which he always suspected of wanting to undermine a sound liberal education for its own vocational ends. His respect for the integrity of the school teacher was matched only by his deep distrust of the intentions of industrialists. Unavoidable financial pressures upon working-class parents might sway them in favour of short-term goals to increase their employability. He thus favoured government action on the curriculum and other matters in full consultation and accord with the teaching profession. The professional teacher and the 'wise parent' were, in his view, virtually synonymous.

Such an interpretation of Tawney's words was scarcely acceptable to the politicians and Department of Education and Science (DES) officials of the 1970s and 1980s who wished to place the blame for alleged declining standards of literacy and numeracy, and the nation's economic ills, upon state schools. Tawney would have raised questions about the evidence for the former and about the role of the independent schools in the latter. The Labour politicians of the late 1970s did not. The 'complaints from industry' were taken as adequate evidence; Callaghan noted in his speech that an initial step towards remedying the situation had already been taken through the setting up of the Taylor Committee to look into the government and management of schools with the intention of bringing together 'local authority, parents and pupils, teachers and industry more closely'. The initial terms of reference made no mention of parents but Bernard Donoughue persuaded the Prime Minister to include reference to parental involvement. In 1977 the Taylor Committee duly reported in favour of increasing the powers of school governing bodies (at the expense of teachers and others) through changing their composition. It recommended equal membership for parents, teachers, LEAs and the community at large (especially employers). Making teachers more accountable and increasing parental rights had an immediate appeal to Conservative governments in the 1980s but they were objectives which appeared to some educationists to come into conflict by the end of the decade. The idea of increasing parental influence on and within schools fitted in well with Conservative policy of increasing consumer choice during their first two periods of office from 1979 to 1987. The 1980 Education Act gave parents the right, within limits, to choose their children's schools in the light of statements about policies, the curriculum and examination results which each school was legally obliged to publish. Thus schools were made more 'accountable' to the community. The rights of parents who had children with special educational needs were strengthened in the 1981 Education Act. LEAs were given the responsibility of preparing a statement analysing special educational needs and provision with parental involvement and right to appeal. This provision included the requirement that, whenever it is practicable, pupils with special needs should be integrated into the general system of schooling, something which parents could press for. A further measure to increase parental choice and involvement was the voucher scheme, favoured in particular by Keith Joseph as Education Secretary, but which was shown in pilot tests to be impractical and expensive and was eventually dropped. The scheme was opposed by Labour for it allowed parents to cash their vouchers in the private sector. The high point in extending parental rights and influence came in the 1986 Education Act. Following on from the Taylor Report of 1977 and the report of 1984 on parental influence at school, *A New Framework for School Government*, the 1986 Act extended the participation of parents and others on governing bodies. The governing bodies were given increased powers over the curriculum including sex education, and in relation to school discipline and preventing political indoctrination. The Education Secretary could also require the regular appraisal of teachers.

After 1986 the Government became less concerned with widening local consumer choice and parental influence and more concerned with extending central control over the school curriculum. The 1988 Education Act imposed a common curriculum on state schools, thus reducing curricular choice and curricular emphasis. To some educationists, the imposed uniformity of a National Curriculum removed much parental choice; the state had assumed the role of the 'wise parent'; Conservative politicians generally saw the National Curriculum as broadening rather than diminishing choices; in their view most parents wanted a broad and balanced curriculum such as that offered by the National Curriculum. They believed that what concerned parents most was the quality of teaching. The results of the national tests which went with the common curriculum and which schools were legally obliged to publish in their prospectuses would, according to this view, be a good guide about the quality of teaching in a particular school. This information, together with other details about school life contained in the prospectus, would enable parents to make a more informed choice of school for their offspring. As parents could 'vote with their feet', teachers were still ultimately accountable to school governors who, under the 1988 Education Act, were given more control over their resources and were given the task of policing the National Curriculum, including its teaching.

In one sense, the 1988 Education Act had met Callaghan's requirement that teachers 'must satisfy the parents and industry' that what they were doing met 'their requirements and the needs of their children'. It took the curriculum out of the hands of teachers and others and put it into those of the State which acted as the 'wise parent' or 'wise industrialist'. To those who were less favourable to the extension of central control, it took away those powers over an essential area of school life, the curriculum, which the 1980 Education Act had placed in the hands of local parents, industrialists, teachers and others. The local partnership promised by the 1980 Act had to all intents and purposes been taken away when the 1988 Education Act turned school governors into policemen for the National Curriculum.

MONITORING THE USE OF RESOURCES

What is the best way of monitoring the use of resources in order to maintain national standards of performance?
... Whether there are more efficient ways of using the resources we have for the benefit of young people. (Callaghan, 1976)

Callaghan's Ruskin College speech carried the central message that educational resources were not infinite and that ways should be found of using the limited resources more effectively. The theme of value for money was not new. Three years earlier in the wake of the oil crisis the Conservative Chancellor of the Exchequer, Anthony Barber, marked the abrupt end of the era of educational expansion with a £200 million package of education cuts. Though the cuts were never fully implemented the lesson was as clear to Conservative Education Secretary, Margaret Thatcher, as it was to her Labour successors, Reg Prentice, Fred Mulley and Shirley Williams, that the education world must obtain the best value from its limited resources. Towards the end of 1976 Britain's economic position worsened. The Labour Government was forced to borrow money from the International Monetary Fund which demanded in return severe restrictions on public expenditure. Education could not remain immune from cuts; it must thus make the best use of its resources. The notoriety caused by the William Tyndale case and the initial findings of Neville Bennett's research into teaching styles seemed to confirm in the nation's mind that educational resources were not being put to their best use, and in particular that the basics were being neglected. It was against this backcloth that the Prime Minister raised his questions about educational resources, their monitoring and use. The case for government intervention was being laid as much in the area of the use of resources as in that of the curriculum. The Yellow Book, which the DES had compiled at the Prime Minister's invitation, provided him with sufficient selective evidence about the nation's schools to merit greater intervention by the DES and Inspectorate.

The impression left by Callaghan's speech that resources and the curriculum needed to be more carefully regulated in the national interest had an instant appeal to the Conservatives who returned to office under Mrs Thatcher in May 1979. Against a background of grave economic problems, expenditure on education was squeezed still further with its percentage of the GDP falling from 5.7 in 1980–81 to 5.1 by 1986–87. This, coupled with the Government's ideological commitment to introducing the principles of the marketplace into the running of schools, led to greater emphasis on the local management of resources to achieve greatest value for money. It was the extension to education of the move to give the customer a greater say in the management of resources that was said to lie at the heart of the privatisation of industries such as gas and British Telecom.

The local management of resources went hand in hand with growing parental participation in the running of schools. Baker's Education Act of 1988 obliged local education authorities to delegate budgets to all governing bodies of secondary and primary schools with 200 or more pupils. Under the Act:

> The governing body of any school which has a delegated budget:
> (a) shall be entitled, subject to any provision made by or under the scheme, to spend any sum made available to them in respect of the school's budget share for any financial year as they think fit for the purposes of the school; and (b) may delegate to the head teacher, to such extent as may be permitted by or under the scheme, their power under paragraph (a) above in relation to any part of that sum.[20]

The overall budget for the nation's schools was centrally controlled but each school could spend its own portion as it wished. As parents and others from outside the world of education played an important part on governing bodies it was thought that this would lead to a closer check on how resources were allocated and used. In some respects this was a return to the system in operation a hundred years earlier for the schools of the mass of the nation's children, the Board Schools (see pp. 52–53), which Labour had championed as examples of local democracy against the attacks of the Conservative Party. A century later it was the Conservatives who were championing the cause of local democracy as a means of trying to ensure what Callaghan had called 'more efficient ways of using resources'.

TEACHER EDUCATION AND TRAINING

> *The curriculum 5 to 16; the assessment of standards; the education and training of teachers; school and working life.* (Agenda for the Great Debate 'Educating our Children', 1976)

Callaghan's Ruskin College speech launched the Great Debate; it did not aim at defining all of its areas. By the time Shirley Williams, the Education Secretary, had firmed up its key themes for an agenda for debate, an additional item had appeared on it: the education and training of teachers. The regional conferences of February and March 1977 were asked to consider under this heading, (i) the steps that can be taken to ensure that all teachers receive the in-service training and education they need at various stages of their careers; (ii) the academic and professional requirements that need to be provided for teachers' initial training and, in particular, the implications these have for entrance requirements.[21] That teacher education and training appeared on the agenda, and in this form, was not surprising. It was an area of concern that had figured prominently in the 1960s when there was growing criticism of the Area Training Organisations (ATOs) – its supervisory bodies, of the teaching and curricula of training institutions and of the standard of the teaching certificate. The James Committee was set up by Margaret Thatcher in 1971 to look into these problems. Far from removing the issue of teacher education and training from the agenda, the Committee's report and the reactions to it gave the matter a higher priority and helped indirectly to lead to its position of prominence in the Callaghan debate.

The remit of the James Committee was wide-ranging, its recommendations novel and far-reaching.[22]

Dear Secretary of State,
You appointed this Committee with the following terms of reference:

'In the light of the review currently being undertaken by the Area Training Organisations, and of the evidence published by the Select Committee on Education and Science, to enquire into the present arrangements for the education, training and probation of teachers in England and Wales and in particular to examine:

(i) what should be the content and organisation of courses to be provided;
(ii) whether a larger proportion of intending teachers should be educated with students who have not chosen their careers or chosen other careers;
(iii) what, in the context of (i) and (ii) above, should be the role of the maintained and voluntary colleges of education, the polytechnics and other further education institutions maintained by local education authorities, and the universities and to make recommendations.'

Its recommendations, while not accepted in their entirety by educationists, highlighted areas of concern. One of these was the variety in the nature and length of teacher education and training. The starting point in tackling these issues was the proposal that 'given an appropriate educational base, the professional training of all teachers should be the same in length and structure, however different in its emphases and the details of content, and that pre-service higher education and professional training for all school teachers should extend over at least four years'. On the age-old debate over the relative merits of concurrent courses (where academic studies were undertaken alongside professional training) and consecutive courses (where professional training followed the successful completion of academic study), the James Committee came down largely in favour of the latter. It proposed a cyclical structure, the first cycle being courses of study for a higher education award/degree or its recommended Diploma in Higher Education, followed by the second cycle of professional training leading to a BA (Education) and thus an all-graduate profession, with the last cycle being career-long, in-service provision with a teacher entitlement equivalent to one term release for every seven years of service (eventually to be five) for approved in-service activities. This novel system was to be operated locally by new bodies (Regional Councils for Colleges and Departments of Education) in the place of Area Training Organisations and under the national supervision of the National Council for Teacher Education and Training.

These proposals were intended by the James Committee to meet the changing needs of a system which had developed considerably since the McNair Report of 1944 (see pp. 177–181 of this book). In particular, they aimed to give colleges of education a wider role, a wider clientele and a more secure position in the field of higher education. However, they should also be seen against a background of growing public concern about trainee teachers, training institutions and serving teachers which lasted well beyond the 1970s. The first cycle was intended to raise the academic standards of those entering training institutions and to avoid the confusion of objectives of some existing courses, especially the three-year Certificate of Education, which attempted to give, at one and the same time, an academic education and a professional training. The academic education was also given in isolation from the general body of students, something which was deemed to be disadvantageous and which the Dip.HE was designed to overcome. Professional training began with the second cycle, lasting two years, and aimed not at training in general but to prepare trainees for their first teaching post. To this end trainees would spend their first year largely in training institutions and their second mainly in school as salaried licensed teachers, with an induction programme designed by the licensed teacher and a specially appointed professional tutor and supported by the school and a local professional centre. The second cycle was thus aimed at improving the quality of teaching in training institutions through giving them a more limited focus and improving the quality of teaching in schools through giving trainees careful guidance and support under experienced, practising teachers. The 'sink or swim' attitude prevalent in the 1950s or 1960s was out of date in the increasingly complex world of teaching in the 1970s. The award of BA(Ed.) to all those who successfully completed these two years heralded the dawn of the era of the all-graduate profession. The third cycle, which of all the cycles met with the most general acclaim, was aimed at maintaining a high quality of teacher and teaching through in-service provision designed particularly to update teachers' knowledge and understanding of developments relevant to the full range of their duties.

The James Report was presented to the Education Secretary in December 1971 but its proposals, especially those relating to the second cycle, were too novel and controversial to gain full governmental approval. In its response, *Education: A Framework for*

Expansion, published a year later, the Conservative Government accepted six of the main objectives of the report:

1 a large and systematic expansion of in-service training;
2 a planned reinforcement of the process of induction;
3 the progressive achievement of an all-graduate profession;
4 the improvement of the training of teachers in Further Education;
5 the whole-hearted acceptance of the colleges of education into the family of higher education institutions;
6 improved arrangements for the control and coordination of teacher training and supply, both nationally and regionally.[23]

Significantly, the White Paper turned first to in-service training, and approved the James Committee's recommendations except for 'making express entitlement' to such training 'a matter of contract between a teacher and his employer' on the grounds of the 'practical difficulties' to which a contract might give rise.[24] Induction programmes for new teachers involving part-time release and a reduced teaching timetable were welcomed, provided that adequate financial support was possible, including cover by supply teachers. The idea of a new BA(Ed.) degree was rejected in favour of strong government support for a new three-year course incorporating educational studies leading both to a BEd. degree, validated by existing bodies, and to qualified status. The concept of the all-graduate profession was thus preserved and the view that there should be substantial supervised practical experience in the classroom was reaffirmed. Such courses did not rule out, but could incorporate, Diploma of Higher Education courses. Significantly for the eighties and nineties, reference was made to making special provision for mature students, including shortened courses. The Government backed the idea that one of the main providers of such courses, the colleges of education, would have to change their role, at least in part. Few would remain isolated training institutions, whereas

> . . . some colleges either singly or jointly should develop over the period into major institutions of higher education concentrating on the arts and human sciences, with particular reference to their application in teaching and other professions. Others will be encouraged to combine forces with neighbouring polytechnics or other colleges of further education to fill a somewhat similar role.
>
> Many of the 160 colleges are, however, comparatively small and inconveniently located for development into larger general purpose institutions. Some of these will continue to be needed exclusively for purposes of teaching education with increasing emphasis on in-service rather than initial training. Some may seek greater strength by reciprocal arrangements with the Open University on the lines of the experiment recently initiated. Others may find a place in the expansion of teachers' and professional centres. Some must face the possibility that in due course they will have to be converted to new purposes; some may need to close.[25]

The James Committee's idea of a common system came into being in

August 1975, ending the system that had resulted from the McNair Report thirty years earlier. This development also helped to shift the emphasis away from concurrent courses where academic subjects were studied during professional training to that backed by James of a consecutive arrangement in which professional training followed after and was separate from 'academic' study. By 1982 more students were accepted for consecutive than concurrent courses. The BEd. developed into an 'integrated' programme over three or four years, with informal divisions shifting the emphasis from academic to professional in the later years.

The inclusion of teacher education and training in the Great Debate signalled its importance to the Labour Government's educational agenda. In the wake of Callaghan's public expression of concern about the quality of teaching and declining standards of literacy and numeracy, it could scarcely be omitted. An obvious starting point of government intervention was the standard of literacy and numeracy of those entering the profession; hence, in August 1978 the Labour Education Secretary announced that 'O' level or its equivalent in English language and Mathematics would be required of all entrants from 1983. But Labour did not hold a monopoly of concern over this area; in that year the succeeding Conservative Government published its White Paper *Teacher Quality*, which emphasised its 'vital concern' with matters connected with teacher supply, initial training, appointments and career development. It laid down three basic requirements. In order to ensure that teachers had 'full subject knowledge' and thus avoid 'slavish adherence' to textbooks it recommended that the higher education and initial teacher training should include at least 'two full years' course time devoted to subject studies at a level appropriate to higher education. A second requirement was that initial training courses should give adequate attention to teaching methods across the ability range, with language work and Mathematics being given substantial attention in primary training courses. This second requirement was reinforced with a third, that relevance to classroom practice of such teaching methods should be reinforced by the students' practical experience in school, the involvement of practising teachers in training courses, and staff in training institutions engaging in classroom teaching on a regular basis. To improve the quality of entrants to training courses, it was recommended that practising teachers should be involved in their selection and that special consideration ought to be given to those people who had experience of areas outside education, such as industry and commerce.

Teacher Quality set the pattern for many developments in the 1980s and early 1990s. The criteria against which all courses were to be reviewed and the body which would employ them, the Council for the Accreditation of Teacher Education (CATE), were announced a year after the publication of the White Paper. Training institutions and their staffs were subject to close checks. CATE was unable to consider courses for accreditation until training institutions were visited (in the case of universities) or inspected (in the case of the public sector) by Her Majesty's Inspectorates (HMIs) and a report produced by them. The views of the local community – especially those of industry and commerce, local authorities and schools – were to be heard through the creation of a local committee for each institution. These local committees were involved in the early stages of the vetting procedure. Courses of initial teacher training were to be extended to 36 weeks and those who taught on them had to satisfy CATE that they had acquired recent and relevant teaching experience in schools. The overriding aim of the reforms was to make professional studies more practical, systematic and balanced with a closer partnership between training institutions, the community, LEAs and schools. Accreditation by CATE was obligatory for courses to remain in operation; any amendments to courses which CATE required had to be undertaken within a given period.

By the beginning of the 1990s all teacher training courses had been scrutinised by CATE. The Government did not take the completion of this process to mean that it could devolve responsibility for teacher training courses to the training institutions. It took the opportunity offered by the completion of the task to assert its faith in CATE, albeit in reconstituted form, and to reaffirm the Education Secretaries' responsibilities. The DES document outlining future arrangements for initial teacher training stated unambiguously that, 'The Secretaries of State believe that they should continue to exercise responsibility for approving courses of initial teacher training as part of their overall responsibility for the quality of education in maintained schools.'[26] The new decade was to begin with the imposition of a more precise set of criteria. Thus from 1990 local committees had a more clearly defined and greater role in the scrutinisation of courses, were to cover more than one institution and were to report annually to CATE. Teacher trainers were expected to return to the classroom for one term in every five years by 1992/93, and the National Curriculum which they would gain experience in teaching for the first time would provide a major focus for training courses. Thus teacher training entered the 1990s with a more clearly defined role, with more even quality and with trainers more in contact with the practical realities of the classroom. The moves towards a common system had been swifter than the members of the James Committee could ever have envisaged in 1972, and fell in with government thinking about the need for increased government involvement in all spheres of education.

The governments of the eighties were as anxious to exercise close control over the intake to the teacher profession as they were over the quality of initial training. One of the virtues for government of the short, consecutive training courses, such as the Postgraduate Certificate of Education (PGCE), was the greater speed with which intake could be adjusted to demographic change, financial constraints and other factors. While this may account in part for the continuing reluctance of governments to extend the PGCE course to two years, the priority given to controlling intake helped both to reduce the problem of unemployment among newly qualified teachers and to switch resources to shortage areas. In October 1977 5.7 per cent of those with university PGCEs were still seeking a post compared with 17 per cent in the public sector. In 1982, although many primary school teachers were unable to find a post, training institutions were asked to step up their intakes by 1986/87 to meet a predicted shortfall, though additional resources were by no means certain. The ability to direct resources to shortage areas, especially Modern Languages, Technology, Mathematics and Physics, was a major result of closer government control. This enabled, for example, students pursuing teacher training courses in Physics, Maths and Design/Technology to be given a higher grant to attract them to such courses. This measure introduced by the Conservative Education Secretary, Kenneth Baker, aroused little controversy although his more radical plans to attract what he termed 'the right number of teachers of quality' at a time when the number of young graduates was falling and the primary pupil numbers were rising were much more controversial.

To meet a range of problems associated with teacher supply in the 1990s, Baker advocated a three-fold plan of attack. The first two, retraining teachers and encouraging former teachers back into the profession, were well tried and tested strategies. The third, which he termed 'new and more flexible routes into teaching', aroused much controversy. These were the licensed teacher scheme for people over 26 who had completed successfully at least two years in higher education and the articled teacher scheme aimed at new graduates not wishing to undertake the one-year full-time PGCE. Both schemes involved school-based training with entrants earning a salary rather than receiving a much smaller student grant. With pilot schemes destined to begin in 1990 the first of the schemes was attacked by the teaching unions for undermining the concept of the all-graduate profession, and both schemes were seen as attempts to revive the era of raw recruits who, with little or no training, were expected to manage the intricacies of the National Curriculum. These schemes were, however, additional and not the sole means of attracting graduates and experienced people to the profession and had the merit of meeting the problems of young graduates with large overdrafts who wished mainly to train in the workplace as their peers in other professions were doing.

Thus, in the twenty years following the James Report, teacher training had changed more fundamentally than in the previous twenty years. It entered the 1990s with strong pressures to move more towards school-based training which had been the chief characteristic of the nineteenth-century system. The Government were well on the way to introducing a national curriculum in training institutions using CATE as the enforcing agency, when attention moved swiftly towards the idea of a school-based system. Alternative strategies included that of replacing the 'PGCE-plus probationary year model' with a two-year initial grade contract at a salary a little less than Main Grade with 50 per cent of the first and 85 per cent of the second year based in schools.

The issue of teacher training which was belatedly included in the 'Great Debate' became a key area of educational debate throughout the eighties and into the nineties. Increased government control of the curriculum and of the quality of training institutions was one of the major achievements of Conservative governments of the eighties. In particular, the advent of 'Baker days' to provide for in-service training and education was a welcome development which helped to regularise in-service provision.

HIGHER EDUCATION

I have been concerned to find that many of our best trained students who have completed the higher levels of education at university or polytechnic have no desire to join industry. Their preferences are to stay in academic life . . . or to find their way into the civil service. (Callaghan, 1976)

Except for teaching training and education, higher education did not figure prominently in either Callaghan's speech or the Great Debate. The narrow and restricting role which he ascribed to it, that of servicing the needs of British industry, stood in sharp contrast to the grandeur and breadth of the Robbins vision, born of the swinging sixties. Had R. H. Tawney, from whom Callaghan claimed 'to have derived a great deal of (his) thinking', still been alive[27] he would have raised the more searching question of 'Why, despite the massive expansion of higher education urged by the Robbins Report of 1963, did the pernicious and stubborn influence of social class still deny to the working classes adequate access to higher education?' In his view the British economy would never thrive while the university system failed to tap much of the nation's talent. For Tawney the major issue was not how to increase industrial recruitment but to ensure that 'our best trained students' were truly representative of the most able, irrespective of social class. This kind of question occupied Labour politicians less as the sober seventies gave way to the austere eighties. Those that concerned Labour and Conservative politicians most were contained in Callaghan's speech and were to do with increased accountability, managing change at a time of financial stringency and tying higher education more to the economic needs of the country.

The Robbins Report had recommended that 560,000 places should be provided in higher education by 1980/81 for some 17 per cent of the relevant population compared with 216,000, 8 per cent of the population, when the report was published. By 1979 Robbins was already in retreat; the White Paper of that year planned for 500,000 places in 1982/83, 14.5 per cent of the relevant population. The Robbins vision ended with the 1981 White Paper which avoided numerical estimates of places and gave warning of a 10 per cent cut in expenditure over the following two years. It concluded, 'This is likely to oblige institutions to review the range and nature of their contribution to higher education with increased competition for places, but the government expect institutions to admit, as they have done this year, as many students as they can, consistent with their academic judgement.' Oxford University was particularly anxious to stress that despite government cuts which meant fewer places overall, students from state schools still occupied nearly half such places and that it was still pursuing schemes to attract more candidates from comprehensive schools. Critics pointed out that the statistics of 49.7 per cent of the total (for 1982/83) disguised great differences between colleges, and that as the independent sector educated only around 18 per cent of the relevant population its share of about 50 per cent of the places still left it very much over-represented. For those who were concerned with the broader issue of working-class access to university education the statistics for the years 1982 to 1987 made disheartening reading (Table 1.4).[28]

The move towards replacing grants with loans also raised questions about its effects upon the social make-up of the student body. It was an issue which caused heated debate throughout the eighties, and especially when the Government White Paper on the subject was published in 1988 with the intention of the scheme being in place for the academic year, 1990/91.

Table 1.4 ***Social class of university entrants***

Social class	*Percentage of candidates*					
	1982	*1983*	*1984*	*1985*	*1986*	*1987*
Professional	21.7	21.1	19.5	18.5	18.2	18.2
Intermediate	47.8	47.3	47.3	47.4	47.6	47.1
Skilled non-manual	9.6	9.4	10.6	11.1	11.5	11.8
Skilled manual	13.9	14.0	14.1	14.0	13.8	14.1
Partly skilled	6.9	8.9	7.2	7.6	7.6	7.5
Unskilled	1.1	1.3	1.3	1.3	1.4	1.3

Substantial numbers of parents were said to be failing to make their contribution to the grant and a system of loans would give students a stake in their education. Fears were expressed that the resulting debts would discourage people from applying for university unless they were wealthy and that those who took on such debts would be looking for more vocationally oriented courses which could alter the whole nature of British university education. By the end of the decade universities were closer than ever to introducing private fees for tuition. As the Vice-Chancellor of Strathclyde University declared in 1989: 'The unthinkable is no longer the unthinkable; the climate has changed.'[29]

The Annual Conference of the Committee of Vice-Chancellors and Principals in that year were divided on the issue of whether they should raise extra funds by charging students tuition fees which were paid at the time by the government.

Certain institutions of higher education in the 1980s were increasingly forced to look elsewhere for finance. As early as 1967 the Labour Government decided on differential fees for home and overseas students and by 1975 there was growing support for the idea that overseas students should pay the full cost of their fees. In order to raise revenues, higher education institutions looked increasingly towards the overseas market so that, for example, by 1987 9 per cent of students attending universities were from overseas. Links were also strengthened with industry, even by those institutions that were geographically disadvantaged. The University College of North Wales, Bangor, for example, as distant as it was from major industry, developed the kind of initiatives which Callaghan favoured in 1976, in the fields of research contracts from major UK companies, commercially orientated units such as horticultural services, and science parks or their equivalent where industry and higher education met directly to discuss and provide for specific needs. These kinds of activity were shaping much of the future of universities by the 1990s. To combat the dwindling number of applications for Science undergraduate courses a suggestion was put forward by the British Association for the Advancement of Science on the verge of the nineties that British Science degree courses should be made less difficult to bring them in line with those in the United States and Europe. This could also involve extending courses at British universities and polytechnics by a further year, an idea to which the Universities Funding Council gave consideration. There was, however, a growing concern that such initiatives were changing the traditional nature of a university education and were also having an impact upon its traditional clientele, the 18–21 age group. The moves to replace grants with loans and to strengthen links with industry and commerce, coupled with the desire to compensate for what was expected to be a dip in the number of 18 year olds entering university, led institutions of higher education to consider taking in more mature-age students. Marketing became the name of the game in the 1980s. Even the newer universities of Sussex, York, East Anglia, Essex, Lancaster, Kent and Warwick – opened between 1961 and 1965 and dubbed the 'magnificent seven' because of their innovatory curricula – found that the pressures common to all universities were causing them to be less distinctive. The only independent university in Britain, the University College of Buckingham opened in 1976, found itself with problems in the eighties partly because of the closer ties with industry of the funded universities. They were competing in a market where their competitors had 'their capital free and their customers (were) heavily subsidised'. The Open University, also a child of the seventies, had, because of its clientele, shown an adeptness at marketing its

products. Set up to cater for mature students studying part-time without necessarily having formal qualifications, it was able to respond more quickly than many conventional universities to government policy.

It was unlikely that the Conservative Government's desire to open up universities to market forces would have left the conditions of service of staff untouched. In particular, the issue of academic tenure gained more prominence. Seen by some opponents as a pernicious device which gave lecturers a job for life and thereby protected lazy and incompetent lecturers from dismissal, and by others as a means to protect lecturers from the market forces, it was defended on the grounds that the academic freedom it bestowed was vital to research and teaching. Its abolition in 1986 for new appointees and the challenge to those who already held it in at least one test case was evidence of the new forces at work in higher education in the 1980s.

The polytechnics founded in the 1960s to meet the precise needs which Callaghan identified in his Ruskin College speech were by no means immune from the forces of change. The country's thirty polytechnics faced swingeing cuts in the early 1980s. They also found it difficult to meet fully the social and vocational aims which Anthony Crosland hoped would mark them out as a more relevant form of higher education. In particular, they found it difficult in the 1970s to fill all their places in Science and Technology and developed courses in non-technological subjects. This did not alter the fact that their centres of gravity were still firmly in professional and technological education. It thus appeared strange to them that the Conservative governments of the eighties – which, like Callaghan, were concerned with the regeneration of industry – should have cut their budgets so savagely.

ADULT EDUCATION

Among the adult colleges, Ruskin has a long and honourable history of close association with the trade union movement. (Callaghan, 1976)

Callaghan chose the occasion of a foundation-stone laying ceremony at Ruskin College, Oxford's adult residential college, to launch the national debate, yet neither he nor Shirley Williams included adult education in its agenda. This seemed to confirm adult education's traditional, peripheral position in the British education system. This omission is surprising for two other reasons. Firstly, Tawney, for whom Callaghan cherished a deep respect, had played a major role in raising the status of adult education within the Labour movement, particularly through his pioneering university tutorial classes for the Workers Educational Association, and later as its president. Secondly, and of more immediate relevance, was the fact that the Labour Government had, in 1969, given a higher public profile to adult education through its appointment of the Russell Committee to engage in a wide-ranging review of adult education. Its terms of reference (see pp. 181–182) were

... to assess the need for and to review the provision of non-vocational adult education in England and Wales; to consider the appropriateness of existing educational, administrative and financial policies, and to make recommendations with a view to obtaining the most effective and economical deployment of available resources to enable adult education to make its proper contribution to the national system of education conceived of as a process continuing through life.

While the emphasis on 'non-vocational' would seem to be out of keeping with the central message of Callaghan's speech, the Committee's sensible definition of the term, in fact, made its report of immediate relevance to the Prime Minister's chief concern, the needs of industry. What made a course of study vocational or not, the Russell Report declared, was nothing inherent in it but the student's motive for taking it; 'if he takes it to qualify for a job it is vocational; if he takes it for the pure love of learning it is not, whatever the subject'. Thus courses concerned with industrial relations for both employers and employees came within the orbit of its enquiry. Of equal importance to the economic health of the nation, however, was the satisfaction of 'non-vocational' needs. Improving technical education alone would not lead to national well-being. These and other points made in the report had not made sufficient impact by 1976 to warrant the inclusion of adult education in the national debate.

However, the Russell Report had an impact in other ways. At the same time as the Callaghan Government was preparing the Ruskin College speech it was negotiating with such bodies as the Workers' Educational Association (WEA) to rescue them from the financial crisis caused by cuts in national expenditure and inflation. The price of financial help was the commitment to a decisive shift away from liberal studies to what had become known as 'Russell-type work'; that is, the three priority or 'special aspect' areas of industrial studies, social and political education and work with the disadvantaged. As in other areas of education, and despite Russell's broad definition of 'vocational', there was some concern about developing these special areas at the expense of the traditional, liberal and academic studies. Yet these were never mutually exclusive in the 1980s, with some stress upon access courses to higher education as well as classes in basic literacy and numeracy which combined easily with the more 'vocational' courses.

THE GENERIC ISSUES

The preceding survey has identified many of the central issues in the contemporary debate and has provided some of their immediate historical context to encourage an informed discussion of those issues. It has also served another purpose. By reference to the views of R. H. Tawney who belonged to an earlier generation of politicians than Callaghan's, it aimed to show that these issues have long preoccupied educationists in a variety of forms. We can thus identify a series of basic or generic issues which have been at the forefront of education during this century and earlier. Before examining the historical evolution of these generic issues, which is the aim of the following chapters, it would be helpful for discussion to summarise what they are. The order in which they appear is that in which they have appeared in the preceding sections. Clearly, in discussion they may well be grouped differently.

Generic issues: a checklist

1. Central government and the curriculum:
   - the relative powers of central government, local education authorities and teachers in relation to the school curriculum.
2. Schools and the basic skills of literacy and numeracy:
   - literacy/numeracy and the primary/secondary school curricula
   - educating for employment
   - education and industry.
3. Progressive education:
   - the definition of progressive education
   - research conclusions and progressive education
   - the 3Rs and progressive education.
4. Industry and education:
   - education and Britain's industrial decline
   - curricular links between industry/commerce and education
   - representation of industry/commerce on governing bodies
   - industrial placements
   - examination reform and practical skills
   - teacher training and industry
   - specialist provision (e.g. City Technology Colleges).
5. Public examinations:
   - the need for publication examinations
   - common examinations at 16+
   - broadening the sixth-form curriculum.
6. The education systems:
   - the independent sector
   - change within the comprehensive school and without
   - assisted places
   - grant-maintained schools
   - the impact of parental choice on the nation's schools
   - sixth forms, sixth-form colleges, tertiary education.
7. Teacher accountability and parental rights:
   - the reform of governing bodies
   - parental involvement in the classroom
   - accountability and adequate resourcing
   - consumer choice
   - educational vouchers
   - the National Curriculum and parental choice.

8. Monitoring the use of resources:
   - the need for monitoring
   - the methods of monitoring
   - marketplace economics applied to schools
   - the outcomes of monitoring.
9. Teacher education and training:
   - the all-graduate profession
   - concurrent and consecutive kinds of training
   - school-based and college-based training: balance and organisation
   - in-service education and training
   - teacher sabbaticals
   - government control of teacher training
   - attracting teachers from industry and commerce
   - licensed teachers
   - areas of teacher shortage
   - teacher numbers and class size
   - the qualifications and experience of university/college lecturers on training courses
   - 'Baker days'.
10. Higher education:
    - the aims of a polytechnic and university education
    - attracting graduates into industry
    - social class and access to higher education
    - alternative sources of finance
    - student grants or loans
    - the Open University: entry without qualifications
    - academic tenure.
11. Adult education:
    - the aims of adult education
    - the priority which should be given to non-vocational courses.

QUESTIONS

The preceding summary of contemporary issues in education provides a basis for the more precise formulation of questions to meet the needs and particularly the perspectives of individual discussion groups. The author does not intend to formulate such questions at this stage but believes that they will arise naturally from the summary. However, it would be helpful for the maximum utilisation of the following chapters if such questions fell into two categories; firstly, those illustrating the more recent forms that such issues have been taking, and, secondly, those seeking to elucidate the essential nature of the educational debate about these issues. The updating tasks will help to ensure that participants make full use of the historical context of Part One of this book; the generic tasks will encourage selective reference at an early stage to Part Two.

NOTES AND REFERENCES

1. *The Times Educational Supplement*, 22 October 1976, p. 1.
2. See B. Donoughue, 1987, *Prime Minister: The Conduct of Policy under Harold Wilson and James Callaghan 1974–1979*, Jonathan Cape.
3. In the parliamentary debate over the Crowther Report in March 1960. See p. 63 of Chapter 2 for a fuller discussion.
4. See pp. 52–59 for the historical details.
5. See p. 101 for a fuller discussion.
6. Speech to North of England Education Conference, *The Times Educational Supplement*, 1 April 1980.
7. The 1980 Education Act, Sections 1–4.
8. C. B. Cox and A. E. Dyson, 1971, *The Black Papers in Education*, Davis-Poynter.
9. *Mathematics Counts*, 1982, HMSO, p. lx
10. Ibid., p. 25.
11. *The Times Educational Supplement*, 7 October 1988.
12. *The Times Educational Supplement*, 7 December 1984.
13. Black Papers, p. 26.
14. Quoted in The Open University's *The William Tyndale File* (Course E200, sections 12–15), 1981.
15. N. Bennett, 1976, *Teaching Styles and Pupil Progress*, Harvard University Press.
16. *Report of the Consultative Committee on The Primary School* (1931), HMSO, p. 75.
17. W. S. Fowler, 1988, *Towards the National Curriculum*, Kogan Page, p. 60.
18. Black Papers, p. 21.
19. *The Times Educational Supplement*, 8 January 1988.
20. *The Times Educational Supplement*, 29 July 1988.
21. See paragraphs 4 and 4.11 of the conference paper *Educating our Children*.
22. *Teacher Education and Training* 1972, HMSO, p. 111.
23. *Education: A Framework for Expansion* (December 1972), HMSO, p. 16.
24. Ibid., p. 18.
25. Ibid., p. 44.
26. Future arrangements for the accreditation of courses of initial teaching training: A Consultation Document (May 1988), DES.
27. He died in 1962.
28. UCCA Statistical Supplement to the 22nd and 24th Reports, 1983/84 and 1986/87 (published by UCCA).
29. Reported in *The Times*, 28 September 1989.

PART TWO

Generic Issues in Education

CHAPTER 2

The debate over the curriculum, 1839–1976

The principal theme of this book is that current debates in education can only be fully understood in the light of their historical development. Nowhere is this more true than in the case of the continuing debate over the curriculum. An understanding of the principal features of the development of the curricular debate is of more than incidental value. The concepts used in the current debate are historical in the sense of being given their meaning during the evolution of our education system. They carry with them certain values which are derived from either the recent or the more distant past. This applies no less to the term 'national curriculum' than it does to the principal ideas about the curriculum.

LEADING FROM THE CENTRE: INNOVATION OR TRADITION?

... its (the national curriculum's) purpose is educational ... it is not concerned with the distribution of power. (Kenneth Baker,. January 1988)[1]

The development and implementation over the last decade of a government-directed curriculum for state schools, sometimes mistakenly called a national curriculum, appear to many educationists and politicians to run contrary to over fifty years of educational practice. Despite Kenneth Baker's assertion that his Education Act of 1988, and in particular its clauses concerning the state curriculum, were concerned with educational not political aims, few educationists believed that the new order in education had not brought with it a radical shift in the relationships between teachers, local education authorities and central government. That relationships had changed, and changed dramatically, was particularly evident to teachers and administrators who had come into education under the regime established by the 1944 Education Act. The debate which was intensified by the 1988 Education Act was not centred on the issue of whether the Education Secretary was acting beyond his powers in establishing a state curriculum; the Act had bestowed such powers upon him; the debate was focused upon the issue of whether or not he was stepping outside the traditional role of education secretaries and their predecessors, ministers of education and presidents of the Board of Education. The question really revolves around the meaning of the term 'traditional' role. Viewed from the mid-twentieth century, his position and powers seemed to have been radically transformed under the 1988 Education Act; seen from an earlier perspective, that of the first decades of the twentieth century, Baker appears to have embarked on the restoration of ministerial powers, largely abandoned in the 1920s, rather than upon an unprecedented aggrandisement of central power. Whether or not educational secretaries of the late 1980s and 1990s are seen as acting beyond their historical role depends then upon how far back in the history of the nation's schools one goes–to 1944, by which time it was recognised that the curriculum was not directly in the hands of the Minister, or to the years before 1926 when it was.

THE FIRST NATIONAL CURRICULA AND THEIR EVOLUTION, 1839–1926

The first national curricula operated within a very different education context from that of today. The fact that there were two national curricula, not one, which covered pupils often of the same age group, indicates that education was organised on very different lines. These differences are perhaps most quickly appreciated by reference to the diagram on page 109[2]. As with the current National Curriculum, independent schools were not obliged to follow its stipulations, but those sectors of education under state control were. During the years when the first national curricula were in operation there were two distinct sectors requiring two different sets of regulations. These were secondary and elementary education. Unlike the present education system which is organised as separate stages (primary, secondary, etc.) in a continuous process, education up to the 1944 Education Act was organised on parallel lines. The vast majority went to elementary schools; a small privileged minority went to secondary and other schools. Despite these substantial differences in the educational contexts, it is instructive to look at the evolution and content of the first national curricula.

That which covered elementary schools dated from 1839 when the government first expressed an interest in the kind of elementary education that it had subsidised since the first state grant to education in 1833. In a concern to have value for its money. the Whig Government of the day set up a Committee of the Privy Council to lay down the guidelines for elementary education and to supervise their implementation. The first state curriculum to emerge from this body was defined in terms akin to the areas-of-experience model. It stipulated that

Four principal objects should be kept in view, viz.

1. Religious Instruction.
2. General Instruction.
3. Moral Training.
4. Habits of Industry.[3]

A quarter of a century later these regulations were redefined using a subject-based curriculum model. In 1862, a revised set of regulations introduced the payments-by-results system. Such a system made teachers directly accountable to their employers and was intended to make maximum use of resources. As its architect, Robert Lowe, reported to the House of Commons in 1863:

I cannot promise the House that this system will be an economical one and I cannot promise that it will be an efficient one, but I can promise that it shall be one or the other. If it is not cheap it shall be efficient; if it is not efficient it shall be cheap.[4]

A closely detailed, subject-based model was introduced to ensure that the Government's wishes were meticulously carried out, with teachers' pay in part being geared to the number of pupils who were successful in passing a carefully supervised set examination. A brief extract from the Revised Code of 1862[5] illustrates the closeness with which classroom activity was regulated.

... Every scholar for whom grants are claimed must be examined according to one of the following standards:

	Standard I	*Standard II*	*Standard III*
Reading	Narrative in monosyllables.	One of the narratives next in order after monosyllables in an elementary reading book used in the school.	A short paragraph from an elementary reading book used in the school.
Writing	Form on black-board or slate, from dictation, letters, capital and small manuscript.	Copy in manu-script character a line of print.	A sentence from the same paragraph, slowly read once, and then dictated in single words.
Arithmetic	Form on black-board or slate, from dictation, figures up to 20; name at sight figures up to 20; add and subtract figures up to 10, orally, from examples on black-board.	A sum in simple addition or sub-traction, and the multiplication table.	A sum in any simple rule as far as short division (inclusive).

But the regulations did not become tablets of stone. By the 1920s this first national curriculum had become much broader in terms of the subjects included and the kinds of teaching approaches and objectives covered. The subject-based model was maintained for older children but the strictly utilitarian skills-based approach of the 1862 Revised Code was rejected. Subjects for older children were defined in terms of attainment targets which bear comparison with those of today's National Curriculum. Attainment targets for younger children related to areas of experience rather than to single subjects. The latter were covered in five brief paragraphs[6] which contrast sharply with the rigidly prescriptive detail of their equivalent 'standards' in the 1862 regulations.

ELEMENTARY EDUCATION CODE, 1922

Younger Children

1. The principal aim of the School in relation to younger children should be to provide opportunities for the free development of their bodies and minds, and for the formation of habits of obedience and attention.
   (a) Physical exercises should take the form of games involving free movement, singing and breathing exercises, rather than of set drill.
   (b) The younger infants should be encouraged to employ their eyes, hands, and fingers in suitable free occupations, and the teacher, by talking with the children, by encouraging them to talk to her and to ask questions, and by telling stories to them, should lead them to form ideas, and to express them in simple language of their own.
   (c) For the older infants the above exercises should be supplemented by short lessons, in which the children are trained to listen carefully, to speak clearly, to recite easy pieces, to reproduce simple stories and narratives, to cultivate their powers of observation, to do simple things with their hands, to begin to draw, to begin to read and write, to acquire an elementary knowledge of number, to practise suitable songs, and to sing simple musical intervals.
   (d) Instruction in sewing and knitting may be given to the older infants, but care must be taken to avoid fine work and injury to eyesight.

The subject-based curriculum for 'older children' sought to do two things. It attempted to distinguish elementary education from secondary education without giving it a vocational bias. To achieve this goal it defined the eleven-subject curriculum largely in terms of practical skills. The subjects listed were: English Language; Handwriting; Arithmetic; Drawing; Practical Instruction in Handicraft, Gardening, Domestic and other subjects; Observation Lessons and Nature Study; Geography; History; Singing; Hygiene and Physical Training; and Moral Instruction. To assist further comparison between the first mass curriculum for pupils up to the age of 14 and the current National Curriculum, it would be worth while to look at the detail in which some of these subjects were presented. Today's core subjects, English and Mathematics, were presented as follows:

The English Language, including practice in speaking with clear enunciation, exercises in continuous oral narration, reading for information both silently and aloud, and written composition. Throughout the course the reading books used by the children should include pieces of literary merit, some of which should be learned for recitation. In the higher classes silent reading should be the rule rather than the exception, and the scheme of instruction should include a wide course of reading under suitable guidance, with the aim of creating a capacity for systematic study and a taste for good literature. Instruction in grammar should be confined to the higher classes. If given, it should be directed to enabling the children to understand the structure of the sentences which they speak, read, or write, and the functions of the several words in those sentences, and should be as free as possible from technicalities.

Arithmetic, including practical work in measuring and weighing, oral exercises, written exercises (which should be of a varied character, and should not infrequently involve the application of more than one arithmetical operation) and, in the higher classes, practice in explaining the processes used. The principles and advantages of a decimal system of weights and measures should be explained to the older children; and the use of literal symbols in working simple problems may with advantage be taught in the higher classes.

Practical instruction should be given in mensuration, and should include drawing to scale; the older boys should learn the use of compasses and protractor; and such practical instruction should be correlated as far as possible with handwork.

Today's foundation subjects, Geography and History, were defined more in terms of content than skill.

Geography, based upon elementary notions acquired through observation lessons, nature study, and descriptive lessons, and leading to a general knowledge of the Earth and its peoples, and a more detailed knowledge of the British Isles and the British Dominions beyond the seas. Where possible, the geography of the chief foreign countries should also be taught in some detail. The children should learn to use good maps, to make their own simple sketch maps, and in the higher classes to draw maps to scale.

History, which should include, in the lower classes, the lives of great men and women and the lessons to be learnt therefrom, and in the higher classes a knowledge of the great persons and events of English History and of the great persons and events of English History and of the growth of the British Empire. The teaching need not be limited to English or British History, and lessons on citizenship may be given with advantage in the higher classes.

Science was not classed as a separate subject in the elementary curriculum, although it was in the secondary curriculum. Moral instruction was carefully, defined as follows:

Moral Instruction should form an important part of the curriculum of every elementary school. Such instruction may either (i) be incidental, occasional, and given as fitting opportunity arises in the ordinary routine of lessons, or (ii) be given systematically and as a course of graduated instruction.

The instruction should be specially directed to the inculcation of courage; truthfulness; cleanliness of mind, body, speech; the love of fair-play; consideration and respect for others; gentleness to the weaker; kindness to animals; self-control and temperance; self-denial; love of one's country; and appreciation of beauty in nature and in art.

The task of the Board of Education's inspectors was that of scrutinising a school's syllabus and checking teacher's lesson notes rather than, as earlier, to supervise tests. The emphasis was not so much upon assessment as upon the delineation of subjects. 'Every Time Table must be hung conspicuously in the school, and must bear upon it the Inspector's signature'. Parental rights were restricted to being able to read this document 'at any reasonable time *outside* the ordinary school hours'. The main purpose of these regulations was to maintain the elementary character of a type of education designed largely for working-class children and to distinguish it from secondary education which was the privileged province of children largely from the middle classes.

The national curriculum for secondary school children was also defined in subject terms.[7]

> ... The Course should provide for instruction in the English Language and Literature, at least one Language other than English, Geography, History, Mathematics, Science and Drawing, with due provision for Manual Work and Physical Exercises, and, in a girls' school for Housewifery. Not less than 4½ hours per week must be allotted to English, Geography and History; not less than 3½ hours to the Language where only one is taken or less than 6 hours where two are taken; and not less than 7½ hours to Science and Mathematics, of which at least 3 must be for Science. The instruction in Science must be both theoretical and practical. When two Languages other than English are taken, and Latin is not one of them, the Board will require to be satisfied that the omission of Latin is for the advantage of the school.

These regulations laid down in 1904 by Robert Morant sought to ensure that the new secondary schools created under the 1902 Education Act adopted the traditional grammar and public school model. Created for the small minority of the nation's children who attended secondary schools, they deliberately avoided a broader academic or vocational curriculum. The detailed prescription of hours was dropped in 1907 but the secondary regulations remained in place until the introduction of free secondary education for all with the 1944 Education Act. The traditional grammar school curriculum was not deemed a suitable model for all the types of secondary school that came into existence after the Second World War, so the 1904 regulations were dropped.

THE ABANDONMENT OF THE COMPULSORY CURRICULUM FOR ELEMENTARY SCHOOLS, 1926.

The compulsory curriculum for the mass of the nation's children was abandoned without fanfare of trumpets in 1926. For the first time since the state became involved in elementary education nearly a century earlier, teachers in elementary schools were given a large measure of autonomy over what was taught, provided that, according to the 1926 regulations, they accepted that 'courses of education and training must be in accordance with a suitable curriculum'. Not only did the Conservative Government of the day avoid giving publicity to this change of policy, even the educational press, including *The Times Educational Supplement*, failed to notice this important development. The *Morning Post* of 22 May 1926 stood alone in its recognition of 'A very remarkable omission of curricula. The Board is wisely leaving the framing of the course of instruction in the elementary schools to the Local Authorities and to the teachers.'[8]

The way in which the first national curriculum came to an end is important to the debate about the current National Curriculum. The fact that the change came about by a simple omission rather than by a well-publicised announcement by Eustace Percy, the then President of the Board of Education, enabled the myth to develop that the teaching profession had highjacked the curriculum and then proceeded to turn it into what a later Minister of Education called 'a secret garden' (pp. 63–64). In fact, it was not a case of the teachers in the twenties seizing the curriculum but of the government quietly relinquishing control of it. *The Times Education Supplement* might not have noted 'the omission of the curricula' in 1926, but at the time of the Callaghan speech it exposed the myth that its abandonment was the direct result of teacher action.[9]

> But there is no reason why the professionals should accept the myth that they stole the curriculum; in truth the teachers were left carrying the can for the public curriculum because the politicians and public were only too happy to turn it over to them.

Why the government relinquished its control over the curriculum is as important to the current debate as the manner in which the first national curriculum came to an end. To some extent it was a natural progression. Elementary school teachers had been allowed to treat the listed subjects as they thought fit within, of course, the letter of the law; they could even depart from the set syllabus, although any 'considerable departure' had to have the approval of the Board of Education. They were thus not subject to the detailed lesson by lesson, hour by hour, control prevalent in some continental countries. With the growing power and professional organisation of teachers it seemed a natural progression for government to hand over the curriculum.[10] But their esteem was not that high with government that this was likely to occur without other reasons for such a changed in policy. One possible explanation was the high cost of maintaining a national curriculum. An insufficiently funded, centrally controlled curriculum could well have provided opposition parties with ammunition to attack the government at election time, and so give education a higher position on the election agenda than the government would have wished. An under-funded national curriculum was an electoral liability. C. P. Trevelyan, Percy's Labour predecessor at the Board of Education, spoke out in the Commons in July 1926 against the general revision of regulations, especially concerning building and staffing standards. He argued that the omission of reference to such standards removed the obligation to maintain minimum standards. This, he claimed, arose from the government's desire to save money. To consider reducing funding to a level below which minimum standards could be maintained was to provide the Labour opposition with valuable electoral propaganda. To remove central control over standards, possibly including the school curriculum, was a tempting move, especially in times that demanded financial stringency. Furthermore, with the attention of the educational world focused on the Hadow enquiry into *The Education of the Adolescent*, this move could be undertaken without attracting a great deal of attention. As R. H. Tawney commented at the time, changes in government policy were no longer heralded with a fanfare of trumpets but were hidden away in government circulars.[11] Furthermore, the retreat from a national curriculum was not total. The Code of 1926 continued to specify the need for schools to teach 'Practical Instruction'. The distinction between the practical nature of the elementary school curriculum and the liberal nature of the secondary school curriculum could be preserved, while freeing government from the cost necessary to ensure minimum standards in a range of subjects. The class basis of the curriculum of each type of school remained inviolate, while any excessive expenditure on elementary education was avoided; two basic tenets of Conservative education policy were thus observed.

A further reason for the Conservative Government's abandonment of the compulsory curriculum in 1926 was advanced by John White in the Doris Lee Lectures in 1975. This reason is worth considering because it surfaced again in a slightly different form during the debate over the 1988 Education Act. The compulsory curriculum was (and is) important as much for what it excluded as for what it included. In the 1980s the Conservative governments were concerned about what they saw as the introduction into schools of left-wing studies such as peace studies. The National Curriculum was seen in part by education secretaries in the 1980s as an instrument for excluding what the government believed to be undesirable subjects from the classroom. The counter argument put forward during the 1988 debate was that a national curriculum under a government of a different hue could be used for entirely different purposes, even for the introduction of those areas of study of which the existing government disapproved. Political control of the curriculum was thus a double-edged weapon. This is precisely the argument that White puts forward for Percy's ending of the compulsory curriculum in 1926. White argues that Percy perceived the Labour Party and its newly devised educational policies as a threat. With secondary education for all inscribed on Labour's banner, and Tawney's strong liking for a liberal education, Percy, White alleges, could well have feared that a compulsory curriculum could be used to deliver to working-class children that kind of liberal education hitherto reserved for the children of the middle classes. Though Tawney actually believed in curricular diversity at this time – that kind of diversity advocated by the Hadow Committee of which he was a prominent member (see pp. 116–117) – the threat was nevertheless regarded by Percy as sufficiently real to merit the destruction of the vehicle, the National Curriculum, which could make it possible. Though Labour could resurrect the National Curriculum when in office, at least the Conservatives would not make it easy for them by keeping it in existence. White goes on to argue that while freeing the curriculum from parliamentary control, Percy strengthened more indirect methods of controlling the curriculum.

If Percy had any doubts about the wisdom of ending the compulsory curriculum, they were likely to have been removed by the kind of threat to the established order embodied in a resolution put forward at the Labour Party's Margate Conference in 1927.[12]

That this Conference, convinced that a unified non-class system of Education is impossible till Education is democratically self-governed and controlled, and convinced that recent publications by the Labour Party and Trades Union Congress insufficiently recognise this and fail to go far enough to prepare for the reorganisation of Education in conformity with Workers' Control in all industry, instructs the National Executive Committee to set up, in order to determine the part Education must play in abolishing the present and creating a new Order of Society, a competent Workers' Committee of Inquiry on the following lines:

(a) To prepare a definite scheme of self-government, with democratic control of administration.
(b) To prepare recommendations on the best methods of teaching and of securing true discipline in schools.
(c) To prepare a report as to how far the present books, pictures and other materials used in schools, and the predominant methods of teaching and disciplining children, foster a bourgeois psychology, militarism and imperialism; and as to how far, under a workers' administration, this attitude towards, and outlook on life might be cultivated.

While the above resolution is extreme in tone and content, it serves to illustrate the uses to which a national curriculum can be put.

In 1926 the government relinquished direct control over the curriculum followed by the majority of the nation's children, inaugurating an era in which teachers had much say in what was taught. The curriculum was said, with more than a little exaggeration, to have become 'a secret garden' thereafter.

THE ERA OF 'THE SECRET GARDEN', 1926–88

Very few people can now remember the era of the first compulsory curriculum. Those who serve the education system today have been educated and gained their professional experience under a different regime, one in which central government rarely, if ever, intervened directly in the curriculum. The tradition that the curriculum was a matter for the professionals and not for the politicians was so quickly established after the government's retreat in 1926 that it has come to be regarded as the natural and only British tradition. This was due in no small measure to the activities of eminent educationists who immediately stepped into the vacuum left by the government's departure to assert teachers' rights. Support for the teaching profession came from an unexpected quarter, the Board of Education's own Consultative Committee on Education. Even prior to the government's departure from the field, this prestigious advisory body had gained the right in 1923 of deciding its own areas of investigation. What began in 1924 as a rather mundane investigation into post-elementary education emerged in 1926 as a major statement on structural and curricular reform. This was quickly followed up by far-reaching proposals about the curriculum of the primary school (1931) and the nursery and infant school (1933) (see pp. 70–71). The teaching profession was fortunate to have such outspoken defenders of its rights as R. H. Tawney, Ernest Barker, Miss E. R. Conway of the NUT, Lynda Grier and Emmeline Tanner. Above all, Percy Nunn,[13] who had established himself by 1926 as a respected authority on curricular matters, was an ardent defender of teachers' rights and was listened to by government in a way in which few educationists are today. Although Eustace Percy, the President of the Board of Education from 1924 to 1929, held different views about the school curriculum, and especially about the place of technical education within it[14], he did not attempt to intervene to impose his views in the face of certain opposition of Nunn, a convinced supporter of the liberal tradition. Had Percy translated his views about technical education into practical proposals and restored government control over the curriculum to impose them, he would have predated the Thatcher TVEI by half a century. With such a group of eminent advocates of the liberal tradition waiting in the wings when the government let fall the national curriculum, such a restoration would have been extremely difficult. The curriculum remained firmly in the hands of local education authorities and teachers. The tradition of curricular autonomy and government consultation continued in the war years. The Norwood Committee which reported to Butler, the last President of the Board of Education, in 1943 wished to strengthen teachers' control of the secondary school curriculum by the radical step of giving the profession control over the School Certificate Examination (see pp. 96–99). It declared that

> in the interests of the individual child and of the increased freedom and responsibility of the teaching profession, change in the School Certificate examination should be in the direction of making the examination entirely internal, that is to say, conducted by the teachers at the school on syllabuses and papers framed by themselves.

But Butler steered clear of curricular matters, except for the matter of religious instruction, during the Second World War. The following extract from a letter from R. A. Butler to the author[15] shows his willingness to consult with the Labour party on major matters of educational policy.

THE MASTER'S LODGE,
TRINITY COLLEGE,
CAMBRIDGE, CB2 1TQ.
TELEPHONE 58201

Our Ref: G/3 29 November 1973

Dear Mr Brooks

In reply to your letter, R.H. Tawney did not actually work with me in the sense that we shared an office but I had several talks with him about the Education Bill in which he stressed the importance of free secondary education for all.

I naturally respected his views because it would have been impossible to get the Bill through Parliament without the respect of prominent Labour men such as ~~Aneurin~~ Bevan, and to get Tawney's assistance was a tremendous help. I do not think he went into more detail beyond that which I have described, but perhaps this will help you.

J.R. Brooks Esq.

* Butler deleted Aneurin and altered Bevan to Bevin

However, Butler's Education Bill, which came before Parliament in 1944, left the door open for the possible restoration of government control of the curriculum. It declared the duty of the Minister of Education to be 'to promote the education of the people of England and Wales and the progressive development of institutions devoted to that purpose and the secure the effective execution by local authorities, under his control and direction, of the national policy'. This definition was clearly open to a centralist interpretation, a fear of which lay behind the following objection raised by a Member of Parliament while Butler's Bill was under discussion in the House of Commons in February 1944.[16]

EDUCATION BILL
8 February 1944

CLAUSE 1. Appointment of Minister in charge of education.
Sir Joseph Lamb (Stone): I beg to move, in page 1, line 12, to leave out, 'under his control and direction.' ... there is a principle involved here which I want to discuss. Most people will be aware that there is a widespread feeling of apprehension among the public that those powers which have been granted to various Departments during the war, for war purposes, may be retained after the war. That would be very undemocratic. We wish to be assured that behind this Bill there is no intention to start a new procedure which many of us would have to resist very strongly. The words which I propose to leave out specify that the local education authorities shall be under the control and direction of the Minister.

Lamb's concern that any extension of the Minister's powers would upset the partnership that had grown up in education was shared by several Members of Parliament. It could have led to the restoration of government control over the curriculum. Butler, however, was anxious to allay fears that his Bill signalled a change in direction and stressed the importance of maintaining 'the spirit of partnership'.

The President of the Board of Education (Mr Butler)
... I have welcomed the attitude shown by many Members that it is desirable, now that we have the great opportunity, that there should be the necessary powers to see that a national policy for education is carried out. I, for one, am not at all ashamed of these words, to which the Government attach particular store. First, I can reassure the Hon. Members who have taken this point of view, that we do believe, to use the words of Gladstone, that 'Here indeed exists the true excellence of English government, with all the parts of it affirming a mutual check upon each other'. While I should expect the administration of an area to be under the administration of the local authorities, I would expect them to have control in their area, just as I should expect them to work with me. The whole success of this Measure depends upon the completion of the scheme of reorganisation. Without reorganisation, you cannot have a proper form of free secondary education for all. I do propose that the central authority shall lead boldly, and not follow timidly, and that in no sense shall we take away the spirit of partnership which we desire from the local authorities.

The importance of the last paragraph, with its emphasis upon leading boldly from the centre, was not lost on Lord Roche when the debate reached the House of Lords. He was particularly anxious to maintain the tradition of bodies such as the Board's Consultative Committee being largely responsible for matters relating to the curriculum; that is, for leaving the school curriculum to the 'experts'.

[Lord Roche]

The Bill itself is a piece of machinery and administrative order, and naturally it does not go into contents of education. The Councils are obviously intended to do that. The curriculum is one most important matter; everything depends on what the children are taught. A second matter of which they will no doubt take cognizance – there may be others – is how the children shall be taught. These are matters for experts. Many of us may be able to deal with the practical matters of administration, but these educational questions are undoubtedly matters for experts.

Lord Roche believed that matters relating to the curriculum were best resolved by bodies or 'Councils' of educationists set up by government. Such bodies consisting of experts with a variety of beliefs would then help formulate policy, if necessary. Though Butler favoured curricular reform by administration rather than by legislation, he nevertheless left the door open for the latter at some possible future date by maintaining a discrete and ambiguous silence about the particular powers of Ministers. But in the years immediately following the Second World War few doubted that the curriculum was a matter for local authorities and teachers, not for central government.

The 1944 Education Act heralded a new era in education with ministerial attention focusing particularly upon the structural forms which secondary education for all would take. The creation of new secondary modern and grammar schools became the major preoccupation of government in the immediate post-war years. What was to be taught in these and other schools was not given a major priority by government, thus encouraging the belief that Percy's retreat from the compulsory curriculum in 1926 was not an aberration but a permanent feature of government policy. Furthermore, the broader educational debates of the 1950s and 1960s were concerned more with the common school than with the common curriculum. There seemed little reason for government to involve itself directly in matters relating to the curriculum. It is important to note, however, that even when the comprehensive school occupied the centre stage of educational debate in the early 1960s, David Eccles, the Conservative Minister of Education, was reasserting government interest in the curriculum. Although the immediate occasion was the debate on the chapter of the Crowther Report concerned with the sixth form, nevertheless his speech had a wider significance. It was a skilfully worded speech stating that the curriculum was not a no-go area for government – it was not a 'secret garden' – and hinting that it was the teaching profession which had turned it into such. As this speech was to begin a gradual shift in the Government's attitude towards the school curriculum it is worth looking at it more closely.[17]

21 March 1960
Education (Report of the Central Advisory Council)

Sir D. Eccles.
I turn to the chapter in the Report on the sixth form. I regret that so many of our education debates have had to be devoted almost entirely to bricks and mortar and to the organisation of the system. We hardly ever discuss what is taught to the 7 million boys and girls in the maintained schools. We treat the curriculum as though it were a subject, like the other place, about which it is 'not done' for us to make remarks. I should like the House to say that this reticence has been overdone. Of course, Parliament would never attempt to dictate the curriculum, but, from time to time, we could with advantage express views on what is taught in schools and in training colleges . . . the section in the Report on the sixth form is an irresistible invitation for a sally into the secret garden of the curriculum.

In the same field of sixth-form work, the Secondary School Examinations Council is studying the arrangements for examinations at the advanced level of GCE. On this I must, again, sound a note of warning. The value of a reform of GCE can be fully realised only if the universities and their faculties shape their entrance requirements so that the schools are given the best chance to broaden the curriculum, while maintaining adequate specialisation.

Although the main area of attention was the sixth-form curriculum – particularly, what was seen to be its overspecialised nature – the speech was couched in broad terms which left the gate of the 'secret garden' open for possible entry by future governments. In reality, however, education was rarely on the Cabinet agenda of either the Labour or Conservative governments of the sixties and seventies. The post of Secretary of State for Education was not usually occupied by a politician of senior status before the 1980s and there was no concerted or deliberate effort to intervene directly in the curriculum by either politicians or DES civil servants. This made the Ruskin College speech by Prime Minister Callaghan, noted more for his interest in foreign affairs and economics than in education, all the more surprising. Risking the wrath of the National Union of Teachers and the displeasure of Shirley Williams, his newly appointed Secretary of State, he called for a public debate on education, including the curriculum, in language not too dissimilar from that of Eccles in 1960. But he had taken the issue an important step further. He had linked the government's concern for the curriculum with the issues of teacher accountability, standards of literacy and numeracy and the needs of British industry. By so doing he had ensured that it became a key item on the political agenda of the 1980s and 1990s. Politicians of the right and left were coming to show some common areas of concern, particularly the curriculum. The Great Debate was intended not just to lower the walls of the 'secret garden'; its aim was to make 'the garden' public property. It was thus rather curiously left to a Conservative Government to 'nationalise' the school curriculum on the very grounds that Callaghan initiated the debate. Intervention was justified on the grounds of the failure of the existing system to deliver a uniform and relevant school curriculum; the more aggressive ministerial styles of Conservative education secretaries of the 1980s, especially that of Kenneth Baker, ensured that Callaghan's initiative was not allowed to drop.

Let us sum up the four relevant historical points highlighted in this section. Firstly, the compulsory curriculum has a long history and was an integral part of the development of state schooling at the elementary and secondary levels virtually from the beginning. Secondly, the Conservative Government in 1926 relinquished its direct control over the curriculum of the masses in a discreet manner. While the reasons why it did so are a matter for conjecture, the manner in which the teachers and local authorities came to control the curriculum is not. The curriculum was not seized by teachers and local education authorities but abandoned by government. Thirdly, the 1944 Education Act left the door open for future intervention by Ministers, but the tradition had quickly established itself by 1944 that the curriculum was not primarily a matter for ministerial intervention. Fourthly, the National Curriculum established by the 1988 Education Act can be traced back to Callaghan's Ruskin College speech and the Great Debate, and was signalled to a lesser extent in the debate over the Crowther Report in the 1960s.

A LIBERAL EDUCATION FOR ALL

It seems inconceivable to many that secondary education for all in Britain could be interpreted in any way other than a liberal education for all. Initiatives of the 1980s and 1990s, such as the TVEI and City Technology College aroused controversy precisely because they appeared to run contrary to this widely held and strongly entrenched view. The aim of this section is to explain the origins and continuing strength of this dominant curricular ideology. Its historical development in the early years of this century shows how peculiarly British was the interpretation given to it then and later. Some of the influences which helped to define secondary education are fairly well known; this section will deal only briefly with these. The way in which secondary education for all came to be interpreted as a liberal education for all is less well known; this section will deal more fully with this aspect because of its significance for the contemporary debate.

In his Ruskin College speech Callaghan expressed his immense debt to R. H. Tawney who first laid down the main lines of Labour's education policy in his book published in 1922, *Secondary Education for All*. What is perhaps surprising is that though Callaghan's speech was largely concerned with curricular matters, Tawney, even in 1922, had nothing new to say on the subject. His radicalism – like that of the TUC in the 1890s, the Bradford Chartists in 1916[18] and many socialists of the inter-war years – was confined to the reconstruction of the education system; it did not extend to the curriculum. The reason for this is very relevant to our present theme. The concept of a liberal education for all was arrived at before Tawney put pen to paper to draft the first main statement about secondary education for all. This predating is of more than simple historical interest. The fact that it was defined in a rather different historical context, in the debate over continuation education just before and during the First World War is important to a full understanding of its meaning.

The idea that a secondary education meant liberal education was already established by the time that the debate over continuation schooling was underway, but the idea that secondary education for all meant a liberal education for all was not. When confined to the small percentage of mainly middle-class pupils few doubted that a secondary education should mean a liberal education. The public and grammar schools provided the model for the new secondary schools created under the 1902 Education Act and the Board's regulations from 1904 onwards reinforced this model. The First School (Certificate) Examination introduced in 1917 further enhanced the prestige of this kind of education. What most educational reformers of the pre-war years demanded was not that such schools should be abolished but that their doors should be opened further than the 25 per cent the Free Place Regulations of 1907 allowed. But this was not secondary education for all, only a demand for secondary education for the most able working-class children, a demand which seemed to receive some kind of official sanction in the Report of the Departmental Committee on Scholarships and Free Places. This report, published in 1920, recommended extending the percentage of free places from 25 to 40.

The main growth point of the idea of secondary education for all came from elsewhere, from the discussions over the nature of continuation education, and was associated initially not with Tawney but with Percy Nunn, who in the years just prior to the First World War was Professor of Education and Vice-Principal of the London Day Training College, later the University of London Institute of Education. It was he more than any other educationist of this period who first defined for the Labour movement, and then for the reform movement in general, the broad characteristics of a liberal education for all. This definition was formed within a very specific historical context and carried the marks of its origin forward for the next fifty years. Nunn entered the debate over continuation education in 1916 as an unrepentant vocationalist and emerged from it in 1918 as an ardent liberalist. His influential position on the Hadow Committee which enquired into adolescent education between 1924 and 1926 gave him the opportunity of gaining some form of official sanction for the idea of a liberal education for all.

Unlike Tawney, who went to the trenches in 1914 as a volunteer with nigh fatal results, Nunn was excused military service on the grounds that his work in education made him an 'indispensable' member of the

London Day Training College. Nunn was an acknowledged expert on mathematical and science education in the years up to 1914 and developed an interest in vocational education as an offshoot of his research. Like many educationists of his time he was drawn into discussions on one of the principal items on the educational agenda of the immediate pre-war years, part-time continuation schooling. Continuation schooling was an attempt to give some form of additional education on a part-time basis to former elementary school pupils. The relevance of these discussions to the educational debate of the 1990s is that they raised the issue for the first time of the type of education that should be given to the mass of the nation's 14 to 18 years olds, albeit on a part-time basis. These discussions threw into relief the issue of vocational education because, for most of the week, this age group were in employment, returning to the classroom for only a few hours of supplementary schooling. An examination of the development of Nunn's thinking on the issue of the kind of education which should be made available to those attending continuation schools is important for two reasons. Firstly, it shows how certain basic ideas and attitudes about continuation education under the old parallel systems of elementary and secondary schools were carried over to secondary education under the reorganised system of primary and secondary schooling after 1944. Secondly, it brought to the forefront of discussion a series of related issues about liberal and vocational education which regained their prominence in the years following Callaghan's Ruskin College speech. Up to 1916, Nunn was an ardent supporter of vocational education; he was particularly impressed by the highly specialised technical training offered by London's technical schools, especially at Shoreditch and Brixton. He also accepted the argument that pupils in the last two years of elementary school (that is, over 11+) were 'often unsatisfactory ... because it is not clear to them that their school work is leading to any definite goal'.[19] The solution to this, he believed, was their transference 'to an institution and to a course of instruction obviously designed to fit them for their life-work'. He thus advocated a 'clean-cut in education' at 11+ with a small minority attending secondary schools to pursue a liberal, academic education and the vast majority attending either a technical school with some students pursuing a concurrent apprenticeship, or a central school where in the last years 'the vocational side of the work should be further developed' or a continuation school, full time to 14 and part time thereafter, with a pronounced vocational bias. Working-class education after the age of 11 was thus to be geared closely to the world of employment.

By 1918, Nunn had revised his ideas, largely as a result of a simple but basic reinterpretation of what continuation education should be. As a valued member of the educational community he was invited by Sidney Webb to join Margaret MacMillan, Leach, Tawney and others on the Labour Party's Advisory Committee on Education which met for the first time at the Fabian Society's headquarters in April 1918. In

October 1918 he was asked to join the Committee's subcommittee on secondary education, and in particular was requested to draft a policy statement on the curriculum of the continuation schools. Nunn was thus put in the position of considering continuation education not within the context of a continuation of elementary schooling but as some form of secondary schooling. His well-received memorandum thus started from the basic premise that 'Continued Education is simply part-time Secondary Education'. This redefinition led him to apply to continuation education the unquestioned British belief that secondary education must be a liberal education. Part-time continuation for all was now interpreted not as part-time vocational education for all but as part-time liberal education for all. He thus came to oppose a view of the curriculum he had supported two years earlier. The extent of his conversion is shown in the following extract from his memorandum.[20]

> There will be several rival claimants struggling for admission to, or predominance in, the curriculum. Different schools, set upon securing efficient workers, will demand that it shall be mainly vocational. The advocates of universal military training will desire that physical education should proceed, as far as possible, upon military lines. If Labour is to turn to good account its new educational opportunity it is essential that Labour representatives upon Local Education Authorities should be clear in advance as to the principal objects towards which Continued Education should be directed, and the general lines upon which it should proceed. ... They should, in the first place, resist any attempt to convert Continued Education into a system of specialised technical training. It is important, indeed, to appeal to the interest of boys and girls in practical work. But both on practical and on educational grounds it would be a disaster if it predominated in the new Continuation Schools or set their general tone. On the one hand, the number of boys who require specialised training for industry is far smaller than is usually supposed; nor, since they often change their employment repeatedly between 14 and 18, is it always practicable to offer those who do need it the particular kind of training which they require. On the other hand, to give it predominance in the curriculum would necessarily involve both the neglect of more important subjects and the creation in the schools of a narrow commercial atmosphere. The background of the whole curriculum should be history, geography, literature and elementary science. Scholars should be led to take an intelligent interest in the problems, and to adopt a proper attitude towards the responsibilities, of international, national and municipal citizenship. A sustained attempt should be made to cultivate the love of good literature, and the use of books for learning and enjoyment.

Unlike Callaghan and Conservative education secretaries of the 1980s and early 1990s, Nunn and the Labour Party's Advisory Committee on Education argued strongly against industry and commerce having an influence upon the school curriculum. This arose in part out of a strong dislike of works schools – that is, schools run by employers and on employers' premises. The memorandum asserted 'it is certain that many employers will aim at using their control of the schools to turn continued education into a narrowed and specialised

Fig 2.1 ***The goal of education***

training for the branch of industry in which they are interested, or to give a bias to such general studies as appear in the curriculum'. The positive argument in favour of the liberal curriculum was that a broad physical moral and intellectual training was the means best suited for the development of citizenship. Nowhere is this better illustrated than in book advertisements of the day which were directed at working-class parents and elementary school teachers. Figure 2.1 shows the goal of education, not as the production of the skilled engineer as one would find in similar advertisements of the time in Germany or in the United States, but as the gentleman of aristocratic bearing.

By 1920, Nunn's thinking about the education of the adolescent had moved a stage further. In *Education: Its Data and First Principles* published in that year he looked forward to a full-time secondary education for all adolescents, not to a part-time continuation education for all, to a liberal education for all, not to a quasi-vocational education for all. His statement about the curriculum is a classic summary of the liberal viewpoint.[21]

> In the school curriculum all these activities should be represented. For these are the grand expressions of the human spirit, and theirs are the forms in which the creative energies of every generation must be disciplined if the movement of civilization is to be worthily maintained. Taking the second group first, every complete scheme of education must comprise (i.) literature, including at least the best literature of the motherland; (ii.) some forms of art, including music, the most universal of the arts; (iii.) handicrafts, taught with emphasis either on its aesthetic aspect, as in weaving, carving, lettering, or on its constructional aspect, as in carpentry and needlework; (iv.) science, including mathematics, the science of number, space and time. History and geography should appear in it in a double guise. On the one hand, history belongs with literature as geography belongs with science. On the other hand, they should have a central position in the curriculum as the subjects in which the human movement is, as such, presented and interpreted: history teaching the solidarity of the present with the past, geography the dependence of man's life upon his natural environment, and the interdependence of human activities all over the globe.

This view quickly became the established orthodoxy by 1926 for two reasons. Firstly, Tawney accepted the liberal view as axiomatic in the first detailed statement by Labour of its policy on secondary education for all in 1922. Published as a policy statement by Labour for the general election of the year, Tawney's *Secondary Education for All* dealt with the structural and institutional changes by which such a goal could be achieved. He duly acknowledged Nunn's concept of a liberal, secondary education for all, accepting it uncritically and unquestioningly as the basis of Labour's view of the new curriculum. More important to the broader dissemination of his view was Nunn's presence on the most prestigious government advisory committee of the inter-war years, the Board of Education's Consultative Committee (the Hadow Committee) which reported on 'The Education of the Adolescent' in 1926. Nunn was coopted on to the committee; he was a strong advocate of the break at 11+ and the organisation of secondary education for all 'as a unitary process with its own distinctive character, planned, in its several varieties, as a whole'; he was regarded by the Committee as the expert of his day on the school curriculum. Chapter four of the Hadow Committee's report was largely his, a restatement, in fact, of the ideas he had put forward in his memorandum on continuation education and in his book. He undertook to speak on 'Schools and Curricula' at the Kingsway Hall Conference in October 1927, organised by Tawney and the Workers' Educational Association, to give further publicity to the concept of a liberal education for all adolescents. With the publication of the Hadow Report, the view that adolescent education should not be vocational education but should seek to 'offer the fullest possible scope to individuality' entered mainstream thinking.

The transference of this kind of thinking to primary education was assisted greatly by the publication in 1931 of the second of the trilogy of Hadow reports, *The Primary School*. Nunn, again acting as a coopted member and backed by Burt and Tawney, argued in favour of an abandonment of the elementary school concept under which various subjects had been grafted on to the original stock of the three Rs. They rejected also the concept, supported in the first Hadow Report, of primary education as preparatory education. In place of these two views of education for the under-11 year olds, the Committee argued for a new liberal concept of primary education.

> We see that the curriculum is to be thought of in terms of activity and experience rather than of knowledge to be acquired and facts to be stored. Its aim should be to develop in a child the fundamental human powers and to awaken him to the fundamental interests of civilised life so far as these powers and interests lie within the compass of childhood, to encourage him to attain gradually to that control and orderly management of his energies, impulses and emotions, which is the essence of moral and intellectual discipline, to help him to discover the idea of duty and to ensue it, and to open out his imagination and his sympathies in such a way that he may be prepared to understand and to follow in later years the highest examples of excellence in life and conduct.

The final report of the Board of Education's Consultative Committee in the inter-war years confirmed the view that the way ahead lay in giving all children between the ages of 5 and 16 a liberal education. The committee, now chaired by Spens in place of Hadow, had spent the years from 1935 to 1938 looking at the curricula of grammar and technical high schools. In giving the majority of its attention to the former and in recommending that the latter should be of a liberal character, the committee confirmed the supremacy of the liberal tradition in British education. Nunn's contribution to defining the principal characteristics of the future secondary school curricula was duly acknowledged. The primacy of academic studies within this tradition was further confirmed in 1943 by the Norwood Committee whose cameos of pupil types alone make its report worth studying. It described the highest achiever within the tripartite (grammar, modern and technical school) system as follows.[22]

> For example, English education has in practice recognised the pupil who is interested in learning for its own sake, who can grasp an argument or follow a piece of connected reasoning, who is interested in causes, whether on the level of human volition or in the material world, who cares to know how things came to be as well as how they are, who is sensitive to language as expression of thought, to a proof as a precise demonstration, to a series of experiments justifying a principle; he is interested in the relatedness of related things, in development, in structure, in a coherent body of knowledge. He can take a long view and hold his mind in suspense; this may be revealed in his work, or in his attitude to his career. He will have some capacity to enjoy, from an aesthetic point of view, the aptness of a phrase or the neatness of a proof. He may be good with his hands or he may not; he may or may not be a good 'mixer' or a leader or a prominent figure in activities, athletic or other.
>
> Such pupils, educated by the curriculum commonly associated with the Grammar School, have entered the learned professions or have taken up higher administrative or business posts.

The kind of exaggerated profile used by the Norwood Committee to justify the creation in the post-war world of a separate-school system rather than one based on common schools was not without influence on government officials. The Board's own statement on post-war reform, 'Education after the War', which paved the way for much of the Education Act of 1944, spoke of 'a caste system' existing in education between the liberal 'haves' and the vocational 'have-nots', the former being in secondary schools and the latter being in elementary schools. Education reform should seek to eradicate this division by giving all pupils access to a liberal education of different types. The Education Act of 1944 defined the conditions under which this could be achieved, though it did not lay down whether this secondary school system should be organised on separate or common school lines.

The Labour Government elected in 1945 with a landslide majority had the task of implementing the 1944 Act. The new Ministry of Education, formerly the Board of Education, followed unswervingly the curricular ideology laid down by Nunn nearly thirty years earlier. The Act laid down the requirement that secondary schools should be 'sufficient in number, character and equipment to afford all pupils opportunities of education, offering such a variety of instruction and training as may be desirable in view of their different ages, abilities and aptitudes'. The great demand for grammar education which far outstripped its supply meant that the 11+ examination, intended to select through discrimination, was in fact selection by elimination, with the vast majority of the nation's children destined to enter modern schools. The small minority who were allocated the scarce number of grammar school places could elect to pursue a technical or practical education but those allocated to a modern or technical school could not choose an academic grammar school education. Nor did Labour's curricular policy laid down in *The New Secondary Education* (1947) intend that the latter choice should be offered. The vast majority, unsuited to the 'more exacting' technical education and the 'abstract approach' of the traditional secondary education, were deemed to be suited to the practical curriculum 'rooted in their own day-to-day experience'. Such distinctions were lost on parents who, in greater numbers than the places allocated, wanted a grammar school education for their children.

Just as the secondary school curriculum defined by the 1904 Regulations and reinforced by the 1917 First School (Certificate) Examination set the standard by which adolescent education was judged in the inter-war years, so the grammar school curriculum, stamped with the hallmark of the new, single-subject GCE examination introduced in 1951, provided the yardstick by which all other forms of adolescent education were measured in the post-war years. The GCE examination gave access to the most highly prized form of liberal education, the universities. The other forms of secondary education, without such a ladder, were severely disadvantaged in their demand for parity of status and esteem. The Conservative Governments of the 1980s faced the dilemma of wishing to maintain the GCE by which they believed educational excellence was measured while at the same time wishing to move away from the predominantly literary, academic tradition upon which it was based. Their answer was to construct the fiction that the new GCSE examination kept the equivalent pass standards of the GCE A to C grades when most people realised that GCSE was examining a much broader range of skills than its predecessor and hence direct comparison of grades was impossible. The newly created modern schools set up after 1945 could not adopt such a ploy. Employees and parents demanded that they live up to the standards set by GCE and thus by 1960 nearly 40 per cent of their pupils were entering GCE examination. The Hadow vision of the practical, liberal education for the modern school was too much of a weakling concept to thrive in the harsh economic and social climate of the post-war years. Though the Hadow Committee of 1926 somewhat reluctantly accepted the idea of a leaving examination for modern schools, it feared that it could alter the practical nature of the curriculum. Certainly entering pupils for the GCE examination could have this effect, especially as it was designed for the 20–25 per cent who followed the more academic grammar school curriculum. The introduction of a new secondary school examination in 1965, the Certificate of Secondary Education, was intended to meet this problem. The new examination, designed for the top 40 per cent of the school population and incorporating a mode 3 facility, enabled a broader range of skills to be examined. A pass of Grade 1 at the CSE was to be regarded as a pass at the GCE. This linking of the two examinations, however, seemed to confirm the superiority of the academic over the more practical. There was a clear need for more carefully worked out and implemented initiatives to establish effective curricular alternatives to the traditional dominant, grammar school curriculum. The pace of change – economic, social and technical – and the rapid expansion of knowledge combined to increase the demands for the reform of the curriculum. The moves towards the creation of a national system of comprehensive schools gave further focus to these demands. Control of the school curriculum was rapidly becoming a political matter in the late fifties and early sixties. The *laissez-faire* tradition, which had in effect left the liberal, academic curriculum in a dominant position, was being seriously questioned. The creation in 1964 of the Schools Council for Curriculum and Examinations was a warning shot across the traditionalist bows. The Schools Council responded to requests from outside bodies to engage in curricular research. Table 2.1 shows the extent of its projects in the years to 1978.

Callaghan's speech was thus delivered at a time of considerable curricular interest; his Ruskin College speech expressed the need for modernising the school curriculum while maintaining many of the standards associated with the traditional curriculum; Conservative education secretaries of the eighties accepted his diagnosis of the 'educational problem'.

Table 2.1 ***Schools Council research and development projects 1963–78***

Field of investigation	*Number of projects*	*Cost (£)*
English	22	1,278,376
Humanities	19	1,738,983
Languages	6	1,067,621
Creative studies	10	628,322
Mathematics	15	1,096,909
Science	24	1,008,098
Interrelated studies	24	1,857,937
Special education	5	270,901
Wales	10	600,535
School home and community	5	55,440
School organisation and resources	16	698,28
Examinations	25	767,803

THE LIBERAL, PRACTICAL CURRICULUM

One of the main aims of the preceding section was to show how the concept of a liberal education for all was defined within a particular and somewhat unexpected historical context. It was formed as part of the debate which took place in the years 1909 to 1918 over part-time continuation education for all, and not as one might suppose as part of the debate over full-time secondary education for all in the 1920s. This context was particularly important in that it was accepted from the outset that curricular advance was to be seen not in terms of extending into the classrooms the kind of training relevant to the work in which young people were engaged for most of the week but in terms of a liberal, non-vocational education. However, Nunn, who guided much of the curricular thinking in the inter-war years, recognised from the outset that a liberal education could be of a non-academic as well as an academic kind. What mattered most was that it avoided vocationalism and was directed towards giving opportunities for individuals to develop their abilities and a sense of citizenship. There was a place in education for individuality and the needs of society, but not for vocational training.

In the third part of the Labour Party's 1918 memorandum on continuation education, Nunn writes:

> In order to be liberal, education need not be bookish, and it is important that the new Continuation Schools should appeal to the interests of boys and girls in practical work. This does not mean that a prominent place should be given to specialised technical instruction.[23]

By 'practical', Nunn meant teaching the traditional school subjects, 'with the possible exception of literature', in such a way as to bring out their relevance to the students' own experiences. As this view coloured thinking about non-academic education for the next half century and more, his words are worth quoting in full.

> The proper course for those who desire to give Continued Education a 'Vocational bias' is not, therefore, to endeavour to squeeze it into the curriculum at the expense of other subjects, but to endeavour to secure that all subjects are taught in a manner which brings them into relation with the concrete interests of everyday life. In the case of science and mathematics no difficulty arises. The relation of the former to the staple industries of a district, textiles, mining, the manufacture of steel or engineering can easily be explained. What is called 'Workshop arithmetic', again, involves, in addition to measurements and calculations, the practical reference of which can easily be shown, a certain amount of simple geometrical theory and training in exact drawing. History and geography will gain enormously in educative value if an attempt is made to treat them in the same spirit. It would be easy to work out a course of lessons in these subjects which would show the development of local life and industries, its relation to social and political changes, the industrial independence of one district with other districts and of the nation with other nations, the part played in the past by different regions in the history of the country, the places held today of different industries, such as transport and the extraction of minerals in the economy of the community. The object of such teaching would not be to make a boy a practical miner or a skilled cotton operative, but to use the environment with which he is familiar as a starting-point from which to lead him to a wider outlook. But the miner will be all the more efficient for having learned something of geological science, and the cotton operative for understanding something of the part which the textile industry has played in the social history of his country and in the economy of the world. Approached in such a spirit the possibilities of using local industries and local conditions on the basis of a general education which will be practical without being narrowly utilitarian, are clearly infinite.

When Tawney first popularised the concept of secondary education for all in his book of that title in 1922, he accepted and acknowledged two key elements of Nunn's thinking: firstly, that most students would want a 'practical' rather than a 'bookish' education, and secondly that a practical education, while being relevant to future occupations, should not be vocational. Tawney put it the other way round: such courses should be vocational only to the extent that they needed to convince students that much of their learning was capable of practical application.[24]

This kind of thinking was carried forward to the Hadow Report of 1926 for which Nunn drew up chapter four on the modern school curriculum. In the Hadow Report, Nunn repeated much of the memorandum of eight years earlier; the aims of education were to offer 'the fullest possible scope to individuality, while keeping steadily in view the claims and needs of the society in which every individual citizen must live'.[25] In order to relate the curriculum to 'real life', the report argued that modern school studies should not be 'a simplified edition' of the academic curriculum but should have a distinctive, practical character of their own. They should be 'practical' in two senses, in being related to the students' locality and in providing opportunities for 'practical work'. Given this perspective it was not surprising that the report took the thinking of the memorandum a stage further and recommended the merging of subject boundaries in order to teach common areas of skill or knowledge and to teach some subjects in project form over longer periods of time than was usually devoted to single subjects. The links between the modern school curriculum and employment were to be kept general, a view supported by many employers.[26] The Hadow Committee urged the need to strengthen links between schools and local industries, and reiterated the general view of teachers and many employers that any 'practical bias' should be introduced only in the third or fourth years of a secondary school course and then not 'of so marked a character as to prejudice the general education of the pupils'. With this restatement of a basic point of Nunn's earlier memorandum, the idea of a practical, liberal education for the majority ceased to be simply a demand put forward by Labour and became a fundamental tenet of the broader reform movement. So strongly entrenched by 1941 had this belief become that the Norwood Committee, set up by R. A. Butler to enquire into the secondary school curriculum and examinations, felt confident enough to describe the pupil for whom it was most appropriate, and then to specify an appropriate kind of school for such a pupil, the secondary modern school.

Again, there has of late years been recognition, expressed in the framing of curricula and otherwise, of still another grouping of pupils, and another grouping of occupations. The pupil in his group deals more easily with concrete things than with ideas. He may have much ability, but it will be in the realm of facts. He is interested in things as they are; he finds little attraction in the past or in the slow disentanglement of causes or movements. His mind must turn its knowledge or its curiosity to immediate test; and his test is essentially practical. He may see clearly along one line of study or interest and outstrip his generally abler fellows in that line; but he often fails to relate his knowledge or skill to other branches of activity. Because he is interested only in the moment he may be incapable of a long series of connected steps; relevance to present concerns is the only way of awakening interest, abstractions mean little to him. Thus it follows that he must have immediate returns for his effort, and for the same reason his career is often in his mind. His horizon is near and within a limited area his movement is generally slow, though it may be surprisingly rapid in seizing a particular point or in taking up a special line. Again, he may or may not be good with his hands or sensitive to Music or Art.

The apologetic manner in which the modern school pupil was defined reflected the general view that the practical kind of education, envisaged in the Hadow Report of 1926, fell short of a truly liberal education. Though the post-war Labour Government in its pamphlet *The New Secondary Education* echoed the Norwood view in arguing for 'a course rooted in their own day-to-day experience'[27] for the majority of the nation's children, it nevertheless argued in favour of establishing parity between the 'practical' and academic forms of liberal education. 'No organisation, indeed, will adequately meet the situation that involves the sacrifice of the best interests of one type of child to those of another.' There was some recognition in the pamphlet that the identification of different kinds of secondary education with different types of secondary school was not likely to help achieve the goal of parity of status and esteem, particularly as secondary modern school pupils left school earlier than those in grammar schools and that such schools also lacked established links with universities and other forms of higher education. The creation of a 'campus plan' or multilateral school was seen as a means of avoiding, at least in part, placing practical studies in a subordinate position to academic studies. However, the creation of 'a kind of federation of schools, each one developing its own individual character', really did little to destroy hierarchical distinctions and could be said to exacerbate them especially when 'practical' and academic education took place in separate institutions in such close proximity.

For most local authorities, the future of the 'essentially practical' education lay in the development of a system of secondary modern schools. But as the previous section has shown, the modern schools were subjected to a number of social and economic pressures which militated against the implementation of the Hadow ideal. These pressures, especially from parents and employers, often took the form of a demand for paper qualifications on the lines of GCE. Yet modern schools were able, in part, to develop new approaches to the curriculum. William Taylor, in 1963,[28] described the influence of progressive ideas on the modern school curriculum.

> ... 'progressives' were of a radical social and political persuasion, and saw the future of education and society as requiring much less competition and more cooperation, attempting to place the child, instead of the curriculum or the subject, in the centre of the educational stage and critical of 'tradition'. Ideas such as these were embodied or implied in much of the writing of educational thinkers, and obtained a firm hold on many of those concerned with the training of teachers in colleges and universities. In turn, these teachers took with them some aspects of the new approach into the schools, and signs of this are easily found in existing practice; new methods of teaching the basic skills; a new attitude towards the spontaneous expressive activities of the child; the introduction of composite subjects such as 'social studies', of new and more 'natural' crafts, such as clay modelling; the attention given to the practical subjects and education through the senses rather than the intellect; and a change in the attitude towards information and facts and a recognition of the importance of experience: all are manifestations of the spirit of the 'new education' as it has worked out in contact with the existing elements of the curriculum.

But, he adds,

> Progressive ideas at the secondary level have always encountered the pressure of social realism; occupational and vocational selection and choice begin to operate at the age of eleven, and, as the Modern school has discovered, when

some types of secondary school are part of the selection and training machinery, there is no status to be obtained by contracting out of the system. In recent years, the Modern school has tried to win its status by 'participating' rather than by contracting out, and its advanced and examination courses can be viewed in this light.

Though the modern school pioneered new approaches its basis was a curriculum of inequality which retained its inferior status even when translated into the comprehensive school. The tradition of the academic curriculum based on traditional subjects retained its precedence over the more experimental and practical curriculum which focused on contemporary problems and grouped subjects. This division was reflected in the examinations for which pupils were entered at the end of their courses. Callaghan's Ruskin College speech recognised that the introduction of a national system of comprehensive schools did not, in itself, achieve a realignment of the curriculum. The recognition by Shirley Williams of the need for examination reform, not just of the examination system but also of what was examined and in what priority, was a key step towards establishing the importance of practical skills within the liberal tradition, a point which the GCSE sought to emphasise.

TECHNICAL AND VOCATIONAL EDUCATION

A century before Mrs Thatcher announced TVEI in 1982, a royal commission enquired into technical and vocational education. Both TVEI and the Royal Commission were brought about by concern over the nation's economic decline in the face of foreign competition. The commission concluded in its reports (1881–84) that one of the ways forward was to empower local authorities 'to establish, maintain and contribute to the establishment and maintenance of secondary and technical (including agricultural) schools and colleges'. Again by coincidence, exactly a century before Baker's Education Act clipped their wings, local authorities in the form of county councils were created under the Local Government Act of 1888 to help make such provision. It appeared that the administrative machinery was being put into place to facilitate the massive expansion of technical education which Britain so desperately needed. Nor was pressure lacking. In 1887 a group of MPs led by A. H. D Acland and T. H. Huxley launched the National Association for the Promotion of Technical and Secondary Education, a forerunner of TVEI. In 1889 NAPTE achieved its first notable success, the Technical Instruction Act, which empowered the newly created county and county boroughs to implement the recommendations of the Royal Commission's report. With a sound administrative and financial basis it appeared that the course of technical and also vocational education was set fair. All that appeared to be needed was a sufficiently generous definition of the term 'technical education'.

This was provided by another Act[29] in the same year. Technical education was defined to include instruction in

(i) Any of the branches of science and art with respect to which grants are for the time being made by the Department of Science and Art;
(ii) The use of tools, and modelling in clay, wood, or other material;
(iii) Commercial arithmetic, commercial geography, book-keeping, and shorthand;
(iv) Any other subject applicable to the purposes of agriculture, industries, trade or commercial life and practice, which may be specified in a scheme, or proposals for a scheme, of a joint education committee as a form of instruction suited to the needs of the district.

It appeared that the nation's urgent economic needs could be met, in part, with effective programmes of educational reform and that the golden age of technical, and indeed vocational, education was about to dawn. What then caused this first major state initiative to fail to achieve its aims and necessitate the launching of similar initiatives a century later? In brief, the answer lies in the fact that the ship of technical and vocational education, apparently so soundly financed and managed, was swamped by the rising tide of liberal education very shortly after it set sail. To maintain the nautical metaphor, and to state the argument more forcibly, its failure could be seen to be due to its being torpedoed, albeit possibly inadvertently, by the Board of Education's own regulations of 1904 governing secondary education (see p. 56). These regulations created an unreal and unnecessary division between secondary and technical education which has bedevilled technical education in one form or another since 1904.

That such a division was unnecessary was evident from another report of this period, that in 1895 of the Royal Commission on Secondary Education. It rejected a distinction which has since become so much a part of educational thinking that it has surfaced regularly during the current debates on technical and vocational education. The Commission refused to accept two things: firstly, that the term 'secondary' should be restricted to that kind of education which aimed at 'the culture of character by means of the more humane and generous studies' (p. 134), and, secondly, that it should be denied to 'those practical arts and sciences by means of which man becomes a craftsman or breadwinner'. Whether education could be regarded as secondary or not depended in the Commissioners' view on whether it went beyond basic instruction in the three Rs and encouraged students to learn principles 'by applying them so ... as to perform or produce something, interpret a literature or a score, make a picture or a book, practice a plastic or manual art'. Secondary education was to be defined not in terms of a catalogue of subjects but in terms of what it set out to achieve in terms of understanding and application. By such a definition, training in the classics could have 'as little liberal culture in it as instruction in a practical art'. The Commission thus recommended that ample provision be made for secondary schools of different types including those of a technical and vocational nature.

The Board of Education acquired a great deal of control over secondary education by the 1902 Education Act. Its definition of secondary education flew in the face of the 1895 Royal Commission's general thinking and recommendations. Above all, the 1904 Regulations ignored the rich experience of secondary curricula of a technical and quasi-vocational kind which had evolved in the Higher Grade Schools, Organised Science Schools and Technical Day Schools. As the previous sections have shown, the regulations were based entirely upon the tradition of the grammar and public schools. The concept of a secondary or general education was thus separated from the idea of technical and vocational education and defined simply in terms of a list of subjects with definite allocations of time per week, the administrator's solution to a complex issue. Secondary schools were thus to avoid what was regarded as the besetting sin of the technical and vocational schools, that of concentrating their attention unduly on a particular group of non-humanistic subjects. What is surprising is not that Morant in 1904 chose to identify secondary education with liberal arts subjects but that there was little or no protest against such a definition. This is explained in part by the two general concerns of the reform movement of the pre-war years. The first was the Free Place Regulations of 1907 which created a slender bridge between the elementary and secondary school (see pp. 111–112). Most reformers aimed at widening the bridge to a traditional secondary education, especially for working-class children, and not to destroy what they regarded as the main goal, increased access to a liberal education. The creation of the First School (certificate) Examination in 1917 intensified this drive. The second principal concern of reformers in the years up to 1918 was continuation education which, as we have seen in the previous section, was interpreted as part-time traditional secondary education. Supporters of technical and vocational education thus faced an uphill struggle to establish technical and vocational education as a generally acceptable alternative form of secondary education.

Percy Nunn provides a useful barometer of educational opinion during this period. In 1916 he argued in favour of a break in education at 11+ when the primary stage was to cease and for a variety of post-primary education to include technical schools. Of the latter, he wrote, 'The technical school should retain its pupils until 17+, with a partially concurrent apprenticeship'.[30] Thus technical and vocational education were seen as complementary. By 1918 he had changed his view so that technical and vocation *per se* were denied a place even in continuation education although, as has been mentioned in the preceding section, a 'vocational' or 'practical' bias could be given to teaching many of the subjects listed in the 1904 Regulations. To this extent Nunn was reflecting the official policy on secondary education of the Board of Education as stated in Circular 826 issued in 1913, but against this view was the narrowing and stereotyping influence of the First School (Certificate) Examination which dominated secondary education from 1917 onwards.

The chances of technical and vocational education being regarded as part of secondary education and on an equal footing with liberal arts subjects remained slim. The basic issue was whether the recent but flourishing tradition of trade schools and junior technical schools would be forgotten in the headlong rush towards secondary education for all. These schools were designed to prepare their students either for artisan or other industrial occupations or for domestic employment. These being essentially vocational schools, they seemed at variance with a concept of secondary education which, at best, would allow only of a technical and vocational 'bias' on the lines defined by Nunn. Tawney's *Secondary Education for All* (1922) accepted Nunn's definition and referred to the schemes put forward by Kent and Darlington in support. Tawney (p. 107) concluded that

> I think they [intermediate schools] should be vocational only to the extent needed to convince pupils that much of their learning is capable of practical application . . . To turn those into 'vocational' schools would only result in separating scholars into groups according to probable occupations, which would be little, if any, better than grouping according to capacity to pay fees . . . A good general education is the first essential whatever calling a boy or girl proposes to follow.

Labour's evidence to the Hadow Committee in 1925 summarised its position on technical and vocational education, a position which reflects the orthodox thinking of the party and of most educational reformers of the age. It stressed the need for a wide variety of educational courses for the 70 per cent of pupils who were seen as unlikely to benefit from the existing type of secondary education. Such courses were to include those with a scientific, commercial or technical bias; to this extent it acknowledged that its view was in keeping with that of the Board and it looked forward to the movement to 'raise the status of handwork to that of bookwork'. The Labour Party and the Trades Union Congress (TUC) could feel well satisfied with the Hadow Committee's report on adolescent education (1926) which established the main lines of thinking about the curriculum for nearly half a century. With Nunn as the Committee's expert on the curriculum it was unlikely that the Hadow recommendations would have been much at odds with the mainstream views of Labour and leading opinion.

These early developments are of more than historical interest; they coloured attitudes to technical and vocational education for the next sixty years. So let us summarise the points made so far. Firstly, technical and vocational education developed largely as a form of working-class education outside the fold of the dominant liberal tradition. Secondly, attempts to give it an enhanced status within the liberal tradition were thwarted by the fact that the hegemony of the grammar school curriculum within the state system had already been established by the 1904 Regulations and confirmed by the introduction in 1917 of the First School (Certificate) Examination. The Hadow Committee made the first brave efforts to bring technical and vocational education within the liberal fold, but in acknowledging that it should do 'nothing ... to cripple the development of secondary schools of the existing types' its chances of giving an enhanced status to these forms of education were severely circumscribed. Its strong position within the elementary tradition was replaced by an inferior position within the liberal secondary tradition. Left-wing critics were quick to spot this. At the Labour Party's annual conference at Margate shortly after the publication of the Hadow Report in 1927, a resolution was put forward which denounced the kind of liberal curriculum advocated by people such as Nunn and Tawney as 'bourgeois psychology'. It called for the placing of education under 'a workers' administration' to foster 'a proletarian attitude'. It aimed at enhancing the position and status of technical and vocational education by keeping it outside the liberal tradition. To this extent it was at odds with official Labour policy which sought to achieve this through linking 'central technical schools' with local universities. Thus the resolution called for 'a definite scheme for providing an adequate number of secondary schools of the grammar school type, for the abolition of central schools which were seen to be providing an inferior kind of liberal education for working-class children, and the development of technical institutes for 'agriculture, commerce, the professions, engineering, transport, etc., according to the work the students attending such schools are likely to take up in later life'. The idea that technical and vocational education could flourish best in institutions outside the mainstream liberal tradition reflected part of the thinking behind the development of City Technology Colleges in the 1980s and 1990s.

But the left wing of the Labour movement was not alone in the support it gave to technical and vocational education in the inter-war years. Support also came from some on the political right, including the Conservative President of the Board of Education from 1924 to 1929, Eustace Percy. Percy had no truck with the left's Marxist ideology but his advocacy of the benefits of such an education was no less strident. The arguments he advanced in 1930 and earlier[31] were those put forward by the Thatcher Government some half century later at the time of the launch of the Technical and Vocational Education Initiative. Both Percy and Prime Minister Thatcher were spurred on by the need of the moment, that of 'a country to be saved' from recession. Though the economic crisis of the early thirties was greater than that of the early eighties, both threw into relief the shortcomings in the provision for technical and vocational education. Percy and successive Conservative education secretaries of the 1980s saw that the way out of recession and the path to future economic stability lay in the increased provision of such forms of education. The handing of the management of TVEI to the Manpower Services Commission in 1982 was, in part, an attempt to avoid what was perceived to be its emasculation if left in the hands of educationists dominated by the liberal tradition. Percy, too, believed that desperate times called for novel and speedy courses of action. In 1930, he condemned the liberal tradition – as represented by the grammar and public schools – as being hopelessly out of date. He attacked those who perceived the democratic movement in education as the acquisition for the working classes of an education suited to gentlemen, and who failed to press for equality of opportunity 'in connection with a profession or craft'. What the times called for was not the true scholar and gentleman but the citizen with technical qualifications and abilities. The technical school and technical college thrust hitherto into the dark corners of the education system should be restored to their former and proper prominence.

Times of crisis usually sharpened concern for technical and vocational education. The 1930s and 1940s were no exception. The Spens Committee, set up in 1933 to look at grammar and technical high schools in the wake of Britain's economic collapse, reported in the shadow of war in 1938, when the nation's industrial shortcomings were all too evident. That Britain was unprepared for war in 1939 was, in part, a result of its lack of long-term planning for technical education. One of its chief providers in the 1930s was the junior technical school, but these schools trained pupils only in sufficient number to meet the immediate needs of local industry. Thus during the Depression they were very few in number and even in 1937, when the economy was improving, there was no rapid increase in their numbers, as Table 2.2 shows.[32]

The Spens Committee urged the expansion of technical education through the systematic development of technical high schools within a tripartite structure of secondary education for all. The Norwood Com-

Table 2.2 ***Comparison of pupils in Britain's schools, 1937***

Age	*Elementary*	*Grant-aided secondary*	*Junior technical, etc.*
1	*2*	*3*	*4*
10–11	566,964	12,165	
11–12	552,388	44,536	
12–13	522,304	80,154	1,135
13–14	530,122	83,902	4,886
14–15	158,303	79,390	11,401
15–16	19,743	73,333	9,037
16–17	2,393	47,718	2,972
Total (11–17)	1,785,253	409,033	29,431

mittee, five years later, with its love of male stereotype, described the type of pupil best suited to such an education.

> The boy in this group has a strong interest in this direction and often the necessary qualities of mind to carry his interest through to make it his life-work at whatever level of achievement. He often has an uncanny insight into the intricacies of mechanism whereas the subtleties of language construction are too delicate for him. To justify itself to his mind, knowledge must be capable of immediate application, and the knowledge and its application which most appeal to him are concerned with the control of material things. He may have unusual or moderate intelligence: where intelligence is not great, a feeling of purpose and relevance may enable him to make the most of it. He may or may not be good at games or other activities.

The central message of both committees was that technical education was too important to be left simply to local initiative, a point not lost on the war-time coalition government. Its green book, *Education After the War* (1941), pointed to Germany's highly centralised system of technical education as part of the reason for its military efficiency. Lord Eustace Percy was asked to chair a special government committee on higher technological education. Its report was published in 1945, the year after the Butler Act placed a duty on local education authorities to ensure adequate provision of technical education at secondary level.

The Percy Report reiterated a point long acknowledged by many educationists, that 'the position of Great Britain as a leading industrial nation is being endangered by failure to secure the fullest possible application of science to industry and this failure is partly due to deficiencies in education'. But would Britain slip back into its old habit of neglecting technical and vocational education once the immediate crisis which highlighted these deficiencies was past? The Labour Government elected by a landslide majority in 1945 could not shed easily its long-standing antipathy to all forms of technical and vocational education. The Ministry of Education's first pamphlet, 'The Nation's Schools', following the thinking of the Norwood Report, expressed the view that about three-quarters of the nation's children would go to secondary modern schools to pursue a 'practical' education on the grounds that 'their future employment will not demand any measure of technical skill or knowledge'. The policy-makers clung to the long outmoded view of British industry employing a vast unskilled and semi-skilled population and relatively very few technically educated workers. Education for the masses could not be presented as 'vocational' and was thus defined as 'practical' with the new secondary moderns being equipped to give a basic training in the use of simple tools with metalwork and woodwork for boys, and kitchen, typewriting and needlework facilities for girls.

Half of the remaining pupils were to go to grammar schools and about half to technical schools. The technical schools started in a position of weakness. As Table 2.3 shows,[33] the decline of secondary technical schools as separate institutions was marked before the drive

Table 2.3 ***Secondary schools and pupils in England and Wales***

	1955	*1965*	*1975*
All maintained secondary schools	5,144	5,863	4,562
Pupils	1,914,814	2,819,504	3,619,302
Maintained technical schools	302	172	29
% of total	5.9	2.9	0.6
Pupils	87,366	84,587	18,049
% of total	4.6	3.0	0.5

towards a national system of comprehensive schools got underway in the late sixties and seventies.

Technical education did not have the strong traditional base of the secondary school from which it could develop in the post-war era. The junior technical schools were not suited to act as such a growth point in that they had recruited pupils at the age of 13, had no sixth forms and did not prepare their pupils for the prestigious GCE examination. They were strangers in the new order brought into being by the 1944 Education Act, and were dominated by the 11+ break and the increasing demand for paper qualifications. In addition, those who manned educational administration belonged to the grammar school – university tradition, and though some were sympathetic to the idea of technical education few had sufficient insight into this form of education to encourage it to develop a secure base. So insecurely established was technical education by the late 1960s that, although many voices were raised in support of grammar schools when they were threatened with extinction in the drive towards comprehensivisation, very few protested against the demise of technical schools.

One of the main opportunities brought about by the introduction of comprehensive schools was the availability within most schools of facilities for technical studies for a wider range of students. Technical education was not intended to be vocational education, but it gave a greater utility to much of the work done within such schools. The tentative introduction of various forms of work experience, of courses linked to Further Education (FE) Colleges, and of community involvement gave the general idea of work experience and technical skills an enhanced status. Though the traditional grammar education still dominated many comprehensive schools, nevertheless by 1976 change was already underway. It was in this changing situation that the Ruskin Speech made its impact, to be reinforced by such publications as *Understanding Industry* by the Confederation of British Industries, the Schools Council Industry Project and later initiatives including TVEI and prevocational education.

THE ECLECTIC, PRIMARY CURRICULUM

One of the arguments put forward in the latter half of the 1980s in favour of the National Curriculum was that it would save the primary school from the worst excesses of progressive education and restore the three Rs to their rightful place in the primary curriculum. Such a view appeared to have the stamp of royal approval when Prince Charles, in between denouncing styles of modern architecture, attacked teaching styles and aims which had neglected the basic skills and had resulted in declining standards of literacy and numeracy. The results of recent educational research tended to support the more subjective impressions of teachers, headmasters, inspectors and training college supervisors that the three Rs still occupied their traditional central position in the primary school classroom, including what was regarded as 'prime teaching time'. Few examples could be found of the type of classroom caricatured in the Black Papers and pilloried in the popular press. One principal reason for these differences is that those who adopt the Black Paper viewpoint tend to assume that the history of primary education is one of the replacements of one type of education or concept of education with another; thus in the late sixties and early seventies the Black Paper authors attacked progressive education, perceiving it to be the latest form of primary education which had superseded all others. The preceding sections have shown, in general terms, a rather different picture, that of the absorption of one tradition by another so that elements of all can still be discerned at work in the modern classroom. The primary school classroom of today is no exception. This section seeks to identify the three main traditions which have influenced and still influence classroom practice.

The first of these traditions has already been described: that is, the elementary tradition out of which primary education emerged rather tardily. Its official reign ended with the abolition of the elementary school regulations in 1926 but it held sway for at least another twenty years thereafter. While it was gradually divested of many of its secondary trappings, such as very large classes and the pupil teacher system, its characteristic emphasis on the basic skills has remained in a prominent position since the nineteenth century. The need to secure smaller classes in order to move away from the mass, formal teaching methods was in itself a long, protracted struggle. The teachers' unions and the Labour movement, in particular, recognised that the grip of the elementary tradition on primary education could be relaxed only if there was a progressive reduction in class size. The following NUT resolution, passed in 1928, and the Labour Party's comments on it, illustrate this concern.

No class in any school, whether infant, junior or senior, should exceed 40 on the roll, and every effort should be made to secure that this maximum is not exceeded.

The Labour Party also believed that an extended liberal education at university level for intending teachers could also help break this strangehold, although here it was a little at odds with the NUT, as the NUT resolution and Labour Party comment reveals.

NUT Resolution

It is desirable that the number of graduates entering the teaching profession should be largely increased, but appointments to post-primary work of every kind should be made with full regard to experience and teaching ability as well as to academic qualifications, and the Board of Education Certificate should continue to be sufficient to qualify a teacher for the headship of a post-primary school.

Labour Party Comment

We agree that the number of graduates entering the teaching profession should be largely increased. While it is desirable that a certain period should elapse before a university degree is made an indispensable condition of appointment to the headship of a post-primary school, we think that the aim should be for *all head-teachers* eventually to have university qualifications.

Despite some disagreement over matters of detail there was general agreement among educationists in the 1920s that the elementary tradition with its class basis ought to be replaced. If the educationists of that decade rejected one very narrow concept of education they were in danger of embracing a second which also had distinct limitations. This saw primary education as preparatory education. It arose from the predominant concern of educationists with adolescent education. R. H. Tawney sketched out the reorganisation of adolescent education along secondary lines in 1922 in his book *Secondary Education for All* and regarded the function of primary education as preparing those under the age of 11 for the kind of liberal education received after that age. The opening paragraph of his book summed up the Labour Party's policy. The reform of education aimed to achieve a system 'under which primary education and secondary education are organised as two stages in a single process; secondary education being the education of the adolescent and primary education being *education preparatory thereto*'. More important for the broader dissemination of this concept was the reiteration of Tawney's definition of primary education by the most prestigious of the Government's advisory committees in 1926, the Consultative Committee of the Board of Education. In its report on *The Education of the Adolescent* it too spoke of the 'desire to mark as clearly as possible the fact that at the age 11 children are beginning a fresh phase of their education, which is different from *the primary or preparatory phase*'. This definition of primary education accepted a basic tenet of the elementary tradition, but whereas the elementary tradition viewed education as preparatory for the world of work, the emerging primary tradition saw it as a preparation for the next stage in education. To this extent the Hadow concept, as promulgated in 1926, shared something in common with the earlier elementary tradition; it also shared something in common with the later developmental tradition in that it laid stress not upon social class but upon developmental psychology. The presence on the committee of the leading psychologists of the age, Percy Nunn and Cyril Burt, helped to ensure that some attention was given to child development, irrespective of parental background. Such a concept also helped to bring the state sector in line with the independent sector which had long exercised considerable influence and which had a strong preparatory tradition. A preparatory education was seen as an essential precondition of secondary education. As Tawney, Nunn, Barker and most of the Hadow Committee had personal experience of the preparatory tradition of the independent sector it was scarcely surprising that their first thoughts on the function of primary education in the new structure were conditioned by their own upbringing.

There was, however, another, more restricted sense in which primary education was seen as preparatory, which paralleled the private sector; and that was in regarding primary education, especially in its later stages, as preparing pupils to sit a selective examination for the secondary sector. On the face of it, the Hadow Committee appeared to favour an examination at the age of 11+ which was intended to achieve 'selection by discrimination rather than selection by elimination'. That is, it appeared to recommend an examination for which there would be no preparation, an examination which aimed to discover pupils' aptitudes and abilities and thus help direct them to the most suitable form of secondary education. As it was not seen, at a theoretical level at least, as a pass-or-fail examination, there was no need for any specific preparation for it. In the introduction to their report, the Hadow Committee took a rather different view. They commented on the subject of an entrance examination: 'But the most pleasant of parks will none the less have an entrance and an exit; and we are disposed to believe that we may safely recommend the institution of an entrance examination, on the lines of the present examination for scholarships and free places in secondary schools.' This examination was, however, peculiarly unsuited to the task which the Committee had in mind, for it was both highly selective (with only the top 25 per cent entering secondary schools) and very much concerned to test only the basic skills. Such an examination would cause teachers to spend a great deal of time preparing pupils not for secondary education but for the entrance examination. The worst features of the Free Place Examination would have thus been preserved. This restricted concept of preparatory education was, in fact, to the fore in the reorganisation of education after 1944 when teachers spent much time in the final years of the primary school preparing their pupils for the 11+ examination, as a result of which a small successful minority went on to receive a grammar school education.

Thus in both forms, preparatory education preserved much of the elementary school tradition. Its emphasis was upon basic skills and it saw pupils in relation to what were believed to be their future, not primarily their immediate, needs.

Yet the Committee that defined the concept of primary education as preparatory education in 1926 redefined it in a very different way four years later. In its report, *The Primary School*, the Hadow Committee pointed to the danger when

> the curriculum is distorted and the teaching warped from its proper character by the supposed need of meeting the requirements of a later educational stage ... no good can come from teaching children things that have no immediate value for them, however highly their potential or prospective value may be estimated.

Having thus condemned the view of the primary school curriculum to which it gave support a few years earlier, it went on to redefine it in a way which appeared very different from both the elementary and preparatory traditions. The breadth of the developmental tradition, to which the Committee now transferred its allegiance, is evident from its statement of the basic aims of the primary curriculum.

> Applying these considerations to the problem before us, we see that the curriculum is to be thought of in terms of activity and experience rather than of knowledge to be acquired and facts to be stored. Its aim should be to develop in a child the fundamental human powers and to awaken him to the fundamental interests of civilised life so far as these powers and interests lie within the compass of childhood, to encourage him to attain gradually to that control and orderly management of his energies, impulses and emotions, which is the essence of moral and intellectual discipline, to help him to discover the idea of duty and to ensue it, and to open out his imagination and his sympathies in such a way that he may be prepared to understand and to follow in later years the highest examples of excellence in life and conduct.

The suggestions made by the Committee for the teaching of the three Rs and other subjects show that developmental or child-centred education was not envisaged to be the creative free-for-all as claimed in the Black Papers. They still remained at the core of the curriculum with the emphasis upon 'the formation of correct habits of speaking and writing' and the 'thorough mastery' of the fundamental rules of arithmetic. In the case of the latter, the Committee laid down the goal that 'these fundamental processes of arithmetic shall become automatic before the child leaves the primary school'. There was a recognition of the need for improved liaison between primary and secondary school and between nursery/infant and primary school to ease problems of transition.

So anxious was Tawney to sink the concept of preparatory education which he had first helped to launch in 1922 that he persuaded the Consultative Committee to extend its enquiry to the infant and nursery school. Its report, published in 1933, stood squarely in the developmental tradition and stressed this by quoting the lengthy passage above from its earlier primary school report. By 1933 it had become self-evident to the Committee that

> no one who has grasped the idea that life is a process of growth in which there are successive stages, each with its own specific character and needs, will dispute the conclusion that the best preparation for a later stage is to base the training during the particular stage on the immediate needs of that stage.

The concept of preparatory education had, by the simple verbal device of apparently stating the obvious, been neatly absorbed into the concept of developmental education, a concept which had been reinforced in both the primary and infant-nursery reports by the use of extensive introductory chapters on child psychology. The process of absorption rather than replacement was complete, with the preparatory tradition having absorbed much of the elementary tradition and the developmental tradition having absorbed elements of both. Thereafter, except for those who wished to simplify concepts for political ends, educationists recognised the difficulties inherent in identifying and analysing the distinct curriculum theories underlying teaching styles and goals.

Historians of education have sometimes failed to recognise the multi-faceted nature of the British developmental theory. Philip Taylor, for example, has commented[34]:

> After the Second World War, 'free activity', 'the play way' and readiness were to become bywords in primary education culminating in the root metaphor of the 1952 Handbook of Suggestions: 'First the blade and then the ear then the full corn shall appear.' Primary education came to be conceived as cultivation.

In practice, although activity methods were employed in the first years of the primary school and pupils were taught a range of subjects of which the Hadow committees of 1930 and 1933 would have approved, the curriculum in the later years of the primary school was greatly influenced by the need to prepare children for the 11+ examination. Figure 2.3 shows a typical primary school report from the period immediately after the 1944 Education Act when education was being reorganised to enable all children to receive a primary and secondary education.

An elementary school child of the inter-war years could be pardoned for wondering if the revolution which had brought about a new structure in education after 1944 had passed the curriculum by. After 1944 pupils were prepared for an 11+ examination not too dissimilar from the Free Place Examination in English and Arithmetic. (Welsh was taught but not tested at 11+ in the schools of Wales.) Other subjects such as Geography, History, Nature Study, Arts and Crafts and Music were usually dropped from the school timetables or given minority time in order that adequate time could be devoted to the examined subdivisions of Arithmetic: mental, mechanical and problems. Achieve-

FLINTSHIRE EDUCATION COMMITTEE

COUNTY PRIMARY SCHOOL
Marine Road, Prestatyn

Report on the work of Ronald Brooks
for the ~~half-year,~~ term, ~~period~~ (mid test) ending Dec 22nd 1950
Standard IV Number in Class 35 Position ....

SUBJECT	MARKS %	REMARKS
Welsh	92	Very Good.
Reading		
Writing		
~~Spelling~~ Language	70	Fairly Good
Composition	80	Good
Comprehension	85	Very Fair
Arithmetic Mental	65	Good
Mechanical	80	
Problems	70	F. Gd.
Geography		
History		
Nature Study		
Arts and Crafts		
Music		
Physical Training & Organised Games		

Attendance V. Good Punctuality V. Good

Progress: Very Satisfactory

Remarks: Keep it up!

Signed .... Class Teacher
[signature] Headmaster

Fig. 2.2 ***A typical primary school report***

ment or lack of it was recorded by a percentage and simple comment. With 11 year olds supposed to be starting to experience what psychologists called 'a rising tide in the veins of youth', it was time to prepare them for the examination which led to the second stage of their education. The curriculum combined some elements of the elementary and preparatory traditions used in the service of a faulty developmental psychology. The narrowing of the primary school curriculum and an excessive emphasis on the acquisition of measurable skills, accompanied in some schools by rigid streaming, remained features of many primary schools well into the 1960s and has led some of those who remember these and other developments to express concern about their recurrence under the National Curriculum.

By the 1960s HMI inspectors were reporting that these effects were lessening, in part because teachers' estimates were increasingly being used to replace externally imposed attainment tests. However, the Plowden Report of 1967 referred to the number of teachers who continued their established routines using 'books of English exercises and of mechanical computation'. There was, however, a steadily increasing commitment to 'child-centred education' in the 1960s as local authorities moved away from the 11+ examination and comprehensive schools became more numerous. In reaction to the excessive use of schools tests and the limited curriculum of many schools in the fifties, the Plowden Committee stressed the need for flexibility, the merits of the topic approach, discovery methods and the value of using the environment as a means of integrating subjects and encouraging curiosity.[35]

> Any practice which predetermines the pattern and imposes it upon all is to be condemned. Some teachers find it helpful in maintaining a balance in individual and class work to think in terms of broad areas of the curriculum such as language, science and mathematics, environmental study and the expressive arts. No pattern can be perfect since many subjects fall into one category or another according to the aspect which is being studied. For young children, the broadest of divisions is suitable. For children from 9 to 12, more subject divisions can be expected . . .
>
> There is little place for the type of scheme which sets down exactly what ground should be covered and what skill should be acquired by each class in the school.

The Black Papers regarded the Plowden Report as a libertarian charter; they failed to realise that most schools tended to adapt current ideas to established practices, and that the primary curricular tradition was not one of immediate and wholesale change to meet the educational philosophy of the moment. It was the absorption of various elements, often incongruous, into a broad working philosophy which was perceived to best suit the needs of particular groups of pupils. If there was continuing concern about classroom revolutions and major shifts in the educational philosophy of the teaching profession, it was only because those who expressed such concern had failed to keep up with educational research or had disregarded its findings. The results of one of the major research projects, the ORACLE project undertaken at the University of Leicester between 1975 and 1980, confirmed what many teachers knew.[36]

> . . . teaching was found to be largely didactic in character. The promotion of enquiry or discovery learning appeared almost non-existent . . . Further, as regards the content of education, a major emphasis on 'the basics' was also found. There was little evidence of any fundamental shift, either in the content of education or in the procedures of teaching and learning.

EXAMINATIONS AND THE SECONDARY SCHOOL CURRICULUM

The speed with which the educational reforms of the 1980s were enacted, together with their radical nature, tended to obscure the fact that they followed the established British practice of piecemeal innovation. With each reform following hot on the heels of the previous one without much thought being given to their overall effect on the school timetable and curriculum, teachers were left wondering when politicians would recognise what was increasingly apparent at school level – namely, how the already overcrowded curriculum could cope with changes such as the GCSE and the National Curriculum. The problems of the overcrowded curriculum, not new, were greatly exacerbated. Only on the eve of the 1990s did the Government turn to consider the problems of implementation. The immediate response was to give priority to the most recent reform, the National Curriculum, and to suggest changes to GCSE which meant the emasculation of the curriculum, the dropping of certain subjects, particularly humanities subjects, the introduction of combined subjects, or the teaching of 'half GCSEs' similar to the 'AS' half-'A' levels. The proposals of the School Examinations and Assessment Council (SEAC) and the National Curriculum Council (NCC) were summarised as follows:

> The first decisions have already been made. Every pupil up to 16 in England and Wales will have to study mathematics, English and the single science covering biology, chemistry and physics.
>
> They will probably also have to continue with a modern language, given the importance of European contacts, and craft design and technology, because of its increasing importance in finding jobs.
>
> As for history, geography, music, art and physical education, children who do not want to continue with them to GCSE will probably be able to drop them at 14 if they have reached level eight on the National Curriculum scale, which some ministers believe is equivalent to a 'good GCSE pass at B or C grade'.[37]

The thinking behind this kind of solution was well in keeping with certain basic features of British educational tradition which came increasingly under attack in the 1960s and 1970s. These were:

> The definition of the curriculum largely in terms of subjects, in part to accommodate the requirements of public examinations.
>
> The placing of subjects into groups.
>
> The arrangement of subject groups into hierarchies.
>
> The attempt to deal with the overcrowding of the school curriculum and examination timetable by eliminating or down-grading whole areas of experience, irrespective of whether or not these were beneficial to the general education of adolescents.

The problems of examinations and the overcrowded curriculum were nothing new to secondary education, and had, in fact, dogged it almost since the advent of state secondary schooling. The war-time coalition

Table 2.4 ***Timetable of a coeducational municipal secondary school, 1922***
(School Hours: 9.30 a.m. to 1 p.m., and 2.30 p.m. to 4.30 p.m.)

Form	V.U.A.	V.U.B.	L.V.R.	V.A.	V.B.	IV.R.	IV.A.	IV.B.	III.R.	III.A.	III.B.	III.C.	II.	I.
Average Age	Y. M. 15 11	Y.M. 16 4	Y.M. 15 8	Y.M. 14 0	Y.M. 14 5	Y.M. 14 3	Y.M. 13 1	Y.M. 13 1	Y.M. 13 3	Y.M. 11 10	Y.M. 12 5	Y.M. 12 7	Y.M. 11 2	Y.M. 10 6
	hrs.	hrs.	hrs.	hrs.	hrs.	hrs.	hrs.	hrs.	hrs.	hrs.	hrs.	hrs.	hrs.	hrs.
Religious Instruction	$\frac{2}{3}$	$\frac{2}{3}$	$\frac{2}{3}$	$\frac{2}{3}$	$\frac{2}{3}$	$\frac{2}{3}$	$\frac{2}{3}$	$\frac{2}{3}$	$\frac{2}{3}$	$1\frac{1}{3}$	$1\frac{1}{3}$	$1\frac{1}{3}$	$\frac{2}{3}$	$\frac{2}{3}$
English Lang. and Lit.	$3\frac{1}{3}$	$3\frac{1}{3}$	$3\frac{1}{3}$	$3\frac{1}{3}$	$3\frac{1}{3}$	$3\frac{1}{3}$	$3\frac{1}{3}$	$3\frac{1}{3}$	$3\frac{1}{3}$	$3\frac{1}{3}$	$3\frac{1}{3}$	$3\frac{1}{3}$	4	$4\frac{2}{3}$
History	2	2	2	2	2	2	2	2	2	2	2	2	2	2
Geography	2	2	2	2	2	2	2	2	2	2	2	2	2	2
Latin	$2\frac{2}{3}$[1]	$2\frac{2}{3}$[1]	...	$2\frac{2}{3}$[1]	$2\frac{2}{3}$[1]	...	$2\frac{1}{3}$[1]	$2\frac{1}{3}$[1]	...	...	...	...	...	...
French	4[2]	...	...	...	...	...	...	...	...	...	...	...	...	...
German	4[2]	4	$3\frac{1}{3}$	$3\frac{1}{3}$	$3\frac{1}{3}$	$3\frac{1}{3}$	$3\frac{1}{3}$	$3\frac{1}{3}$	$3\frac{1}{3}$	4	4	4	$3\frac{1}{3}$	$3\frac{1}{3}$
Arithmetic	$1\frac{1}{3}$	$1\frac{1}{3}$	$1\frac{1}{3}$	$1\frac{1}{3}$	$1\frac{1}{3}$	$1\frac{1}{3}$	$1\frac{1}{3}$	$1\frac{1}{3}$	$1\frac{1}{3}$	2	2	2	$3\frac{1}{3}$	$3\frac{1}{3}$
Algebra	2	2	2	2	2	2	$1\frac{1}{3}$	$1\frac{1}{3}$	$1\frac{1}{3}$	$1\frac{1}{3}$	$1\frac{1}{3}$	$1\frac{1}{3}$	...	...
Geometry	2	2	2	2	2	2	2	2	2	$1\frac{1}{3}$	$1\frac{1}{3}$	$1\frac{1}{3}$	$\frac{2}{3}$	...
Trigonometry	$1\frac{1}{3}$[2]	...	...	$\frac{2}{3}$[3]	$\frac{2}{3}$[3]	...	...	...	...	...	...	...	...	...
Chemistry	$2\frac{2}{3}$[4]	...	$2\frac{1}{3}$[4]	$2\frac{1}{3}$[4]	$2\frac{2}{3}$[4]	$2\frac{2}{3}$[4]	$2\frac{2}{3}$[4]	$2\frac{2}{3}$[4]	...	...	...	...	...	...
Physics	$2\frac{2}{3}$[1]	...	$2\frac{2}{3}$[5]	$2\frac{2}{3}$[1]	$2\frac{2}{3}$[1]	$2\frac{2}{3}$[5]	$2\frac{1}{3}$[1]	$2\frac{1}{3}$[1]	$2\frac{2}{3}$[5]	$2\frac{2}{3}$	$2\frac{2}{3}$	$2\frac{2}{3}$	...	...
Botany	$2\frac{2}{3}$[4]	$2\frac{2}{3}$	$2\frac{1}{3}$[4]	$2\frac{2}{3}$[4]	$2\frac{1}{3}$[4]	$2\frac{2}{3}$[4]	$2\frac{2}{3}$[4]	$2\frac{2}{3}$[4]	$2\frac{1}{3}$[4]	...	...	...	...	...

Nature Study	…	…	…	…	…	…	…	…	…	…	…	…	1⅓	1⅓
Drawing	1⅓	1⅓	1⅓	1⅓	1⅓	1⅓	1⅓	1⅓	1⅓	1⅓	1⅓	1⅓	1⅓	1⅓
Music and Singing	⅔[2]	⅔	⅔[6]	⅔	⅔	⅔	⅔	⅔	⅔	⅔	⅔	⅔	1⅓	1⅓
Housewifery	…	…	…	…	…	…	1⅓[1]	1⅓[1]	1⅓[5]	…	…	…	…	…
Manual Instruction	…	…	…	…	…	…	1⅓[8]	1⅓[8]	1⅓[8]	2⅔[8]	2⅔[8]	2⅔[8]	1⅓[8]	1⅓[8]
Needlework	2⅔[1]	2⅔[1]	2⅔[5]	2⅔[1]	2⅔[1]	2⅔[5]	1[1]	1[1]	1⅓[5]	1⅓[8]	1⅓[8]	1⅓[8]	1⅓[8]	1⅓[8]
Cookery, Laundry	…	…	…	…	…	…	1⅓[8]	1⅓[8]	1⅓[8]	1⅓[8]	1⅓[8]	1⅓[8]	…	…
Physical Exercises:														
Boys	⅔	1⅓	⅔	⅔	⅔	⅔	⅔	⅔	⅔	⅔	⅔	⅔	1⅓	1⅓
Girls	1⅓[3]	1⅓	1⅓	1⅓[3]	1⅓[3]	1⅓	⅔	⅔	⅔	⅔	⅔	⅔	1⅓	1⅓
Games	1⅓	1⅓	1⅓	1⅓	1⅓	1⅓	1⅓	1⅓	1⅓	1⅓	1⅓	1⅓	1⅓	1⅓
Private Study	…	…	1⅓[6]	…	…	⅔[7]	…	…	…	…	…	…	1⅓	1⅓
Journals	…	…	⅔	⅔	⅔	⅔	⅔	⅔	⅔	⅔	⅔	⅔	⅔	⅔
Special Handwork	…	…	…	…	…	…	…	…	…	…	…	…	1⅓	1⅓
Homework	10⅔	10⅔	10⅔	7½	7½	7½	7½	7½	7½	7½	7½	7½	3⅓	3⅓

[1]Latin or Physics may be taken by boys; and Latin or Domestic Subjects by girls. [2]French or Germany may be taken. [3]Trigonometry or Music and Singing, or Physical Exercises may be taken. [4]Chemistry or Botany may be taken. [5]Physics or Domestic Subjects may be taken. [6]Music and Singing or Private Study may be taken in the case of boys. [7]Boys only. [8]Manual Instruction or Domestic Subjects may be taken.

government in 1917 set up one of SEACs predecessors, the Secondary Schools Examination Council (SSEC) to tackle the matter. The SSEC had the task of devising and introducing an examination system particularly for the secondary schools created under the 1902 Education Act and governed by the 1904 Regulations. This body, consisting of LEA, teacher and university representatives, aimed to use the First School (Certificate) Examination to provide a general education quite distinctive from that of the elementary school. The First School (Certificate) Examination was devised as a grouped-subject (as opposed to today's single-subject) examination. To pass the School Certificate candidates had to pass in five subjects, but not any five. In 1917, these five had to include at least one subject from the three main groups, English subjects, Foreign languages (classical or modern) and Sciences/Mathematics. The inferior status of the fourth group (Art, Music and Practical subjects) was confirmed by the stipulation that candidates could offer only one of their five from this group. This system of grouping remained in operation until 1951 although some limited reform was achieved in the inter-war years by relaxing the latter rule to enable more than one subject to be chosen from the fourth group, and by allowing proficiency in either a modern language or maths/science, but not necessarily in both. The principle of the group certificate, however, remained largely at the insistence of the main teachers' union, the NUT. Its purpose was not necessarily to protect the interests of the majority of students; the five-subject requirement served university demands for a pass at credit standard to ensure a general education of high standard before embarking on a narrow degree course. The demand for a pass at credit or university matriculations standard was taken up by many employers, thus placing additional severe pressures on students.

What this meant in terms of timetable arrangements is seen from Table 2.4, which shows the weekly hours of study of a coeducational selective secondary school with some technical bias.[38] Although this was not a typical school of the inter-war period, it offers the best opportunities of comparison with today's secondary schools.

The note of explanation which accompanies the table indicates the hierarchies among and the gender bias within subjects, all of which were underpinned by the examination system.

Note of explanation

The girls have access to well fitted cookery and laundry rooms and in addition to Cookery and Laundry work they study Housewifery and Needlework.

Thus more time is assigned to Handwork subjects than is usually the case, and moreover, these subjects are taught in surroundings which bring the pupil into contact with the outside world.

All pupils take German as the first foreign language. This was determined before the war owing to the bearing of German science on the local industries (in this case mining and iron industries).

The curriculum in the first year is as follows: English, History, Geography, German, Mathematics, Physics (Introductory Science), Handwork, Drill, Music, Games.

The subjects studied in the first year are continued throughout the school course with the exception that, at the beginning of the second year, Introductory Science is replaced by Chemistry (for boys) and by Botany (for girls). Differentiation begins in the second year. The better boys have a choice between Latin or Physics and the more able girls have a choice between Physics, Latin and additional Domestic Science. Only scholars with distinct literary ability are allowed to take Latin. Thus the majority study one foreign language, and, as a rule, those who take up Latin are intending candidates for an Arts Degree or for entry into profession (e.g. law, medicine).

The weaker scholars have no opportunity of studying a second foreign language; instead they devote their time to practical subjects which are potentially vocational.

A committee of the Board of Education which enquired into curriculum differentiation for boys and girls in secondary schools in the early 1920s wanted to use the newly instituted First School (Certificate) Examination to emphasise what it perceived to be the differences in the interests and future occupations of the sexes; the Committee did not think it desirable to attempt 'to divorce a girl's education from her home duties and opportunities'. It also argued that girls should be encouraged to take the examination a year later than boys so as not to place 'undue demands on the girl's physical and nervous force', the Committee having detected a tendency among girls 'to mental lethargy and slovenliness in work'. It did, however, argue in favour of 'a more prominent and established place in the ordinary curricula of schools for ... aesthetic subjects', and for more practical approaches to the teaching of the traditional subjects but there was very little immediate change in these directions. The Board's Consultative Committee thus recommended a more balanced curriculum than the school certificate examination permitted. It also recognised a problem which the examination system helped to create, that of 'the overcrowding of the timetable' which tended to push creative and artistic subjects to the periphery of the curriculum. Interestingly, the first thoughts of the NCC and SEAC in 1989 on the avoidance of timetable overcrowding, quoted earlier, was to do much the same thing.

Throughout the 1920s and 1930s the Board of Education's most prestigious advisory committee, the Consultative Committee, attacked the influence of examinations. Their criticisms have a modern ring to them. The most outspoken, and some would say the most relevant to the 1990s, was that made in its report on *The Primary School* (1930). This has been examined in the previous section (see pp. 89–90). The two main reports relating to secondary education, the Hadow Report (1926) and the Spens Report (1938), made rather different criticisms. The Hadow Report of 1926 recognised how manifestly unsuited was the First School (Certificate) Examination for assessing practical subjects and practical approaches to traditional subjects, and argued in favour of creating a 'new examination framed in correspondence with ... needs. Such an examination was to be optional and was to be in the hands of new examining boards. The Spens Report (p. 257) endorsed the principle that any examination should 'follow the curriculum and not determine it'. It argued that the First School (Certificate) Examination had established standards and broadened the curriculum when it was founded, but by 1938 it had become a restricting influence.

The School Certificate Examination controls the curriculum, and we cannot avoid the conclusion that the requirements of the examination have put a heavy premium on certain subjects to the detriment of others, and have compelled schools, in the interest of pupils desiring to obtain the Certificate, to teach certain subjects to all pupils throughout their course, even when they might be deriving greater benefit from taking alternative subjects or from taking fewer subjects to a higher level.

The Spens Report took up the theme of the unnecessary strain of examinations on pupils, which had been a criticism voiced in the Consultative Committee's Report of 1922. The rigour of preparation for the examination and the importance attached to the group certificate by employers often caused overstrain and excessive anxiety. The Spens Committee also pointed to another fundamental problem, that of one examination serving a dual purpose, as a terminal qualification and as a qualification for entry to higher education. The Committee claimed that the latter was being given unwarranted priority over the former with 'disastrous' results. Subjects which were of no value for matriculation purposes were at a disadvantage; the development of practical and aesthetic subjects thus lagged behind other academic subjects. The Committee concluded that the conjunction of the matriculation certificate (for university entrance) and the school certificate had helped to upset the curricular balance of academic and non-academic subjects, a balance which they believed ought to be maintained. The separation of the two tasks through the employment of two examinations, which the Secondary School Examination Council advocated, was given support by the Spens Committee. They also argued that it was not in the interest of school leavers for the school certificate to record only those subjects in which a credit had been obtained, which was the current practice largely to please employers.

The chief criticism made by the Spens Committee, however, was of the grouped-subject system and of the five-subject requirements. These were seen as severely inhibiting the wider choice of subjects which the teaching profession was said to favour. Spens favoured the idea of 'a compulsory spread', one which lies behind today's National Curriculum, in order to discourage undue specialisation at the adolescent stage of education. While encouraging the lifting of some of the restrictions, the Committee nevertheless argued in favour of a pass in English and in either a foreign language or a science before a certificate should be granted. There could thus be a reduction in the number of subjects on the timetable. This was accompanied by a recommendation for a reduction in syllabus content, the provision of papers corresponding to varying ranges of work in different subjects and a limit of six or seven on the number of subjects offered. The aim of these changes was to maintain curricular breadth while at the same time avoiding overloading students.

Of the two approaches to examination reform – the radical questioning of the whole value of external examinations by the Hadow Committee in its report on *The Primary School*, and the more cautious reform of the school certificate advocated by the Spens Committee – the Norwood Committee in its report in 1943 favoured the former. It took up the view expressed in the 1922 report and that of Spens that the First School (Certificate) Examination dominated and distorted the curriculum and came to a conclusion in line with that of Hadow that examinations should only play a subordinate role in the assessment of pupils. It looked forward to the time when all syllabuses and examination papers were devised and marked by teachers, thus making the formal process of assessment the servant instead of the master of the curriculum. It argued that school records should play a more important role in assessment. Until these ambitious goals were achieved the existing system should be reformed to reduce university and school-certificate domination of the curriculum. The interim reforms favoured were: that the school certificate examination should be run by a body of eight teachers, four LEA representatives, four university representatives, supported by four HMI assessors; that schools should offer their own syllabuses (thus anticipating elements of CSE and GCSE mode 3) and prescribed syllabuses should be lightened in content; and that the examination should be a single-subject not a grouped-subject examination, without restrictions on the number of subjects for which a student was entered. The post-war Labour Government favoured the latter proposal and made the Minister of Education responsible for coordinating secondary school examinations.

In 1951 the single-subject GCE examination was introduced with the consequences that have been examined in the previous sections. The new pass level, however, was to approximate the old credit grade, not the old pass grade; thus, as in the case of the transition from GCE to GCSE in 1988, Ministers could make the claim of raising educational standard at the same time as promoting highly advantageous reform. These reforms seemed to free the curriculum from much of its examination straitjacket but this was not to take into account the influence of the universities. In 1949 the universities had made their view known that they rejected the Norwood stress on school reports and outlined a new matriculation requirement of five GCE passes with at least two at Advanced level. These were to include English, another language, and Mathematics or a Science subject; thus the greater degree of freedom

Table 2.5 ***Percentage of mode 3 subject entries in 1966, 1973 and 1974 (CSE boards)***

Examining board	*1966*	*1973*	*1974*
Associated Lancashire	3.0	10	17
East Anglia	30.8	29	31
East Midland	18.5	24	24
Metropolitan	1.0	6	9
Middlesex	4.4	9	12
North	9.3	28	35
North Western	0.3	5	9
Southern	1.0	12	17
South-East	1.5	6	10
South Western	6.0	13	15
Welsh	0.3	4	7
West Midlands	2.1	6	10
West Yorkshire and Lindsey	49.4	62	69
Yorkshire	3.0	12	19
Total	8.9	16.3	21.0

which was apparently offered under the new certificate was reduced by university entrance requirements which demanded grouping. University influence on the school curriculum was tremendous in view of the shortage of university places, and, especially in that it continued to operate through the examination system; if the Norwood ideas of school records and school-based examinations had been adopted, perhaps university influence over the curriculum, followed by the vast majority of the nation's children and not just the small percentage who went to university, would have been lessened. Successive governments of both political persuasions also wished to increase their control over the curriculum through enhanced representation on the SSEC so that by 1961 all of the representatives of the examining bodies had been removed and government nominees increased in number. But unlike the universities, government had no clear idea of what they wanted from the examination system.

In practice, the control of the curriculum fell more into the hands of the teachers, although university influence, especially on grammar schools and the GCE, remained strong. The major developments of the sixties in public examinations took place largely outside the area of university influence. The Beloe Report of 1960 challenged SSEC policy in advocating the setting up of a new examination, the Certificate of Secondary Education, for 16 year olds for whom the GCE was not suitable. The CSE allowed teachers to align the examination system more with the curricular needs of students than with those of outside groups. Subject panels were teacher-dominated and the mode 3 provision enabled teachers to design and examine syllabuses partly but not entirely in line with the Norwood concept of internal examinations. Table 2.5 shows the take-up of mode 3 in selected years during the first nine years of its operation.[39]

Attempts to reform examinations have always been met with the criticism that such changes represent a lowering of standards. To help meet this criticism a Grade 1 pass at CSE was classed as a pass at GCE; similarly with the introduction of the GCSE examination in 1988, the first three grades of the new examination were claimed to be of the same standard as the first three grades of the old examination, GCE. But the newly created GCSE groups did little to encourage mode 3 submission. This was not surprising as teacher assessment was an in-built feature of the compulsory coursework requirement of the new examination and the examining groups were still establishing mode 1 standards. The GCSE, which appeared to ease much of the tension between curricular needs and public examination, was scarcely under-way before it was confronted with the less flexible National Curriculum.

EXAMINATIONS AND THE SIXTH-FORM CURRICULUM

The education of students who stay on at schools and colleges after the compulsory school leaving age has been a constant concern of educationists. Supplementary Advanced level, examined for the first time in 1989, was but one of the more recent attempts to meet a problem described thirty years earlier in the Crowther Report.[40]

> The argument is not whether specialisation is desirable or unavoidable; it is about when it should begin. In England it begins for many subjects earlier than in any other country.
>
> In this system of specialisation for young people while they are still at school English education is singular. Neither in Western Europe nor in North America is there anything of the sort. Even nearer to home, in Scotland, the schools insist on a much wider spread of subjects in the Sixth Form than we do in England. On the continent of Europe, there is no question of dropping altogether the study of languages or history or mathematics or science, while in some countries Latin as well is kept on the compulsory list for all pupils in the most highly selective schools. There is, it is true, the possibility in the later years of following a course with a bias towards either literary or scientific studies – the situation in this respect (though, of course, at a much higher level of attainment) is rather more like that in the Fourth or Fifth Forms of an English grammar school than in the Sixth. But admission to a university or equivalent institution depends on satisfactory performance in all subjects of the curriculum, and not only in those in the direction in which the curriculum is biased. In the United States, similarly, the 17 year- old in High School takes a wide range of subjects.

The Crowther Report examined an important issue which was not reconsidered when 'AS' levels were under discussion. That was the way in which the sixth form exerted 'a downward pressure' on the school curriculum so that 'in effect, specialisation had already begun before pupils entered post-compulsory education'. Practical and aesthetic subjects were already being pushed to the periphery of the curriculum before students entered the sixth form, thus denying to many the fullest opportunities for a broad sixth-form education. The result of this was the kind of restricted thinking which lay behind such initiatives as 'AS' levels, where broadening the curriculum was seen largely in terms of Science students taking an Arts subject, including languages, and Arts students taking a Science subject, including Mathematics. The Crowther solution put forward in 1959 was a little more far-reaching than the 'AS' level formula in that it recognised that sixth-form students had common needs, irrespective of their faculty. It centred upon the more efficient, aims-orientated use of 'minority time' as well as the need to restructure 'A' level syllabuses and reduce the number of 'A' levels taken. Surveying the use of minority time, it reported that it was either wasted entirely or not treated sufficiently seriously. It recommended a pattern of common and complementary studies, and rejected the idea of 'making it normal for an arts specialist to take one science subject at Advanced level, and a science specialist one arts subject'.[41]

The main common elements, which should be taken by arts and science specialists together, can be summarised under three heads – religious education and all that goes to the formation of moral standards; art and music; and physical education.

The complementary elements should be designed to ensure the 'literacy' of science specialists and the 'numeracy' of arts specialists. By literacy in this context we mean not only the ability to use the mother tongue as an adequate means of communication for adult purposes, but also the development of moral, aesthetic and social judgement. By 'numeracy' we mean not only the ability to reason quantitatively but also some understanding of scientific method and some acquaintance with the achievement of science.

We considered, and reject, proposals to make good these deficiencies either by a 'general course' or by making it normal for an arts specialist to take one science subject at Advanced level, and a science specialist one arts subject.

On the subject of how to raise the status of such studies in the eyes of students who gave their first priority to 'A' level work, the Crowther Committee were less definite.

There are grave dangers in the examination of work done in 'minority time', but some outside influence is probably necessary if schools and pupils are to take it more seriously than at present. The most potent influence is likely to be the knowledge that prospective employers, universities and colleges of advanced technology attach importance to it.

The problem of the sixth form curriculum was one of the first nettles to be grasped by the Schools Council at its first meeting in October

1964. It saw the problem in broader terms than Crowther in that it recognised the need not simply to counter excessive specialisation but to make provision for the growing number of sixth formers for whom the conventional three 'A' level curriculum was inappropriate. Its first thoughts were not too dissimilar from the later 'AS' formulation, especially in the emphasis on 'minor' and contrasting' studies. In one of its first working papers it argued in favour of a pattern of 'A' levels with some minor contrasting study in a different curricular area for some students, with others pursuing a curriculum comprising largely of minor studies in a wide variety of curricular areas. The needs of the increasing number of students who did not intend to go on to any form of higher education and for whom 'A' level courses were not always suitable were further examined in a working paper in 1968. This paper was more radical in its approach to the problem and adopted a way of looking at examinations which became the accepted convention in the 1980s and 1990s; it attacked the traditional definition of examinations in terms of subject content, and, using the model of the German *Arbitur*, stressed the benefits of aims-orientated examinations. In this type of examination there was no detailed definition of subject content, with the consequent 'cramming' which this produced; there was a rigorous exclusion of any questions which require the mere reproduction of facts. The examining board would state the aims of the examination and in response to this each school would submit its own range of questions, from which one would be selected. Candidates would be allowed five hours to answer the question, thus avoiding the race against the clock. The sixth-form curriculum, while still being geared to some form of examination, could thus be sufficiently diverse to cater for a wide range of student needs and teaching styles. Teacher assessments and oral work would form part of the final assessment. These ideas met with a mixed response with Craft, Applied Science and Technology specialists showing a large measure of agreement but History specialists 'not wholeheartedly in support of so much departure from custom'. The Schools Council was entering a minefield, being open to attack from those on the right who regarded any change in sixth-form examinations as a lowering of standards, and those on the left who wanted more radical changes than minor modifications to the sixth-form curriculum.

Its first definite scheme of reform came in 1969. A joint working party report suggested a controversial means of reducing over-specialisation through 'qualifying' examination (Q) in a wide range of subjects in the lower sixth and two or three 'further' examinations (F) roughly of 'A' level standard at the end of the second year. These radical proposals to replace 'A' levels with 'Q' and 'F' levels were rejected partly on the grounds that they would mean students sitting external examinations in three consecutive years, including the GCE 'O' level year. A second bite at the cherry was taken in 1973 when the Schools Council made a proposal to meet the latter criticism with a two-tier set of examinations, normal (N) and further (F) levels, to be sat in the same year. A five-subject curriculum was envisaged with students pursuing three 'N' level courses of half the work of 'A' levels, and two 'F' level courses of three-quarters the work of 'A' level. This was mathematically correct ($3 \times \frac{1}{2} + 2 \times \frac{3}{4} = 3$ 'A' level equivalence) but was likely to increase rather than reduce student overload. It finally foundered after the universities argued that this would lower standards. Thereafter, the reform of the curriculum was related to various schemes to reform rather than to replace 'A' levels, including 'AS' levels and streamlined 'A' levels. Schemes such as the Certificate of Extended Education which were aimed at the new sixth former stood little chance of developing into a fully accepted qualification because they lacked the relationship with 'A' level which was regarded as the hallmark of sixth-form study. The rejection of the Higginson proposals for streamlined 'A' levels left 'AS' levels the chief instrument for broadening the sixth-form curriculum, a somewhat inadequate response to a fundamental problem. The move in the 1990s towards tertiary and sixth-form colleges with access to technical and other courses offers the possibility of a more fruitful answer.

QUESTIONS

1. Explain how the areas-of-experience model differs from the subject-based curriculum model by reference to the development of elementary education in the nineteenth century.
2. How far could the gearing of teachers' pay to examination successes be justified?
3. What were the merits and demerits of the type of syllabus definition of the Revised Code? What alternative forms of syllabus definition are there?
4. Compare the first national curriculum for 'younger children' and for 'older children' with those of today.
5. Compare the roles of the inspectorate of the 1920s with those of today.
6. How was the elementary code designed for what were seen to be the needs of a particular social class?
7. Can there be such a thing as a non-political school curriculum?
8. In what ways did the 1944 Education Act leave open the possibility of future government control of the curriculum?
9. How are educational concepts historically conditioned?
10. Discuss how school subjects can be made relevant to students' own experiences.
11. What kind of education do employers believe schools should offer?
12. In what way does the Norwood Committee's descriptions of the

academic, practical and technical pupil reflect the educational bias of the age?

13. How far do today's debates about technical and vocational education mirror those at the end of the last century?
14. How far was the movement away from the elementary tradition dependent upon reductions in the size of classes?
15. How far should primary education be 'preparatory'?
16. Discuss the merits and demerits of dealing with timetable overcrowding through (a) the elimination of subjects from the timetable and (b) the combination of subjects.
17. Has the idea of a grouped-subject examination certificate any merits?
18. How far does gender influence the choice of examination subjects today?
19. In the light of various schemes put forward over the years, discuss how best sixth-form studies can be broadened.

NOTES AND REFERENCES

1. *The Times Educational Supplement*, 1 April 1988.
2. Viscount Haldane *et al.*, *The Next Step in Education*, 1927.
3. Quoted in J. S. Maclure's *Educational Documents: England and Wales*, pp. 43–4.
4. Maclure, op. cit., p. 79.
5. Maclure, op. cit., p. 80.
6. Code of Elementary School Regulations, 1922.
7. Maclure, op. cit., p. 156.
8. *The Morning Post*, 22 May 1926.
9. *The Times Educational Supplement*, 31 December 1976.
10. Lord Eustace Percy claimed this was the reason in his autobiography: *Some Memories*, 1958, pp. 120–1.
11. *Manchester Guardian*, 18 January 1926.
12. The Labour Party Research and Information Department/Advisory Committee on Education Memorandum 165d, May 1927.
13. Director, University of London Institute of Education (formerly London Day Training College) 1922–36; Professor of Education 1913–36. Author of several books on education, especially *Education: Its Data and First Principles*, 1920.
14. Lord Eustace Percy, *Education at the Crossroads*, Evans Brothers 1930.
15. Dated 29 November 1973.
16. *House of Commons Paliamentary Debates 1943–44*, vol. 396, cols. 1647, 1656, 1657 and 1658.
17. Debates, op. cit., 1960, vol. 620.
18. See B. Simon, *The Politics of Educational Reform 1920–1940*, Lawrence and Wishart, pp. 10, 17, 62.

19. 'The Organisation of Education after 11+', p. 2, *The Papers and Correspondence of Sir P. Nunn, 1907–1918.*
20. Labour Party's Advisory Committee on Education, *Continuation Education Under the New Act*, Memorandum No. 6, 1918.
21. Nunn, 1920, *Education: Its data and First Principles*, Arnold, p. 24.
22. *Curriculum and Examinations in Secondary Schools*, p. 2.
23. *Continuation Education Under the New Act*, p. 2.
24. *Secondary Education for All*, pp. 65, 106.
25. *The Education of the Adolescent*, p. 101.
26. Ibid., p. 115.
27. Reprinted in *Equal Opportunity in Education* (ed. H. Silver), Methuen, pp. 94–101.
28. *The Secondary Modern School*, pp. 91–2.
29. The Welsh Intermediate Education Act 1889, Section 17.
30. 'The Organisation of Education after 11+', p. 4, *Papers and Correspondence of Sir P. Nunn 1907–1918.*
31. *Education at the Crossroads*, Evans Brothers 1930.
32. The Spens Report, p. 105.
33. *Secondary Schools and Pupils in England and Wales 1976*, Volume 1.
34. P. Taylor, 1986, *Expertise and the Primary School Teacher*.
35. *Children and their Primary Schools.* A Report of the Central Advisory Council for Education (England), 1967, vol. 1, p. 152.
36. Quoted in R. Lowe (ed.), 1987, *The Changing Primary School*, Falner Press, p. 13.
37. *The Times*, 26 December 1989.
38. Board of Education, *Report of the Consultative Committee on Differentiation of the Curriculum for Boys and Girls Respectively in Secondary Schools*, HMSO, 1923, p. 188.
39. *Mode III Examinations in the CSE*, Schools Council Publications, 1976, p. 61.
40. *15 to 18.* A Report of the Central Advisory Council for Education (England), HMSO, 1959, vol. 1, p. 258.
41. Ibid., p. 461.

CHAPTER 3

Schools, systems and values, 1900–1990

By the beginning of the 1990s only 165 maintained selective schools had survived Labour's drive towards a fully comprehensive system. In 1965, when Circular 10/65 launched the age of the comprehensive school, their number stood at 1,180. It seemed that the momentum which had carried on throughout the Conservative eighties had left the comprehensive system in an unassailable position. The defeat of attempts in such places as Tameside and Milton Keynes to create new grammar schools appeared to testify to this. Yet in some ways the strength of the comprehensive school system was more apparent than real; on the eve of the nineties some educational commentators were already beginning to speak of a new, post-comprehensive school era and this despite the fact that no political party had launched a direct attack upon the comprehensive school principle. Their conclusion arose from a close reading of educational developments in the eighties and earlier. While Callaghan's Ruskin College speech in October 1976 was not intended as a denunciation of the system which a bill, then awaiting royal assent, was intended to complete, it was not difficult to discern in it a shift in attitudes and values from the heady days of Crosland's crusading zeal (see pp. 124–125). Some of Callaghan's criticisms of educational standards, especially in their links with progressive education, were not far removed from those of the Black Papers of the late sixties and early seventies, and those made by some Conservatives in the 1980s. But of equal importance was his emphasis upon the rights of the consumers; consumer ideology and market forces became the leading political ideology of the eighties with the emphasis upon parental choice and the needs of industry. Perceived national and parental need demanded a wider variety of educational provision from which to choose, ranging from city colleges of technology and other selective schools, to assisted places in the independent sector, and to schools opting out of local authority control as the result of parental votes. Added to these political and ideological forces were financial pressures which were combining to end the reign of Labour's most supported school, the all-through 11 to 18 comprehensive, in favour of tertiary education. It seemed as if the comprehensive age was beginning to appear as an aberration in the British educational tradition of mixed provision, as if the nation was poised for a return to traditional values which the comprehensive school system had barely disguised.

One leading educational commentator, John Rae, had already found a new name for the post-comprehensive school era before its chief characteristics had barely become discernible. Writing at the end of the eighties, he spoke of the new pragmatic age in contrast to the heavily ideologically laden comprehensive and progressive years. In answer to the question, 'How should we organise the school system?', he replied [1]:

> We should approach this question solely from a pragmatic standpoint. No ideology, political or religious, should be allowed to distract us from the main issue: if our future prosperity depends on a well-educated population, not on a well-educated elite, what school organisation will enable us to achieve that goal? When we consider whether grammar schools should be reintroduced or independent schools abolished, whether City Technology Colleges should be established or the school leaving age raised, we must free ourselves from the thought that any principle is at stake. What is right is what will produce the results we need.

He appears to assume that a utilitarian ideology is no ideology at all, that we can have a principle-free or value-free educational system. In fact, his emphasis upon organising our education system to promote national prosperity is something that has been a chief concern of educationists, is one sense or another, since the advent of state education. Others argue that the Thatcherite consumer ideology of the eighties and early nineties was little more than the assertion of class values at worst, or meritocratic values at best, which have characterised much thinking about education since the beginning of this century and earlier: that consumerism is largely a middle-class consumerism, and that true selection or real choice is only open to those who can afford to pay or who are particularly able. Whether the nineties represent a new approach to thinking about our education system, or whether it represents little more than a remix or restatement of earlier ideologies, or whether indeed we can have, as Rae asserts, a value-free education system, can be answered only by or largely by reference to the history of education. This chapter intends to show that (a) no one educational ideology has determined the development of our education system in any of its stages, and (b) although one view of the aims of education may be dominant, as at present, it has never exerted an exclusive influence. It also intends to show that most of the major educational reforms have been promoted on so-called 'pragmatic' grounds.

SELECTION BY ELIMINATION: SOCIAL CLASS AND EDUCATION, 1869–1922

In 1927, Viscount Haldane summed up in a graphic form the problem which the Hadow Report on *The Education of the Adolescent*, published in that year, had tried to tackle.[2] As can be seen from Haldane's diagram (Figure 3.1), the education system then in operation

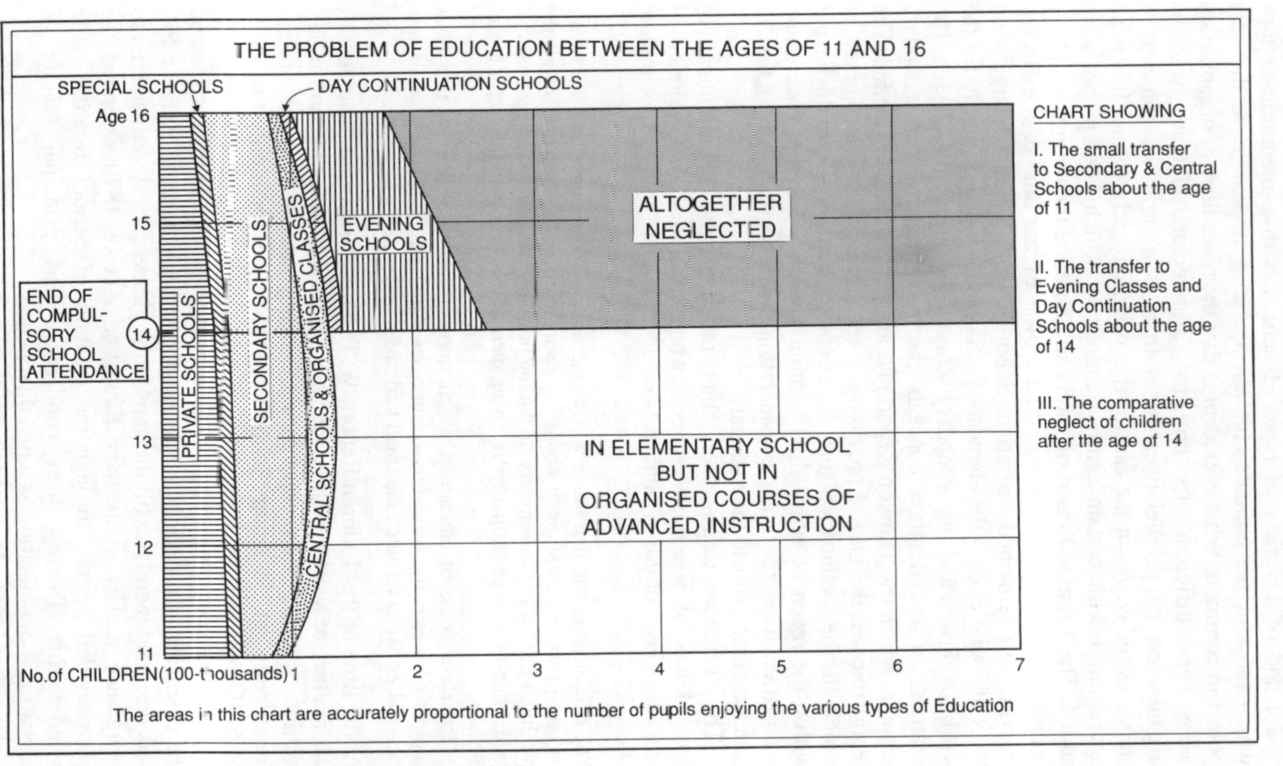

Fig. 3.1 ***Education between the ages of 11 and 16***

bore little resemblance to that of today; the existence of an independent sector and of a variety of types of school with a predominant type which most of the nation's children attended, appear to be the only points in common. What is evident is that the main lines of organisation were very different. Its principal architectural feature was its organisation on parallel lines rather than as a series of consecutive stages as today. As in the case of much British architecture, it was an aggregation with certain central features to which later pieces were added. The Taunton Report of 1868 had identified the main principle of construction, which, while modified a little by the time of the Hadow Report, still remained operative. Schools were organised largely on lines of social class – the elementary schools intended primarily for the working classes and the secondary schools for the middle classes. The neatness of the diagram conceals the fine gradation of secondary schools, which the Taunton Report had argued should be extended. The report rejected the idea of providing 'free . . . schools of every grade, at which the best education that the country could give, would be put within the reach of every child without charge'.[3] Parental choice and occupation were the main consideration, with 'parental obligation to educate being prior to the national'.

The Taunton Commission thus favoured the development of three kinds of secondary school, which excluded the majority of working-class children and reflected divisions within the middle classes.

> The education of the first grade which continues till 18 or past, and that of the second grade which stops at about 16, seem to meet the demands of all the wealthier part of the community, including not only the gentry and professional men, but all the large shopkeepers, rising men of business, and the larger tenant farmers.
>
> The *third* grade of education, which stops at about 15, belongs to a class distinctly lower in the scale, but so numerous as to be quite as important as any: the smaller tenant farmers, the small tradesmen, the superior artisans.

At the time of the Taunton Report, W. E. Forster reported the extent of the neglect of working-class education to Parliament. One and a half million working-class children were being educated 'more or less imperfectly' in elementary schools but this represented only two-fifths of 6–10 year olds and one-third of 10–12 year olds. The majority of working-class children received no education at all. He thus advocated the extension of working-class education in his Education Bill; the Bill was designed merely to fill the gaps in the elementary system and not to reorganise it. His Elementary Education Act of 1870 extended the class-divided system through the creation of School Boards. Little wonder that Tawney later condemned this principal feature of educational organisation as a hereditary curse.

Two developments occurred at the beginning of this century which highlighted the absurdity of the class basis of educational provision and the shortcomings of attempts to modify it. The first was the Education Act of 1902; the second was the introduction of the Free Place Regulations in 1907. The 1902 Act set up LEAs to provide secondary schools and enabled them to fund able working-class pupils who pledged to become teachers to attend them; the second extended the meritocratic principle a little further. The Free Place Regulations stated that,[4]

> In all Schools where a fee is charged, arrangements must be made to the satisfaction of the Board for securing that a proportion of School places shall be open without payment of fee to scholars from Public Elementary Schools who apply for admission, subject to the applicants passing an entrance test of attainments and proficiency such as can be approved by the Board . . . .
>
> The proportion of School places thus required will ordinarily be 25 per cent of the scholars admitted.

It was left to Tawney in the first of his many writings for the Labour Party to point out how these measures served only to indicate the extent of the educational deprivation of the vast majority of the nation's children and the absurdity of the principle upon which such disadvantage was based.[5]

> Except on the theory that the better intellectual 'stocks' are identical with the richer classes, and that the working classes consist of inferior intellectual 'stocks', the probability is that ability is more or less equally distributed over the whole population, irrespective of income. A political statesman, or scientist, or general, or industrial organiser, is as likely to be born in the family of a dock labourer as in that of a millionaire. He is as likely to be born there. But he is most unlikely to be developed.

By no stretch of the ideological imagination could the regulations be seen as creating an educational ladder. What his analysis of elementary school children who had crossed the slender bridge to a secondary school showed was that for many the meritocratic ladder was illusory; for most the greasy pole was the reality.

Age	12–13	13–14	14–15	15–16	16–17	17–18
Number	32,709	36,405	30,732	20,628	11,522	4,905
Percentage	4.68%	5.28%	4.47%	3.08%	1.74%	0.74%

Tawney preferred another metaphor to those of the ladder or greasy pole, that of the Indian rope which ended in nothing. The scarcity of places meant that, at most, just over 5 per cent of elementary school children entered a secondary school. Of those who could adjust to the curriculum and withstand family and financial pressures to leave, few stayed on beyond the first school certificate, which could be cashed in for a white collar job. The regulations, after all, provided only free tuition; the other costs of books, uniform, etc., had to be met. If the regulations were intended to be what Sidney Webb in another context called 'a capacity-catching machine', it was a remarkably unsuccessful and inefficient one.

There were some who went beyond Tawney in their criticisms of the systems. Their opposition to the meritocratic principle was not based on the grounds that it was applied unevenly or that it operated inefficiently; educationists, such as William Leach, objected to it on the grounds that it took no account of the majority of the nation's children. When, during the First World War, Tawney was spearheading the Workers' Educational Association's campaign for a far more effective educational ladder, his reconstruction programme was vigorously attacked on egalitarian grounds by Leach, a Bradford cloth manufacturer and former grammar school pupil. Leach, who was behind the ambitious Bradford Charter of 1916,[6] made an outspoken attack on the WEA reconstruction programme in the Association's 1918 Annual Report. It provides a clear insight into the nature of egalitarian standpoint and is worth quoting at length.

> I have left my only real quarrel with the WEA charter to the last. It concerns the important question of what is vaguely called 'secondary' education. 'Secondary' education seems to be a term invented by superior people to prove to the workman that after reaching a certain point his child need not really go further because all after that is more or less unnecessary luxury – a mere process of mind ornamentation and polishing, and quite unimportant to all that is really vital in equipment. The WEA actually lends colour to this monstrous gospel by framing its demand as follows:
>
> > 'That all children admitted to a secondary school should have reached an approved standard of education, the ground of transfer being the fitness of the scholar for the broader curriculum.'
>
> Oh, I could lecture my friends and drub them for twelve more pages about this wrong-headed docility to accepted but wretchedly false dogmas. The well-to-do parent never asks about his child's 'fitness' for the broader curriculum. He just sees that he gets it, and he pays for fees for it. If he decided that the youngster was scarcely fit to go through it his class would properly ostracise him as unfit to be a parent. Grammar schools don't differentiate between elementary and secondary. They have no use for the words at all. Neither should the WEA. There is not one argument on earth in favour of universal compulsory 'elementary' education which does not apply still more forcibly to universal, compulsory, 'secondary' education. Have done with this stupid call for 'fitness'. The system is still uninvented, the professor is still unborn, to tell us what is the 'fitness' of a child of 10 or 11 or 14. Not until a groundwork in languages, sciences, literature, and the arts is the common heritage of all the population should we tolerate the idea of specialising for anything at all.

But for the most part the Labour movement had another stage to go through before it came officially to endorse Leach's plea for a secondary education for all. A brief consideration of this will help to show how change in education is far more complex than authors such as Rae suggest. Free places in secondary schools were for the able few;

educational advance for the majority was seen by Labour in terms of extending compulsory attendance at elementary school to the age of 14 and of part-time continuation schooling thereafter to the age of 18. This policy was officially endorsed by the Labour Party's Advisory Committee on Education in 1918. Leach opposed such a policy as a sorry makeshift which extended, rather than removed, the class-based systems, and as an inferior substitute for the egalitarian measure of secondary education for all. Tawney and Nunn pressed for both an extension of the free-place system for the able few and for continuation schooling for the majority. Labour, in Leach's view, ought to be 'helping towards (the) overdue demise' of both the meritocratic and class-based systems. Tawney and Nunn sought to achieve some measure of equality through what was essentially an extension of class education, the continuation school; they intended to use continuation schooling as a means of giving access, albeit part-time access, to the kind of liberal education enjoyed by secondary school scholars. Continuation education was thus a part-time liberal education for all (see pp. 68–69). They thus made a distinction between schools as social institutions and the kind of education which they offered. Leach tended to argue that class institutions were incapable of doing anything but reflecting class values and were thus incapable of fostering common values.

By 1922 events had helped to push the Advisory Committee more towards Leach's full egalitarian position. In July 1920 a committee of the Board of Education,[7] with strong NUT representation, argued that the mesh of the meritocratic sieve ought to be widened by increasing the percentage of free places in secondary schools from 25 to 40, by providing maintenance allowances related to the cost of living and not earnings, and by making secondary schooling more attractive to working class students through the provision of 'variation in the type of secondary schools'. Tawney was asked by the Advisory Committee to prepare a brief pamphlet on the Departmental Committee's report.[8] While he was doing that the report of the Geddes Committee on economies dashed the hopes of implementing the clauses of Fisher's Education Act of 1918 relating to continuation schools. Labour was forced to rethink its policies with the General Election of 1922 in sight which could ditch Lloyd George and his predominantly Conservative government. Leach's idea of secondary education for all now looked more attractive as a vote winner that could help Labour gain power, or at least replace the Liberals as the Opposition. Tawney was now asked to revise his brief pamphlet and to produce a more egalitarian statement. In April 1922 his *Secondary Education for All* was published some five months before the autumn election. Tawney was convinced that Labour's restatement of its educational policy meant that it had shed its former meritocratic stance and had arrived at a truly egalitarian position, that his proposals meant that selection by discrimination had replaced selection by elimination.

SELECTION BY DISCRIMINATION, 1922–65: MYTH OR REALITY?

There had been a long Labour tradition of opposition to the élitist and meritocratic concepts of education. In 1897, the TUC demanded that secondary education to the age of 16 be placed 'within reach of every worker's child'. It denounced the scholarship system on lines very similar to those of Leach quoted earlier. What Leach did, however, was to go beyond the slogan of 'secondary education for all' to consider in a preliminary manner the problems of devising an educational system to achieve a large measure of practical equality. The Bradford trade unionists' charter which he helped to draw up in 1916 advocated 'universal, free, compulsory secondary education' to 16 on the basis of a common education. In his criticism of the WEA programme for educational reconstruction he attacked the idea of trying to devise a system to discern special 'fitness' or special aptitudes and abilities at the ages of 10, 11 or 14. Like many reformers of his age he sought a secondary education for all in order to provide access to a common culture. 'Not until a groundwork in languages, sciences, literature, and the arts is the common heritage of all the population should we tolerate the idea of specialising for anything at all.' By implication some of his ideas were at odds with the growing body of opinion which favoured some kind of break and examination at 11+ followed by differentiated education. Though Leach claimed in 1918 that the professor was 'still unborn to tell us what is the "fitness" of a child of 10, 11 or 14', Professor Nunn was working his way towards doing just that. In his comments on the WEA programme Nunn recommended that 'There should be a "clean cut" in education, designed to take place normally at 11+. Pupils should leave the Primary School at this stage to enter either a secondary, a technical, a central or a continuation school.'[9] Leach was advocating a common education in a common school; Nunn argued in favour of a break at 11+ and different kinds of school providing different kinds of education. Labour Party policy which Tawney laid down in *Secondary Education for All* in 1922 aligned itself with Nunn who also served with Leach on its education advisory policy. With the publication of Tawney's book, the slogan 'Selection by discrimination will replace selection by elimination' was born. Leach doubted whether Tawney's proposals would bury the hydra-headed meritocratic principle and assert the supremacy of egalitarianism.

Tawney's view of the nature of change was rather different; he generally believed that the education system developed by shedding previous ideologies and adopting new ones. Thus, he argued that the nineteenth century was dominated by class ideology where

> Secondary education was not built upon primary education, but was parallel to it. There were, in short, not different stages in a single system but different systems of education designed for classes whose capacities, needs and social

> functions were supposed to be necessarily so different as to make a unified system at once impracticable and disastrous.[10]

Writing in 1922, he argued that such a concept of education had long since been abandoned; it had not been public policy for nearly a generation. What had taken its place was selecting for higher education by means of scholarships. The times now demanded a further choice between the scholarship or meritocratic system, which produced an intellectual proletariat, and an egalitarian system which viewed primary and secondary education as stages in a single process through which all normal children ought to pass. Pupils would be examined at 11+, not with a view to ending their education but as a means of discovering their aptitudes and abilities. Such a simplified view of the nature of educational change, where nodal points were reached and new ideologies became operative, fitted Tawney's moral position. Those who opposed the transition to the new educational order – that is, for Tawney, those who were not on the side of the angels – were easily identified. Thus the Geddes Committee, which advocated cuts in educational expenditure, and the Federation of British Industries, which argued in favour of the retention of cheap juvenile labour, were vigorously attacked as 'respectable cannibals preying on the nation's youth'.

In practice, however, Tawney's proposals for secondary education for all did much to ensure the survival of previous ideologies. That this was likely to happen was evident from his arguments, and their relative priority, for reorganising the education system. Unlike Leach, who stressed the common needs of all adolescents (the humanitarian argument), Tawney stressed meritocratic and utilitarian considerations.

> The division of education into 'elementary' and 'secondary', as interpreted and organised hitherto, is educationally unsound and socially obnoxious. It results in (a) a grave waste of talent, (b) the exclusion from the secondary schools of children who ought to enter them, (c) the imposition on the primary schools of the task of educating children between twelve and fourteen, for which they may not be specially fitted, (d) waste and inefficiency arising from overlapping.

He was thus less alert than Leach was to the problem of advocating measures which, though designed to promote greater equality, could, in practice, fall far short of their aims. His book was more egalitarian in spirit than in many of its recommendations. His proposals concerned the abolition of fees, the provision of an adequate system of maintenance allowances and a common leaving age of 16 and marked an undoubted step in the direction of practical equality; yet, at times, he appears to suggest that these measures are valuable in order to ensure that the educational sieve worked more efficiently: 'the wider the field the better the candidates'. The meritocratic system would operate more fairly and more fully if these disincentives were removed which prevented able working-class children from presenting themselves for selection in greater numbers. He was anxious to point out that 'Equality of educational provision is not identity of educational provision, and it is important that there should be the greatest possible diversity of type among secondary schools.'[11] The existing system wasted 'brains and character'. It was little wonder that one of the eminent educationists of the day, Fred Clarke, accused Tawney of seeking to develop the meritocratic principle under the guise of promoting egalitarian reform.[12] Tawney did little to dispel such a view through his failure to confront two key issues: the type of examination by which pupils at 11+ were to be selected for the different kinds of secondary schooling, and the means by which parity of status and esteem were to be achieved between secondary schools. On the latter issue, his comment amounted to little more than a statement of faith that other kinds of secondary school would follow the same lines of general education as (traditional) secondary schools, 'from which I believe they will be indistinguishable when they are in full working order'. If proof is needed of the ability of different, and possibly contradictory, concepts of education not only to coexist in schemes of reform but also to interact, then the Hadow Report on *The Education of the Adolescent* provides it. The Hadow Committee accepted the model for educational advance advocated by Tawney, Nunn and others, of primary and secondary education for all with a transitional break at 11+. This kind of arrangement was intended to eradicate the class-based, parallel systems and to end the meritocratic system by which only very able working-class children received a secondary education. The Committee's ideas on the restructuring of the system was based upon current understanding of child psychology; the 11+ break was justified on the grounds of 'a tide which begins to rise in the veins of youth at the age of eleven or twelve. It is called by the name of adolescence.'[13] The Committee rejected the idea of the all-age 5–15 school, supported by the NUT,[14] on the grounds that this would perpetuate social divisions within education. The all-age school in its view was particularly associated with elementary education and would prevent the egalitarian measure of providing secondary education for all of varying kinds. Yet at the same time as taking this step in the direction of greater equality, when speaking about 'conditions of entry' to the principal kind of school which was its chief concern, the secondary modern school, it adopted a strongly meritocratic position, probably without realising it.

> But the most pleasant of parks will nonetheless have an entrance and an exit; and we are disposed to believe that we may safely recommend the institution ... of an entrance examination, on the lines of the present examination for scholarships and free places in secondary schools.

The Committee admitted that the free-place examination was highly competitive and gave no indication of how it could be adapted to the type of selection by differentiation that it desired; the modern school curriculum was intended to be 'practical' in nature yet access to it was to be determined by performance in 'a written examination ... and also, wherever possible, an oral examination'. How written papers in English and Arithmetic designed for a pass–fail examination could help measure aptitudes and abilities for a 'practical' curriculum was never discussed.

The matter of the school leaving age also demonstrates how meritocratic principles coexisted in Hadow thinking with more egalitarian views. Although some members of the Committee had originally wanted their enquiry to 'assume a leaving age of 16', they accepted in the end and without much protest a reference which restricted them to considering adolescent education to the age of 15. Thus, without any comment about the inequalities which such a system introduced, they advocated a secondary stage 'which, for many pupils would end at 16+, for some at 18 or 19, but for the majority at 14+ or 15+'. As the type of school which kept its pupils the longest, the grammar school, was part of the ladder to the universities and the others not, this magnified the disadvantages which the vast majority would suffer. The Labour Party was alert to the way in which the meritocratic principle was undermining the egalitarian ideal and recommended that the modern schools should also have a direct route to the universities. How this could be achieved without affecting the practical nature of the modern school curriculum or without creating hierarchies within the modern school was never considered. The Hadow Committee pinned its hopes for achieving a large measure of equality among secondary schools through insisting that staffing ratios, teaching qualifications and equipment should be the same for all types. These did little to offset the advantages of the higher social prestige, the higher leaving age and the importance of being a vital rung on the ladder to the universities, which the grammar schools possessed.

For much of the inter-war period the battle for the reorganisation of secondary education found its focus in the issue of the leaving age. Hadow had recommended that it should be raised to 15 in 1932 – a measure which the more radical, egalitarian reformers came to accept only as an interim step to a common leaving age of 16. There were many on the right wing of the three parties who accepted the idea of raising the leaving age to 15, either locally under the 1921 Act or nationally with exemptions under the 1936 Act, as a means of combating unemployment. The 1921 Education Act enabled hard-hit areas to keep children at school longer; the 1936 Education Act enabled those who could find 'beneficial employment' to leave before 15, while retaining at school those who could not. To those on the political left, raising the leaving age primarily as a means of dealing with economic problems was unacceptable and resulted in grave injustices. Tawney argued, for example, that the 'beneficial exemptions' clause of the 1936 Act would result in able working-class adolescents leaving school before the age of 15 and that these were precisely the group who would benefit most from staying on. The meritocratic system would thus fail to function effectively. To others on the left, the exemptions clauses demonstrated that the government was not concerned with the radical reform of the education system to ensure the egalitarian measure of a common leaving age of 16. The more radical thinkers opposed exemptions not because they made the meritocratic system work less effectively but because, by gearing the duration of schooling to the condition of the labour market, the education of all children was being put in jeopardy. In their view the purpose of education was to develop the abilities of all children to the full and not just those of the most able. But even the more limited advance of a leaving age of 15 with exemptions, which was due to come into effect on 1 September 1939, was suspended because of the outbreak of the Second World War. Reformers pinned their hopes on the war years creating a more egalitarian spirit which would flow over into education; and they thus looked at Butler's Act to finally introduce a system of education which provided both diversity and equality.

The 1944 Education Act appeared to resolve most issues while, in fact, settling very few. It introduced secondary education for all within a reorganised education structure of continuous stages but left several issues unresolved. To some these were mere 'loose ends'; to others they involved important matters of principle. The leaving age was raised to 15 without exemptions but with special powers given to the Minister to delay its implemenation for two years; the matter of the leaving age of 16 was deferred, to be settled by Orders in Council when circumstances permitted. Labour argued that this measure was fundamental to equality of educational opportunity but Mrs Keir's 'suggestion for raising the leaving age to 16, three years after it had been raised to 15, at most three years from April 1945'[15] was narrowly defeated in the Commons. Fees were to be abolished in secondary schools with the significant exception of direct-grant schools (see pp. 127–134). The retention of fees in schools receiving grants direct from the Board was regarded as indefensible by Labour. Butler was accused of throwing out the report of the Fleming Committee in deference to class prejudice which sought to maintain social exclusivity in 'these superior kinds of grammar school'. Even after the Butler Act was passed, Labour pursued the matter of direct-grant schools but the only assurance they received from Butler was that 'the Government would provide a common entrance examination for all irrespective of whether they are fee-paying students or not'. He confirmed his belief in the meritocratic principle of 'free access . . . based on ability not income'.

Selection by elimination was not dead. Those who could not pay the fees or gain high marks in the entrance examination were excluded from direct-grant schools. But what of the rest of the system? The war-time government and the Labour governments which succeeded it believed that the tripartite structure for secondary education, proposed by Butler in his White Paper, but not stipulated in his Act, could best provide for the different kinds of aptitude and ability among adolescents. Ellen Wilkinson, Labour's first Minister of Education, pinned her faith on 'parity of material conditions between the different schools leading to parity of esteem'. The more perceptive educationists argued that tripartitism, in its retention of two key features of British educational tradition – the 11+ examination and grammar schools – undermined the egalitarian principle. Even Tawney, who had opposed the alternative structure of multilateral schools on the grounds of their size and the destruction of separate grammar schools which their creation would entail, was forced to admit by 1952,

> The secondary education of the majority of children is now given in the Secondary Modern School. Some brilliant examples of such schools exist; but many still remain, it is to be feared the old elementary schools called by another name. Because of the traditional superiority of the particular kind of secondary school known as the grammar school, the struggle to win a place in it is intense, with the result of disillusionment for those who fail and over-pressure on all.[16]

Tawney's observations about entry to grammar schools and about secondary modern schools contained much truth. The competition for grammar school places was more intense for working-class children than perhaps even he was aware of. Recent research[17] has shown that the chances of working-class boys entering selective schools in the years to 1942 were improving, but grew worse afterwards. For those born between 1913 and 1922 the odds against a working-class child getting into a selective school in comparison with a middle-class child were 3.45 to 1. For working-class children born between 1923 and 1942 the odds were even better, 2.93 to 1. But then the position grew worse, despite the Education Act of 1944. For working-class children born between 1943 and 1952 the odds lengthened to 3.97 to 1. The relative increase in the size of the middle classes and the jump in the birthrate in the late 1940s overwhelmed the increase in selective school places, thus intensifying competition for entry to grammar schools. Parental pressure demanded the increase in grammar school places with their access to the administrative professions, and Britain largely turned its back on technical schools, with their access to industry, which could possibly have relieved some of the pressure. Even the limited expansion of grammar school places was at the expense of technical school places.

Not only did middle-class children do better in the 11+ examination, they also tended to do better than working-class boys in any transfers from secondary moderns to grammar schools around the age of 13, thus tending to reinforce the image of the secondary modern school as 'the elementary school called by another name'. 'It is also interesting, although not perhaps surprising', writes A. H. Halsey *et al.* 'to note that middle-class boys were somewhat more likely to transfer than working-class boys . . . we would guess that many of the transfers were simply children at secondary modern schools who wanted to stay on beyond the minimum leaving age.' For most secondary modern school children there was little hope of a reprieve with their schooling having been decided at the age of 11. The secondary modern school shared the basic social features of the old elementary school, the children of non-manual workers were much under-represented and the children of manual and semi-skilled workers over-represented. This fact was pointed out by the Crowther Committee which examined secondary education in the 1950s. Their report also showed that social class was at work within the secondary modern schools; pupils from more favourable home backgrounds were over-represented in their upper streams and on their extended courses. Subjective and social factors meant that in the continuing sorting-out process in the secondary modern schools even the most able pupils from less privileged backgrounds found it difficult to gain and maintain a place on extended courses. For many the sense of failure at 11+ was reinforced throughout the secondary modern course. The esteem of educational institutions had little to do with equality of resources and much more to do with social origins of its pupils and the degree to which they promoted or did not promote upward mobility. Compared with grammar schools, the secondary modern school largely failed on both scores. Little wonder that it was the parents of middle-class pupils who had failed to gain places in grammar schools in the 11+ examination who were often the most forceful and vocal in their demands for comprehensivisation. This was also true of some Labour MPs who argued with some justification that the grammar schools had failed the working classes and that the egalitarianism promised in 1944 was largely illusory. What Tawney had called 'the vulgar irrelevancies' of class and income still played a major role in determining educational opportunity. It was this which led Anthony Crosland, in particular, to press for a national system of comprehensive schools as a means of ending the class-based tripartite system.

THE COMMON SECONDARY SCHOOL, 1925–90

The idea of a separate school system did not go unchallenged either in the period between the wars, when the Hadow and Spens reports gave such massive endorsement to such a scheme, or in the post-war years when most local authorities implemented a bipartite or occasionally a tripartite, system. In the inter-war years, the principal alternative model which gained support from the teaching unions was that of the multilateral or multibias common schools; in the post-war years, support grew for a much more unified form of common school, the comprehensive school. The former brought all pupils together under one roof at 11+ but maintained parallel streams pursuing different kinds of education, especially after the age of 13. The Spens Report of 1938 explained what contemporaries understood by the term 'multilateral or multibias' school.[18]

> ... the provision of a good general education for two or three years for all pupils over 11+ in a given area, and the organisation of four or five 'streams', so that the pupils at the age of 13 or 14 years may follow courses that are suited to their individual needs and capacity. There would be a common core in these several courses, but they would differ in the time and emphasis given to certain groups of subjects. There would, for example, be a literary and linguistic course; a mathematical and scientific course; and other courses in which the pupils would devote more time to subjects leading on to technological studies, to commercial studies or to practical or artistic pursuits. In this way the ordinary grammar school courses would, it is maintained, be fully provided for, and separate Grammar Schools would not be necessary. The policy of substituting such multilateral schools for Grammar Schools, for Modern (Senior) Schools, and, to some extent, for Junior Technical Schools, has recently been advocated.

While Spens's predecessor, the Hadow Committee, were drawing up their proposals between 1924 and 1926 for a system of separate secondary schools, the teaching unions expressed their concern at the lack of consideration of alternative models. Miss Conway of the NUT advocated an all-age school from 5 to 15, but this was regarded as unlikely to assist the move away from adolescent elementary education to secondary education for all. The Association of Assistant Masters, which in many ways had least to gain from destroying separate grammar schools, put forward the multilateral idea in 1925 for consideration by the Hadow Committee. It saw the multilateral school as a means of achieving a large measure of equality between the various forms of secondary education, which was impossible if the traditional secondary or grammar school existed alongside other types of school. One speaker at the union's annual conference in 1925, aware that the Hadow Committee was likely to pile up evidence in favour of the separate school system which Hadow, Burt, Tawney, Nunn and Barker supported, pointed to the dangers of retaining grammar schools. He declared:

> If secondary schools of various types were set up, it would mean that there would be in secondary schools of the present type a class which was bound to be looked upon as something socially superior to the children who would attend the new schools of the distinct types.

The Hadow Committee set the pattern of official thinking in the inter-war years, with little or no encouragement being given to multilateral schools. The Spens Committee, some twelve years later, could only see such schools as being of value in rural areas. Official opinion was constantly reinforced by the unambiguous advice of the principal psychologist, Cyril Burt. Burt argued that the range of individual differences as revealed by intelligence tests had grown so wide by the age of 12 that pupils should have already been grouped 'according to their capacity, not merely in separate classes or standards, but in separate types of school'.

A growing number of teachers' unions and bodies within the Labour movement thought otherwise, or at least found it difficult to give such categoric support to one kind of system. The National Union of Teachers called for a diverse secondary school system to include large multibias schools on an experimental basis. The National Association of Labour Teachers advocated a system based only on multilateral schools. The Spens Committee supported a much more cautious approach, basing its qualified support for common schools largely on grounds of the 'economy and increased efficiency' which they would offer in sparsely populated areas. Even this luke-warm acceptance ran contrary to official government thinking in the early years of the Second World War when the government guidelines for the future reconstruction of education laid down in the Green Book of June 1941 clearly advocated a tripartite model. With, at best, limited official support for multilateralism, the Labour Party was led to spell out its position more fully. Tawney was called upon in 1943 to prepare a report on the subject to put before the party's annual conference. Using materials supplied by some of the Labour movement's most ardent multilateralists, he produced the fullest case in its favour that had been presented to that date. Though the report was neither completed nor published it reflected a shift in emphasis in the arguments in favour of the common school. It began by stressing the problems of measuring abilities and aptitudes at the age of 11+ and the difficulties of correcting a wrong diagnosis by transfer at 13+. For the first time, the Labour Party engaged in a lengthy discussion of the problems of early selection. 'In the first place, the varying capacities and aptitudes of children cannot be satisfactorily determined at the end of the primary school course, even if, as we have proposed, it lasts longer than at present.' Assessment should be made on a continuous basis throughout the common school. Transfer from one department to another within the same school would be less traumatic, and more common as a consequence, than between separate secondary schools. The main body of argument within the report related Tawney's common culture ideology with what has come to be termed 'the social argument'. Multilateral schools, it was argued, brought together 'in the formative years of adolescence, children of widely different outlooks and prospects, who can share in the study of particular subjects, and in all out-of-school activities and so create for the first time the common social and cultural background which is the basis of a democratic community.' In keeping with his belief in the small community school, Tawney advocated that the common secondary school should not normally exceed 600 pupils. The latter's unrealistic size suggests that Tawney's commitment to multilateralism, like that of many within the Labour movement, was less than 100 per cent. Not wishing to expose party divisions to public gaze, particularly as the Norwood Report and Butler gave support to a separate school system, the Party's research department shelved the uncompleted report quietly and quickly. Tawney accepted Norwood's definition of three broad kinds of ability which were best served by three different kinds of school, and in the growing mood of optimism engendered by Butler's Bill shared the belief that

> There is no reason to suppose that the modern secondary schools will necessarily be regarded as inferior to the more specialised grammar and technical schools. On the contrary, the former if wisely planned are like to provide the education best calculated to give the majority of boys and girls a hopeful start in life.

Forward with Norwood appeared to have become the slogan of Labour's leadership and of many reformers outside the Labour movement.

Despite the strong support among local authorities for developing separate kinds of secondary school, some elected to use the Butler Act as a springboard for introducing multilateralism. London County Council led the way as part of its post-war programme of rebuilding after the blitz. Coventry followed suit as part of a similar programme. Rural areas, including Anglesey which fitted in with the Spens idea of sparsely populated areas, also embarked on what had come to be called plans for introducing comprehensive schools. A Labour government circular defined the following types of common school and laid down a size of 1,600 for multilaterals, much larger than that suggested in the 1943 report. These were:

> *A bilateral school:* one providing for any two of the three main elements of secondary education, that is modern, technical or grammar, organised in clearly defined sides.
>
> *A multilateral school:* one intended to cater for all the secondary education of all the children in a given area and includes all three elements in clearly defined sides.
>
> *A comprehensive school:* one which is intended to cater for all the secondary education of all the children in a given area without an organisation in three sides.

Local authorities such as Middlesex intended to use existing buildings to create smaller schools of half that size. Instead of the large multilateral school providing for the separate streams, it was suggested that a series of small schools would be built offering a common curriculum for pupils up to the age of 13 or 14 on the research report's model. Generally, however, progress towards the development of multilateral and comprehensive schools was slow in the years of austerity following the war.

With the fall of the Labour Government in 1951, the common school issue began to emerge as a matter which divided the political parties. The Conservative Government found it as difficult as the post-war Labour Government had done to sanction the destruction of grammar schools to create comprehensives. Labour, now in opposition, found it less difficult at both a local and national level. Labour was moving away from the Spens concept of multilateralism as an experimental type of school alongside others such as grammar and modern schools, to the idea of supporting experimentation with different kinds of common school but with the comprehensive school as the norm. Four kinds of argument were advanced in the 1960s in support of a national system of comprehensive schools. They are perhaps best expressed through a brief analysis of a speech given by Anthony Crosland shortly after he issued Circular 10/65 which initiated the centrally coordinated move away from tripartitism to comprehensive secondary education. Shortly after Labour's return to office under Harold Wilson in 1964, Crosland, the Education Secretary, outlined the reasons for his circular.[19] His first set of arguments were a development of those based on equity and justice advanced in the Party's 1943 report. Selection at 11+ was socially unjust in that it discriminated against slow developers – 'You do not feed a child less because it grows slowly' – and against those with less advantaged backgrounds – 'Life itself is a selective process. But we must allow that process to work fairly; we must allow time for the beneficial influence of education to compensate for the deficiencies of upbringing and early circumstance. To segregate at 11+, to divide the unselected goats from the carefully selected sheep, was thus unjust.'

His second set of arguments stressed the benefits to democracy of the cross-fertilisation of ideas and experience, and of the more harmonious relationships between social classes, that would result from common schools. Separate schools, he argued, exacerbated social divisions; the common school would 'reduce the sense of social division and increase the sense of social cohesion'. This would be to the nation's benefit in that it would help to create a society where people would understand each other better 'because they can communicate'. This second argument was linked to a third, the benefit to the nation's economy – the improved understanding and communication between classes, reflected in better management–shop floor relations, which would be advantageous to economic progress. Furthermore, as the proportion of relatively inexpert and unskilled jobs declined, it became even more absurd to make segregated, educational provision for 'a fixed 25 per cent of top ability' with the resulting 'frightful waste of latent talent'.

Crosland's fourth set of arguments revolved around a range of practical considerations. The evidence of the very limited reliability of 11+ selection procedures was becoming obvious; the philosophy which underlay the Hadow and Norwood reports and the 1944 Act – that we were faced with children who differed from each other genetically and permanently and who therefore needed to be educated in separate schools – was increasingly shown to be erroneous by research and observation. The increasing number of students taking 'O' level examinations in secondary modern schools showed that overlap was both necessary and possible. Many middle-class parents were not willing to accept a secondary modern education for their children if they failed the 11+ examination, especially as evidence was growing of 10–12 per cent wrong allocations on the basis of transfers alone. The fact that more and more students were staying on beyond the statutory leaving age also bore witness to the inadequacies of a segregated system. Although Crosland's Circular 10/65, issued in July 1965, regarded the all-through comprehensive school as 'the simplest and best' means of translating the comprehensive ideal into practice, it allowed various forms of reorganisation. The principal types are indicated in Figure 3.2.

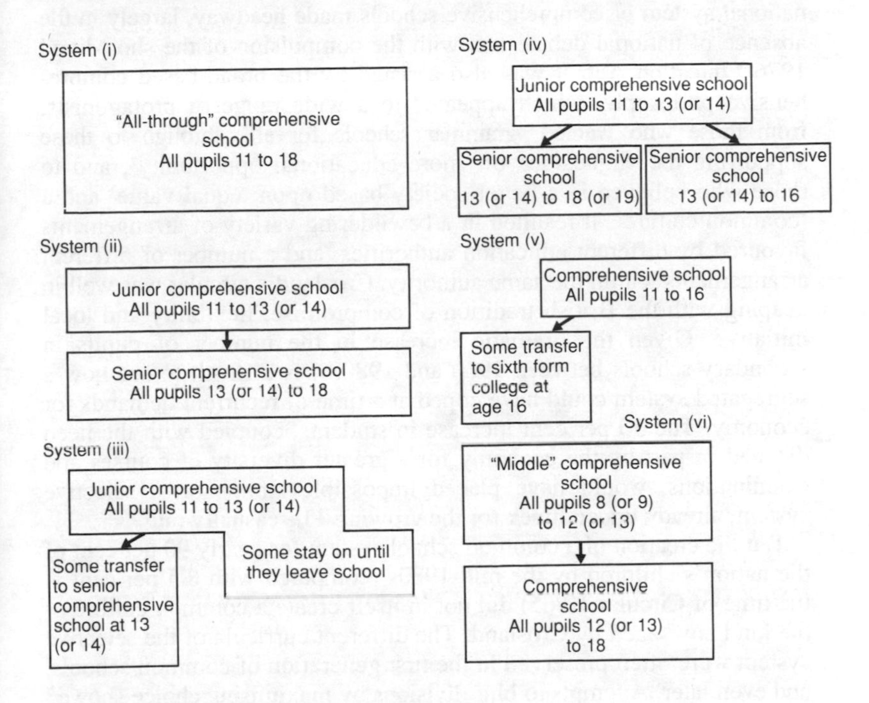

Fig. 3.2 ***Various comprehensive systems***

While the Newsom Report, *Half Our Future*, published two years prior to Circular 10/65, had avoided discussing whether a divided school system could itself be responsible for some of the problems of the average and less than average ability 13–16 year olds, Crosland had no doubts on the matter. He issued a second circular (Circular 10/66) reinforcing pressure on laggardly authorities to comply. This circular made it clear that the DES would use the control of building programmes to favour authorities that were going comprehensive and to penalise those that were dragging their heels. In 1970 a bill was introduced to compel reluctant local authorities, such as Surrey and Cheshire, to fall into line but the return to power of a Conservative government in June 1970 gave them renewed hope. The new Secretary of State, Margaret Thatcher, issued Circular 10/70 which gave LEAs greater freedom to make their own decisions. This circular stressed the value of the mixed system of selective and comprehensive schools on the basis of offering parental choice; the consumer ideology developed in the 1980s and early 1990s was thus being counterposed to the egalitarian ideology of the 1960s. If comprehensives were academically strong, then parents would support them; if not, then grammar schools would provide for the able.

Despite such support for a mixed system, the move towards a national system of comprehensive schools made headway, largely in the absence of national debate and with the compulsion of the short-lived 1976 Education Act. It was also assisted by the broad-based comprehensive philosophy which appealed to a wide range of protagonists, from those who wanted 'grammar schools for all', through to those supporting the vague idea of 'more educational opportunity', and to those who believed in a better society based upon 'equal value' and a 'common culture'. It resulted in a bewildering variety of arrangements favoured by different education authorities, and a number of different arrangements within the same authority. Crosland's circular was well in keeping with the British tradition of compromise, flexibility and local initiative. Given the dramatic increase in the number of pupils in secondary schools between 1960 and 1980, it is difficult to see how a segregated system could have coped at a time of recurrent demands for economy. The 50 per cent increase in students, coupled with the need dictated in part by the economy for a greater diversity of courses and examinations, would have placed impossible strains on a selective system, already under attack for the growing 11+ casualty rate.

But the creation of a common school system for nearly 90 per cent of the nation's children by the mid-1980s (compared with 8.5 per cent at the time of Circular 10/65) did not in itself create a common culture of the kind envisaged by Crosland. The different curricula of the selective system were often preserved in the first generation of common schools, and even later. Attempts to blur divisions by maximising choice showed that the 'hidden curriculum', which still crudely categorised students, was widely operative. Research into comprehensive schools that existed in 1974,[20] showed that many comprehensive schools still fell far short of a 'comprehensive' intake; many were virtually secondary modern schools in their ability and social class ranges. The idea of a common culture through a common curriculum rather than through further institutional reorganisation gained favour, and was given support in Callaghan's Ruskin College speech. The Conservative governments delivered such a curriculum for rather different reasons; the alleged decline of basic skills could be arrested and reversed by a national curriculum. It would also enable central government to extend its powers to bring what it regarded as errant local authority to heel. Such curricular reform offered no direct challenge to the comprehensive system and could be interpreted as offering support to it through imposing greater curricular uniformity through which the highly elusive common culture could be achieved. In theory, a common culture could have been achieved in selective schools but massive differences in aims, resources and above all in expectations were translated into two very different curricula. The common curriculum delivered in a common school system would seem to offer a better chance of success, but it is not something upon which many teachers are likely to wager their next pay rise.

DIRECT-GRANT SCHOOLS, 1926–76

The implementation of a comprehensive policy by Labour in 1965 left the selective, fee-charging grammar schools, which received their grants direct from central government rather than from local authorities, in an anomalous if not extremely vulnerable position. Direct-grant schools were a diverse group, a few being large and highly selective regional grammar schools and many being local grammar schools, akin in their curriculum and social make-up to maintained grammar schools. Largely middle class with very few children of unskilled and semi-skilled workers, largely independent foundations which drew upon State funds, and selective in an age which valued the common school, they could be seen as a group of schools which could frustrate the movement towards comprehensive education. It appeared to Labour both illogical and self-defeating to continue to give financial support to schools outside the State system. Thus, shortly after Labour returned to power in 1974 it gave the direct-grant schools the choice of either going comprehensive, or forgoing State aid and becoming fully independent. Direct-grant schools would have been consigned to the museum of educational curiosities had it not been for the 1988 Education Act which permitted schools to opt out of local control and obtain direct funding from central government under certain conditions thus, in effect, recreating direct-grant schools, though of a non-fee charging kind. The financial and political attractions of direct-grant, or to use the newly coined term 'grant-maintained', status to schools were considerable, especially when local plans for closing sixth forms to create tertiary colleges were being drawn up. Although a legal judgement in the opening months of the 1990s went against those who sought grant-maintained status simply to preserve sixth forms when local plans favoured tertiary or sixth-form colleges, nevertheless grant-maintained status had a strong pull, especially as schools were obliged under local management schemes to take responsibility for much of their expenditure in any case. However, without the additional fees which direct-grant schools had been able to charge there were likely to be considerable dangers facing those who succumbed unwarily to the temptation of opting out of local authority control. An examination of the evolution of direct-grant schools thus has a great deal of relevance to the current debate over grant-maintained status.

The origins of direct-grant schools are more complex than those of grant maintained schools. Under the 1902 Education Act local authorities were given considerable powers to create or maintain secondary school places. They were able to provide and maintain new schools, to give aid to schools not provided by them and to pay the fees of pupils at schools not controlled by them. The aided schools could also receive grants through a separate channel after 1904, that is, from the Board of Education direct. Thus, if a voluntary body controlled a school it could receive grants from the central government, or from the local authority, or from both. Circular 1381, in 1926, simplified the situation. Henceforth secondary schools run by voluntary bodies could draw their grants from either source but not both; this created the direct-grant list of those who elected to receive their financial assistance from central government. By 1942, when the Fleming Committee began its enquiry into those schools, they represented only about 15 per cent of the nation's secondary schools.[21] The distribution of pupils between the three types of schools in 1942 can be seen in Table 3.1.

Table 3.1 ***Distribution of pupils between secondary schools in 1942***

Type of school	*Number of schools*	*Number of pupils*
Maintained schools	793	303,986
Aided schools	381	124,536
Direct-grant schools	232	85,681
Total	1,406	514,203

The war years with their stronger egalitarian impulses, offered the first real opportunity of reforming direct-grant schools when the nation was considering introducing free secondary for all. The war-time government's first full statement on educational reform denied any major place to such schools in the drive towards secondary education for all. Its Green Book, *Education After the War*, published in June 1941, indicated general government thinking to 1944, that while they constituted 'a special problem' nothing needed to be done about them. 'To deprive them of their fee income would mean their disappearance, and it is suggested, therefore, that the present arrangement should continue whereby in recognition of State aid they offer an appropriate percentage of free or special places (p. 11).' Some within the Labour movement were beginning to think otherwise. Tawney's memorandum on the public schools, written for the Labour Party in January 1941, was the first shot across their bows. His analysis of the social exclusiveness of independent schools and its harmful effects, threw the weight away from the educational argument and more towards social and political concerns.

There may be a good deal to be said for preserving schools outside the national educational system, on the ground that their existence is favourable to initiative, experiment, diversity of educational type and other desirable features. There is nothing whatever to be said for preserving schools whose distinctive characteristic is that they are recruited almost exclusively from the children of parents with larger incomes than their neighbours. The co-existence of a public educational system, providing for nine-tenths of the children, and a private educational system providing for the children of the rich, is injurious to both. Children think of themselves and of each other as their elders show what they think of them.

His memorandum fired discussion within the ranks of Labour; by the time the Fleming Committee began its enquiry in 1942 some of the more radical members of the usually moderate WEA, of which Tawney was President, were drafting a memorandum to put before it based on the social argument for reform. In their evidence to the Committee, Green, Shearman and Lady Simon argued that the only way to settle what the Green Book had called the 'special problem' was to bring everyone up to the age of 16 within the non-fee-paying state system; only by such a measure could real equality of opportunity be established. During the presentation of their oral evidence a committee member raised the educational argument of the advantage of retaining the direct-grant schools' high tradition of scholarship, however expensive it might be; the WEA Secretary, Harold Shearman, replied in a curt manner that it was not possible to separate educational and social issues. 'Socially, the concentration on a privileged few was indefensible; traditions were not necessarily always useful.'

Butler believed that this was little more than the 'ritual fire and fury (by Labour) about social exclusiveness and privilege' and believed that the appointment of the Fleming Committee would remove much of the real heat from the debate over public schools in general and direct-grant schools in particular. But neither the Labour movement nor the Fleming Committee was willing to let this happen for long. Butler's White Paper made no mention of the direct-grant schools, the issue having, he hoped, been quietly shunted into the Fleming Committee siding. The TUC pointed to this omission and to the way in which the subsequent Bill could be improved by eliminating fees in direct-grant schools, thus turning them into something akin to today's grant-maintained schools. Much to the President's displeasure, the Fleming Committee thought likewise. Under Scheme A, direct-grant schools would change radically; the requirement of a minimum percentage of Free or Special Places would disappear, and 'all schools ... would be made accessible to pupils without regard to income'. In practice, this meant that local education authorities would have the right to reserve places in direct-grant schools up to a number agreed between the governors and local authorities; the remaining places would be free or assisted. The Board was to pay the school the difference between the approved fee and fees from parents, if any. Capitation grants would be discontinued. The report was regarded by Butler as being 'sensationally ingenuous'; Fleming was accused of lacking both impartiality and humour but his report could not simply be shelved. The need for some kind of political consensus meant that the 1944 Education Act had to take some cognisance of it. Under the Act, at least 25 per cent of direct-grant places were to be 'free' and to be filled by pupils from the state sector; local authorities could reserve at least another 25 per cent but not necessarily for state scholars. The Fleming recommendation that fees should be remitted for the remaining places was accepted only in respect of day pupils, not boarders. Furthermore, capitation grants were to continue being paid to direct-grant schools. Table 3.2[22] shows the principal differences that existed after 1944 between local authority schools and direct-grant schools, and provides a basis for comparison between the latter and today's grant-maintained schools.

Table 3.2 ***Differences between LEA and direct-grant schools after 1944***

Item	*LEA SECONDARY*	*Direct grant*
Governing body.	Instrument made by LEA Composition of board of governors for decision by LEA.	Either one-third of governors must be appointed by the LEA(s) or the majority must be representative e.g. MP, certain officers of local authorities or governors appointed by local authorities or parish meeting.
Ownership of premises.	School site, buildings and playing fields owned by LEA.	School site and playing fields owned by trustees
Maintenance and use of the premises	LEA meet the cost and determine the use subject to any powers delegated to the governors.	Governors responsible for the maintenance and determine the use. Cost met from: (a) fees paid by parent or LEAs; (b) grants from the S. of S. (c) other income of the foundation (if any).
Tuition fees.	None.	Fixed by governors subject to approval by S. of S. Paid by LEA for free or reserved places. Paid by parents for residuary places but remitted according to income scale approved by S. of S.
Religious worship and instruction.	Day must begin with non-denominational worship. Instruction according to 'agreed syllabus' (non-denominational). Parents may withdraw pupil from both or either.	Worship every day (not necessarily at beginning). Otherwise as for aided schools.

Table 3.2 ***Cont'd.***

Item	*LEA SECONDARY*	*Direct grant*
Capital expenditure.	Met and controlled by LEA.	Met by governors. Approval of S. of S. required. No grants from S. of S. for capital expenditure.
Admission of pupils.	LEA responsible.	25% of places must be 'free places' offered either by LEAs or governors to pupils who have spent 2 years at maintained primary schools. Further 'reserved places' must be offered to LEAs which need not be taken up). The total of 'free' and 'reserved' places may not exceed 50% without the agreement of the governors. LEAs are responsible for the selection of pupils for 'free' or 'reserved' places which they take up (subject to the pupils being suitably qualified). Governors' free places and residuary places are the responsibility of the governors.
Secular instruction.	Under control of LEA except in so far as delegated to the governors and/or head.	Under control of governors except in so far as delegated to head.
Appointment of teachers	Under control of LEA unless delegated to governors.	Under control of governors but S. of S.'s power to approve fees, enables him to influence total numbers.

Abbreviations: LEA–local education authority.
S. of S.- Secretary of State for Education and Science.

One of the last acts of the war-time government was to invite the direct-grant schools to apply for inclusion in the list under the revised terms. This reduced their number from 231 to 160; 35 decided to become independent, 160 were accepted and 36 applications were rejected. In 1957 the list was reopened and a further five formerly independent schools were added; by 1968, when the Donnison Committee began its enquiry into the most effective methods by which such schools could 'participate in the movement towards comprehensive reorganisation', their number stood at 179. As single-sex, selective grammar schools catering largely for the middle classes, it was difficult to see how, without a total change of character, they could participate. Furthermore, there was considerable variation in the existing links between the local authorities and direct-grant schools as Table 3.3 shows.[23]

Not all LEA places were filled by pupils from state primary schools; only 38 per cent of residual places were occupied by ex-primary scholars.

Table 3.3 ***Local education authority places in direct-grant schools at January 1968***

Percentages taken by LEAs	*Day schools* Roman Catholic	*Other*	*Boarding schools*[1]	*Total no. of schools*
Under 20	–	1	7	8
20–24	–	2	5	7
25–29	1	11	1	13
30–39	1	24	5	30
40–49	–	20	7	27
50–59	2	14	1	17
60–69	6	10	2	18
70–79	6	6	2	14
80–89	12	3	–	15
Over 90	28	2	–	30
Total	56	93	30	179

Source: Department of Education and Science returns for January 1968.
[1] Schools with 25% or more boarding pupils.

Such a mismatch between the aims and ideals of comprehensive and direct-grant education was not easily overcome, especially as the latter was geared primarily to academic study for university and further education. The highly specific goal of direct-grant schools in 1967–68 compared with the maintained sector is evident from the statistics given in Table 3.4.[24]

Given this divergence of purpose it was difficult to imagine any kind of compromise that would have left direct-grant schools with anything resembling their former powers and status. Their argument that, compared with other schools in the independent sector, their social composition was far more varied was more valid than it was effective with the commissioners (see Table 3.5). [25]

The commissioners upheld the legal right of voluntary bodies to provide efficient private education paid for by parents, but argued that all day schools, including direct-grant schools, receiving public funds from either central or local authorities should take part in the movement towards comprehensive reorganisation. As all day schools should not charge fees, the majority of the commissioners argued that the direct-grant arrangement should cease. Direct-grant boarding schools could either join the ranks of the existing 151 maintained schools with

Table 3.4 ***Destination of school leavers, 1967–68***

	Percentages								
	Direct grant			*Maintained grammar*			*All maintained (including grammar)*		
	Boys	Girls	Total	Boys	Girls	Total	Boys	Girls	Total
Universities	47.9	29.1	38.5	25.6	13.2	19.5	6.1	3.1	4.6
Colleges of Education	3.9	21.5	12.7	4.8	18.5	11.6	1.4	5.1	3.2
Other full-time further education	23.1	23.4	23.2	13.2	19.4	16.3	7.8	10.6	9.2
Temporary employment pending further education	–	–	–	1.7	1.2	1.4	0.5	0.4	0.5
Employment or destination not known	24.9	25.8	25.5	54.6	47.7	51.2	84.2	80.7	82.5
Total	100.0	100.0	100.0	100.0	100.0	100.0	100.0	100.0	100.0
Number of leavers	7,374	7,179	14,553	52,920	52,240	105,160	288,980	271,910	560,890

Table 3.5 ***Social composition of direct-grant schools, 1967–68***

		All direct-grant schools %
I and II	Professional and Managerial	59.6
IIIa	Other non-manual	12.8
IIIb	Skilled manual	20.1
IV and V	Semi and unskilled	7.5
Number where father's occupation stated, excluding those not classifiable		12,716
Total number of leavers		14,553

boarding pupils or possibly become integrated in the independent-school sector with a least half of their boarders supported by public funds. Such boarders would be drawn from a wide range of ability and would be selected on grounds of boarding need. In the case of schools which had boarders and day pupils, local authorities should take up day places with pupils drawn from a broad social and ability range.

The Donnison Commission reported to Edward Short six months before Labour fell from power in June 1970. The return of a Conservative government with Margaret Thatcher as Secretary of State for Education left the direct-grant schools in a more secure position. The return of Labour in 1974 led to the reopening of the matter; in March 1975, the Education Secretary, Reginald Prentice, urged the schools to enter the maintained system. If they were unwilling to do this their grants would be phased out from September 1976. Prentice hoped that they would become an integral part of the comprehensive school system; the Roman Catholic schools did so but most of the others elected to become independent. While many Conservatives regretted the ending of the direct-grant list, it was not possible to reopen it when the Party returned to power in 1979. The assisted places scheme which came into existence under the 1980 Education Act enabled some of the former direct-grant schools to accept able scholars from the State sector in return for public funds; the Government's argument was that many comprehensive schools were not meeting the needs of very able children of small means and thus public assistance ought to be given for them to attend schools in the independent sector. The Education Act of 1988, in allowing schools to opt out of local authority control and to receive their finance direct from central government, reintroduced direct-grant schools in a modified form: grant-maintained, non-fee-charging schools.

INDEPENDENT SCHOOLS

Independent schools in general, and public schools in particular, are a perennial topic of discussion but such discussion is more intense at some times than at others. In the 1980s and early 1990s the issue of State funding for 'assisted places' in the private sector aroused strong feeling. What is perhaps forgotten is that this idea has found acceptance in the past with those on the political left as well as those on the political right, but for rather different reasons. To the former, assisted pupils have been seen in the past as fifth columnists, as a means whereby through the gradual increase in their numbers, through a policy of progressive infiltration, the status, role and social composition of independent schools were to be radically altered. To those more on the political right, the assisted places scheme was not an exercise in social engineering but a way by which children of limited means could benefit from private education in centres of academic excellence. The issue of independent schools, and especially public schools, has a habit of quickly emerging from the wings to the centre stage of debate, as in the 1960s, or of returning to the wings with equal speed as other issues take precedence.

The steps taken by Anthony Crosland in the 1960s to abolish grammar schools did not stop short of the private sector. The direct-grant schools and the independent schools, but especially the more prestigious of their number, the public schools (which belonged to the Governing Bodies' Association or the Headmasters' Conference), were left in an exposed and vulnerable position. In the age of the common school, independent schools appeared more than ever one of the main bastions of social privilege and social divisiveness. Their position would have not been quite so precarious had it not been for a crusading socialist at the DES, for a Secretary of State, Anthony Crosland, who had expressed his inability 'to understand why socialists have been so obsessed with the grammar schools, and so indifferent to the more glaring injustice of the independent schools'.[26] Within a few weeks of issuing Circular 10/65, Crosland announced to the House of Commons his intention of setting up a committee to recommend a national plan for integrating public schools with the maintained sector. This was a far cry from the terms of reference given by Charles Trevelyan, the first Labour President of the Board of Education, to a committee on private schools in December 1930 when their improved efficiency rather than integration was the principal concern. These two views illustrate something of the range of opinion on the issue of public school reform.

Public school reform has rarely been high on Labour's educational agenda. Generally, the Labour movement adopted three approaches to the issue. In the drive for secondary education for all in the inter-war years, the public schools were not seen as being capable of making any significant contribution. This view was expressed in 1922 in Tawney's *Secondary Education for All*. 'In the main, except in the matter of inspection, they stand by their own choice apart from the general system of public secondary education, and need not be taken into account in considering how that system can be improved and extended.' There was no intention of removing the freedom of parental choice to spend their income on private education if they so wished, nor of integrating them with the state system. Labour's concern was, in fact, to improve their efficiency, to ensure that they met certain basic standards of education and accommodation, hence Tawney's emphasis upon 'inspection'. It was this second view which led Trevelyan during Labour's second period of office from 1929 to 1931 to set up a departmental committee 'for the purpose of securing that the children attending such schools receive an adequate education under suitable conditions'.[27] The idea of compulsory inspection was seen by many independent schools as the thin end of the legislative wedge. No independent school hitherto had been compelled to undergo inspection by a public authority, although a small number had elected to do so voluntarily. This position was unacceptable to the committee chaired by Chuter Ede, a prominent Labour politician and later Parliamentary Secretary to Butler, but the Departmental Committee's moderate recommendations went about as far as public and political opinion would allow them to go in the early 1930s. It reported that 'a small proportion are so defective that they are harmful to the mental and physical welfare of their pupils' and that 'a larger proportion are seriously weak and inefficient'. Although the majority were seen to be above serious reproach, the Committee nevertheless recommended the compulsory inspection of all schools. The Committee was seen by some as going beyond its brief in making recommendations also for the compulsory inspection of the curriculum, but with a true British compromise this was confined to 'efficient instruction in reading, writing and arithmetic, of a scope and standard suited to the child's (children's) age and capacity'. Some members wanted to inspect the whole curriculum but even the inspection of the three Rs was strongly opposed by many public school witnesses. The only choice the private sector was to have was by whom they were to be inspected, the Board or local authorities. Inspection could lead to closure, although with the right of appeal, and only after the school was given six months to remedy matters. Such inspection was to take place at regular intervals and was not to be a once-and-for-all operation.

There were some who, while accepting the concern for the physical and educational welfare of independent school pupils as perfectly legitimate, adopted a third and far more radical approach to public school reform. This group also took its lead from Tawney who attacked the inequalities reflected in and perpetuated by public schools in his book *Equality*, published in 1931 while the Departmental Committee was sitting. His criticisms have formed the basis of much left-wing thinking and policy from then to the present time, including those of Crosland. Tawney's concern was 'the restriction of leadership to particular classes, with special opportunities and connections which is only gradually being undermined by ... wider educational provision'.[28] Public schools with their traditional links with the older universities

Table 3.6 ***Schools attended by certain members of different professions***

The following figures are compiled from *Whitaker's Almanack* for 1927 (for 1926 as regards Governors of Dominions), the *Stock Exchange Year Book* for 1927 (for Directors of Banks and Railways), and *Who's Who*.

		Educated									
		English public schools				*Welsh, Scottish & Irish schools*					
*Professions**	*No. for whom information is available*	*One of the fourteen principal schools*	*Others*	*Total*	*English school other than public schools*	*Welsh*	*Scottish*	*Irish*	*Total*	*Privately or Abroad*
Bishops (63)	56	38	14	52	4	–	–	–	–	–
Deans (30)	24	13	6	19	4	–	–	–	–	1
Lords of Appeal, Justices of Court of Appeal and High Court (39)	25	11	6	17	1	1	4	–	5	2
County Court Judges, Recorders, Metropolitan Magistrates, Stipendiary Magistrates (215)	156	75	47	122	20	1	1	3	5	9
Home Civil Servants (members of 20 Departments receiving £1,000 a year and upwards) (455)	210	70	82	152	29	1	10	4	15	14
Members of Indian Civil Service (English names only) (105)	41	17	16	33	1	–	5	–	5	2
Governors of Dominions (65)	47	21	9	30	14	–	–	–	–	3
Directors of 5 Banks (165)	82	53	9	62	5	–	7	–	7	8
Directors of 4 Railway Cos (9-)	50	32	5	37	2	–	7	–	7	4
Total	691	330	194	524	80	3	34	7	44	43

*The figures added in brackets in this column indicate the total number in each category.

were very much a part of the restricting process (Table 3.6). Public schools were not 'easily accessible to the public, but schools from which the great majority of the public are precluded from entering'. This was a theme which he illustrated in *Equality* and in a confidential memorandum which he prepared for the Labour Party in 1941 just before the Fleming Committee began its enquiry into the 'means whereby the association between the Public Schools . . . and the general education system of the country could be developed and extended'.

In his memorandum Tawney raised the question of whether the public schools were really worth troubling about when the number of schools which raised the 'problem' in its most acute form hardly numbered more than 60 to 70 and had a population of not much over 25,000. Even halving their fees would still have left them inaccessible to the majority. He answered his question strongly in the affirmative.

> The system of educational privilege which they represent; the social and political power which they wield as the training-ground of the plutocracy; their hold on the higher posts in the professions, which, though no longer the virtual monopoly that till recently it was, has by no means ceased to count; the indirect influence which they exercise on educational thought and policy, make their position in the life of the country somewhat similar to that formerly occupied by the two older Universities. It would be fanciful to suggest that the results of reconstructing the 'public school system' are likely to be as far-reaching as were those which flowed from the reform of Oxford and Cambridge; but it would be superfical to dismiss them as of negligible importance merely on the ground of the small number of schools and pupils concerned.[29]

If they could not be ignored, how should they be treated? Should the 'natural' forces of a declining school population, an improving state system and war taxation be left to bring about their extinction just as catastrophic natural forces had brought about the demise of the dinosaur? Tawney argued that any system which produced a race of social mandarins, isolated during youth from natural and easy contact with the life of other young people, ought to be reformed; he was not willing to advocate their abolition on the grounds of the high academic standards and model liberal curriculum which they offered for the emerging state secondary schools.

> A well-grounded dislike of certain other features of these schools ought not to cause that fact to be overlooked. The quality of the staffs at some 'public' schools is extremely high. The conditions under which boys and masters work are probably more favourable than those at most other schools. The tyranny of examinations is certainly less pronounced than at many secondary schools. More encouragement is given to boys to follow their own bent, and there are ampler facilities for enabling them to do so. The intellectual level of the abler pupils from public schools who pass to universities is probably above that of any other group of boys in the country. At the same time, a one-sided and clever-silly intellectualism is, on the whole avoided; self-reliance is encouraged. Within narrow class-limits, a genuine training in social responsibility is given.[30]

He thus favoured reform not abolition, positive intervention not a *laissez-faire* policy, for it was by no means certain that left on their own they would fade away. Some public school headmasters such as Frank Fletcher had already brought the issue into the public arena, and urged public schools to become less exclusive through admitting more able pupils of small means, possibly at public expense. Tawney considered this as one of four possible ways of breaching the walls of privilege. The others were turning such schools into direct-grant schools, channelling grants through local authorities or setting up a public school equivalent of the university grants committee. Without coming down in favour of any particular scheme he stressed that any grant of public funds should not be unconditional, that inspection should be obligatory, that they should comply with the Board's secondary school regulations and that they should accept a certain percentage of students of limited means. However, for Tawney, it was ability rather than any other consideration that should decide who attended such schools. There were clear limits to his egalitarianism, not perhaps unexpected from a former Rugby scholar and Professor of Economic History: 'They must not merely admit a few pupils from elementary schools as a matter of grace, but must be equally accessible to all boys intellectually qualified to profit by them without regard to the means or occupation of their parents.' He did not see the public schools as complete meritocracies; he did not suggest that the less able but wealthy should be debarred from them only that the more able of limited means should be admitted. On the key question of the proportion of such pupils to be admitted he suggested for day and boarding schools a minimum percentage not less than 50 per cent to bring about 'a real change in the tone and atmosphere of such schools'. He believed that this would lead to substantial changes, to public schools ceasing to be the monopoly of a small well-to-do class. However, given his unwillingness to force such an arrangement on public schools who did not apply for public funds, it was unlikely that any of the fourteen principal schools in Table 3.6 would have been greatly affected and the heartland of the system of privilege would have remained largely untouched.

Tawney's views were too extreme for some and not radical enough for others. Chuter Ede, who had chaired Labour's 1930–32 enquiry and who acted as Butler's Private Secretary in the Second World War, is said to have pleaded with a WEA deputation 'almost with tears in his eyes for caution on this question as so many of the public schools were doing such useful work'; he was against abusing the freedom of parents to choose their children's schools.[31] Harold Shearman and Lady Simon of the WEA held more radical views than either Chuter Ede or Tawney. When asked by the Fleming Committee in 1942 about whether it would be an advantage to retain the public school tradition of scholarship, Shearman replied that it was not possible to separate educational from social issues. 'The concentration on a privileged few should be ended.' Lady Simon clarified how that was to be achieved by bringing all public schools, and especially boarding schools, under local authority control to be used as local need dictated; on the issue of freedom of choice, another WEA representative, Ernest Green, argued that 'the present freedom to choose was available to only a small minority of parents'. On the matter of inspection, this was only acceptable as an interim measure until 'such policy of the common school could be realised'. Most of the WEA representatives were against the policy of limited 'infiltration' advocated by Tawney, and were 'not interested in seeing schools of the Public school type preserved'. An additional argument which was advanced was that single-sex boarding schools exercised an unhealthy influence during the impressionable years of adolescence. Tawney, who was the WEA's president but who was in the United States at the time, would scarcely have agreed with the oral evidence given to the Fleming Committee. This brief examination of Tawney's position and of those of his WEA colleagues illustrates many of the arguments used then and now in the debate over the public schools.

Those who shared the views of Ernest Green and Lady Simon pointed to the way in which nineteenth and twentieth century developments had combined to undermine the original intentions of many of the founders of the first public schools – a fact which the Fleming Report acknowledged. The Report, published in 1944, showed the complete reversal of the role of the public schools from their original inception in the fourteenth century when, like Winchester, they were founded for the 'poor and needy' with a few special places reserved for the 'sons of noble and influential persons (and) special friends' who could offer some kind of protection.[32]

> We allow, however, sons of noble and influential persons, special friends of the said college, to the number of ten to be instructed and informed in grammar within the said college, without charge to the college, so that by occasion thereof prejudice, loss or scandal in no wise arise to the Warden, priests, scholars, clerks or any of the servants of the same.

But the Committee had no intention of forcing the public schools to revert to their original role. Like Tawney, it merely wanted to offer the opportunity to the day and boarding schools to associate themselves with the general system, thus leaving those not in dire need of state assistance to turn down the invitation. Scheme B put forward by the Committee recommended that the Board should provide bursaries to public schools for those 'who have been previously educated for at least two years at a grant-aided Primary School'. But its immediate aim, like Tawney's, was not to swamp the public schools and so change their social composition. The initial minimum of reserved places for those schools electing to take part in the scheme was to be 25 per cent; thereafter, however, there was to be a gradual shift towards 'equal accessibility and no child, otherwise qualified, shall be excluded solely owing to lack of means'. Intellectual ability, assessed on the basis of the primary schools' record, was to be a key factor in the selection process for transfer at 11, although transfer at the age of 13 was not to be restricted to those attending grammar schools; it was to include transfers from multilateral schools. Given that the public schools, themselves, had asked Butler to set up the committee it was unlikely that it would have come up with the more radical proposals supported by some members of the WEA. As in the case of state secondary education, Tawney had anticipated the general line of recommendation.

For a few brief years the issue of the public schools had risen fairly quickly and fairly high up the educational agenda. However, it was unlikely to sustain its position for long. Too late for its recommendations to be considered for inclusion in the 1944 Act and of too little interest for the post-war Labour Government in the years of austerity, the Fleming Committee's recommendations, like the public school issue, quickly receded from public gaze. The Labour Government upheld the principle of freedom of choice and stood against any attempts to coerce the independent sector into some fuller relationship with the general system. For many within the Labour Party, as within the nation as a whole, the public schools were simply not seen as a problem. On the contrary, to some people they represented the path which the State sector should follow with their high academic reputations and their position within an educational market based upon consumer choice.

Yet with growing evidence of the continuing social exclusiveness of independent schools, public school reform was always a cause awaiting a champion. Table 3.7 illustrates the degree of exclusivity in 1967–68.[33]

Table 3.7 ***Social composition of direct-grant schools, 1967–68 compared with other types of schools (in percentage terms)***

Father's class	*Secondary modern*	*Compre-hensive*	*Technical*	*Non-HMC*	*Grammar*	*Direct grant*	*HMC*
I, II	26.6	1.5	10.2	8.8	35.1	6.2	11.8
III, IV, V	59.1	1.3	12.9	3.3	19.6	1.8	2.1
VI, VII, VIII	74.7	1.6	11.4	0.5	11.1	0.6	0.3
All	63.5	1.5	11.7	2.5	16.9	1.6	2.4

I, II Managerial and higher grade professionals, supervisors (13.7% of the population).
III, IV, V Clerical, artisan, foreman (31.4% of the population).
VI, VII, VIII Skilled, semi-skilled, unskilled manual (54.9% of the population).

Anthony Crosland, Labour's Secretary of State from 1965 to 1967, had already spoken out against what he perceived to be their 'glaring injustice' in *The Future of Socialism* a decade earlier; the terms of reference which he gave to his Public Schools Commission in 1965 were far more extensive and radical than both those of Labour's Departmental Committee in 1930 and the Fleming Committee which aimed at 'developing and extending the association between the Public Schools ... and the general educational system'. Its terms of reference were far more precise and ideologically explicit:

(a) To collect and assess information about the public schools and about the need and existing provision for boarding education; forms of collaboration between the schools (in the first instance the boarding schools) and the maintained system.
(b) To work out the role which individual schools might play in national and local schemes of integration.
(c) If it so wishes, and subject to the approval of the Secretary of State, to initiate experimental schemes matching existing provision with different types of need.
(d) To recommend a national plan for integrating the schools with the maintained sector of education.
(e) To recommend whether any action is needed in respect of other independent schools, whether secondary or primary.

In some ways the Public Schools Commission carried on where its predecessor, the Fleming Committee, left off by recommending that schools who voluntarily wished to integrate should be encouraged to do so, and that by the end of about seven years assisted pupils from the state sector should fill at least half of their school places. But, unlike Fleming, it stressed that such pupils should not just be the academic high-fliers; they should admit a wider range of ability and the co-educational principle should be extended. It went further in attacking the less obvious subsidies given to public schools in the form of tax relief; those which did not serve a 'truly charitable purpose' would lose their 'fiscal and similar reliefs'. This would lead, in the Commission's view, to the progressive integration of public schools. But the commission side-stepped the issue of how particular, reluctant public schools were to be integrated, arguing that this needed some prior general administrative settlement.

What perhaps is most valuable to the present and future debate about the public schools are the positions adopted by various bodies on the issue of the public schools in general, and their social exclusivity in particular. The Governing Bodies' Association and Headmasters' Conference in their evidence to the Commission argued that public schools were and are the products of social division, of a class-divided society. They reflected rather than generated class divisions.

> ... we hardly think that we can reasonably be supposed to be the cause of the class system as it exists in this country: that system is a result of the complexities of history and the distribution of wealth, and we are ourselves a product of it. Nor can any complex society exist without some form of social grouping. What is presumably meant by the charge against us is that some features of the social groupings in this country are undesirable and that we make them worse. We are at least entitled to ask how we do this. Our own experience is that children's social attitudes are basically determined by their home backgrounds, and that education, though it may have some effect, works on already processed material.

> Some parents may indeed have social aspirations when they send their children to public schools, but in general we believe that the schools successfully challenge the pretensions of such parents.[34]

The NUT in its evidence to the commission argued that such schools both reflected and perpetuated class divisions.

> This divided education system reflects the division in British society itself. As long as the strong class system remains it is certain that a class-based school, such as the public school, will tend to remain, to reflect and to seek to perpetuate it. The public school of the mid-nineteenth century reflected the characteristics of the aristocracy: since then the influence of the thrusting upper middle class can be seen: tomorrow it could well be that, if unchanged, or changed in the wrong way, the public schools will reflect the rising influence of the meritocracy.

The Women's Liberal Federation claimed that public schools reflected, perpetuated and promoted class divisions.

> Although the social range in many public schools is considerably wider than is generally recognised, the presence of manual workers' children is rare and the atmosphere is predominantly middle and upper middle class. At this age children begin to notice social differences more acutely and there is often an atmosphere of hostility between boys at a public school and other boys in the town. This divisive effect is reinforced by the attitude of parents who are proud of having managed to send their son to a public school, and may tend to cut off a boy from previous local friendships. He may not think himself 'superior' but contemporary non-public school boys will expect him to be, so the divisive effect will be felt in any case.

Whatever the perception educationists had or have of the public schools, few have favoured or favour their outright abolition, if only because the divisive influences were so deeply embedded in society that they would have contrived other divisive arrangements. 'The public school problem' was thus possibly both real and insoluble. Even the compromise solution put forward by the Public School Commission did not lead to much political action. By the time of Callaghan's Ruskin College speech the public school issue had again slid down Labour's educational agenda; declining educational standards and the declining economy were wrongly seen as matters relating to the State sector of education only. The 1980s saw some revival of interest in public schools because of the assisted places scheme. But this aroused little or no heated discussion of 'the public school problem' itself, merely this particular form of relationship between the state and the private sector. The diversion of public funds to the independent sector at a time of financial restraint in the state sector was the principal ground of opposition, although this was sometimes accompanied by the objection that assisted places were taken up more by middle-class than working-class pupils. The more fundamental issues said to lie at the heart of 'the pubic school problem' await the occasion which, once again, will bring them to the forefront of the educational debate.

QUESTIONS

1. Discuss the factors which could help to explain the declining numbers of ex-elementary school pupils staying on at secondary school (page 111).
2. Identify the concepts of education which Leach supports and attacks in his criticisms of the WEA charter (page 112).
3. Did changes in our education system result from shedding old ideologies and adopting new ones?
4. Discuss the relative merits and demerits of raising (or lowering) the school leaving age (a) locally or regionally, (b) nationally, with exemptions for certain groups of student, and (c) nationally, without any exemptions.
5. Does a system of separate secondary schools inevitably mean a class-divided educational system?
6. How far have comprehensive schools promoted the mixing of students from different social classes?
7. Can education compensate for what Crosland called 'the deficiencies of upbringing and early circumstance', and if so, which system is best suited to achieve this?
8. How do direct-grant schools differ from the grant-maintained schools of today?
9. Why have government committees been reluctant to make recommendations about teachers' qualifications in the independent sector, and is such reluctance justified?
10. In what ways do the uses of the assisted places scheme suggested by some Labour educational reformers in the 1960s and 1970s reflect a different ideology from that of the scheme run by Conservative governments in the 1980s and 1990s?
11. How far is the claim made by Tawney, that ex-public school students dominate national life in its various forms, true today?
12. How far is the argument about 'the freedom to spend one's taxed income as one wishes' as tenable in relation to private education as it is in relation to any other services or goods?

NOTES AND REFERENCES

1. Rae, J. *Too Little Too Late*, Collins, 1989, p. 136.
2. Viscount Haldane *et al.*, *The Next Step in Education*, London, 1927.
3. Maclure, J. S. *Educational Documents: England and Wales*, p. 96.

4. Ibid., p. 162.
5. Labour Party Memorandum on Scholarship and Free Places, 1918.
6. See B. Simon, *Education and the Labour Movement 1870 to 1920*, Lawrence and Wishart, 1974, pp. 346–9.
7. Report of the Departmental Committee on Scholarships and Free Places HMSO, July 1920.
8. J. R. Brooks, 'Secondary Education for All' Reconsidered, Durham Research Review No. 38S, Spring 1977, pp. 1–8.
9. The Organisation of Education After 11 +, *The Papers and Correspondence of Sir P. Nunn 1907–1918*, London Institute of Education.
10. *Secondary Education for All*, p. 61.
11. Ibid., p. 67.
12. *Essays in the Politics of Education*, p. 94.
13. Introduction, p. xix.
14. See the note of reservation in the report by Miss E. R. Conway.
15. *Manchester Guardian*, 15 April 1944.
16. 'British Socialism Today' in *Socialist Commentary*, June 1952.
17. A. H. Halsey, A. F. Heath and J. M. Ridge, *Origins and Destinations*, 1980, p. 64.
18. Spens, op. cit., pp.XIX–XX.
19. In a speech delivered at the North of England Education Conference in January 1966, reprinted in A. Finch and P. Scrimshaw (eds) *Standards, Schooling and Education*, Hodder and Stoughton, 1980, pp. 27–34.s
20. J. Steedman, *Examination Results in Selective and Non Selective Schools*, National Child Development Study, 1983.
21. *The Public Schools and the General Educational System*, HMSO, 1944, p. 33.
22. *Public Schools Commission, Second Report*, HMSO, 1976, pp. 60–3.
23. Ibid., p. 66.
24. Ibid., p. 69.
25. Ibid., p. 77.
26. *The Future of Socialism*, p. 261.
27. Report of the Departmental Committee on Private Schools and other schools not in receipt of grants from Public Funds, 1932, p. 6.
28. *Equality*, p. 29, and *Public Schools*, Labour Party Memorandum, January 1941, p. 11.
29. Ibid., p. 13.
30. Ibid., p. 25.
31. Letter to the author from Ernest Green, 10 January 1974.
32. Fleming Report, p. 7.
33. Halsey *et al*., op. cit., Table 4.4, p. 52.
34. Ibid., vol. 2, p. 154.

CHAPTER 4

Further, higher and adult education since 1900

Further and higher education have been subject to various and confusing definitions. This book uses those of the 1988 Education Reform Act to help reduce such confusion, to sharpen its historical focus and to point up the issues around which the current debate revolves. Further education will thus be taken to include:

- full-time and part-time education for persons over compulsory school age (including vocational, social, physical and recreational training); and
- organised leisure-time occupation provided in connection with the provision of such education.

Higher education will be taken to cover:

- a course for the further training of teachers or youth and community workers;
- a post-graduate course (including a higher degree course);
- a first degree course;
- a course for the Diploma of Higher Education;
- a course for the Higher National Diploma or Higher National Certificate of the Business and Technician Education Council, or the Diploma in Management Studies;
- a course for the Certificate in Education;
- a course in preparation for a professional examination at higher level;
- a course providing education at a higher level (whether or not in preparation for an examination).[1]

TOWARDS TERTIARY EDUCATION AND UNITED PROVISION FOR 16–19 YEAR OLDS

Fisher's Education Act of 1918 and Butler's Act of 1944 had a vision of further education that the Baker Act altogether lacked, yet ironically it was during Baker's period of office that further education began to acquire some of the status which his more illustrious predecessors wished but failed to bestow on it. Fisher's generous vision of day continuation schools and Butler's equally ambitious scheme for county colleges were fatally flawed in two ways. Firstly, they stood outside the tradition most venerated in Britain, the liberal, secondary-university tradition. They thus appeared as loose appendages to the education system which, despite the good intentions of their authors, could be easily discarded in times of economic retrenchment. Further education, especially in its part-time forms, seemed to be the permanent Cinderella of educational provision for the 16–19 year olds, lacking the prestige which went with sixth-form study within the grammar school. Secondly, both were central government initiatives, slow to take root and vulnerable to the harsh economic climate which followed each of the two world wars. Yet the 1980s were also a period when educational expenditure was held closely in check but, by then, several developments had conspired to give an enhanced status to further education. Industry's demand for relays of cheap, adolescent labour, prevalent in the first half of the century, had belatedly given way to a demand for a more technologically skilled workforce. The microchip had done more to change the attitude of industry to post-compulsory education than all of Tawney's moral diatribes. MacGregor, the first Education Secretary of the 1990s, aimed to encourage students to take up vocational forms of further education through such schemes as an entitlement of 16–19 year olds to training vouchers which could be cashed for courses of their choice.

But of equal importance in enhancing the prestige of further education were the moves from the 1970s onwards to combine the provision of all forms of post-compulsory education within one educational institution, the tertiary college. Falling school rolls and strict controls on educational expenditure forced many local authorities to consider concentrating provision for 16–19 year olds, thus bringing together on one campus the mainstream advanced level tradition and its full-time and part-time alternatives. What history and tradition had kept rigidly apart, economic necessity, in the Baker and MacGregor years and after, brought closer together. Baker's scheme for separate city colleges of technology was within the Fisher and Butler tradition of separate development, and this suffered the same basic flaw. Yet at a local level, authorities were moving towards comprehensive but not uniform provision at 16+ within a single institution rather than in separate institutions, even in the face of strong opposition from comprehensive schools to decapitation. The challenge to British tradition thus came not from central but from local government. What the tertiary college is seeking to do is thus best understood by reference to the traditions of post-compulsory education since 1917.

In 1917, while one area of post-compulsory education, the sixth form, was being strengthened with the introduction of the Higher School Certificate, another, part-time continuation education, was being emasculated to appease the industrial interest. In June of that year Fisher issued Circular 1002 which said that the Board would henceforth only recognise the Higher School Certificate in order to reduce the multiplicity of examinations for sixth formers and so improve their efficiency. In contrast, the President, with very little support from the Labour movement, was fighting a rearguard action to stop his plans for part-time further education for those who had formerly attended elementary schools from being wrecked by industrial opposition. The cotton trade led the attack and by a most elaborate juggling performance produced figures to show how dividends would be hit and employment put in peril if young employees had to return to school for continuation education during working hours. Many trade union officials also regarded the idea of part-time education for 14–18 year olds for eight hours a week as unworkable. Labour Members of Parliament were equally unenthusiastic. It was left to people such as Tawney and Nunn to support Fisher's case. Nunn provided a workable scheme and Tawney the emotive argument in support. The former's plan for continuation schooling was flexible.[2]

Full-time attendance should be required until the age of 14 and thereafter part-time attendance, within the normal hours of employment, diminishing annually in amount, until 17+. A certain fluidity in the arrangements should be made possible, and it should be permissible to compound for some of the part-time attendance by an additional year of full-time attendance. The vocational side of the course must as a rule be general in character, but should be made as specific as local conditions permit.

There should be supplementary transferences at 14 from the continuation school to other institutions.

Tawney's condemnation of industry's opposition to such a scheme was scathing.

To suggest that British industry is suspended over an abyss by a slender thread of juvenile labour, which eight hours continued education will snap, that after a century of scientific discovery and economic progress it is still upon the bent backs of children of fourteen that our industrial organisation and national prosperity, and that rare birth of time, the Federation of British Industries itself, repose – is not all this, after all, a little pitiful?

Behind the objection based on the convenience of industry lies another objection based on the theory that all except a small minority of children are incapable of benefiting by education beyond the age of fourteen. It is not actually stated, indeed that working class children, like anthropoid apes, have fewer convolutions in their brains than the children of captains of industry. But they are evidently sceptical as to either the possibility or the desirability of offering higher education to more than a small proportion of them.[3]

While industry's strong opposition to the diminution of its supply of adolescent labour did not prevent the clauses about continuation education in Fisher's second Bill from reaching the statute book, it was fairly clear that they would be jettisoned at the first opportunity. The first major attempt to provide some kind of further education for the mass of the nation's adolescents thus appeared initially successful. The Fisher Act of 1918 stipulated that 'all young persons shall attend such continuation schools at such times, on such days, as the local education authority of the area ... may require, for three hundred and twenty hours in each year'.[4] However, with the economic recession of the early 1920s and the demands by the Geddes Committee for retrenchment, part-time further education was one of the first victims of the economy drive in all areas except Rugby.

While the first national experiment in mass part-time, further education failed, post-compulsory full-time education in secondary schools flourished, fed by a constantly increasing secondary school population. At the time of the economic recession in 1921 the number of pupils in secondary schools stood at 336,836; by the time of the Spens Report in 1938 they had grown steadily to number 470,000. This resulted in an increase in the number of students pursuing sixth-form courses from just over 34,000 in 1934 to over 40,000 in 1937. Success brought its problems, including the attractiveness of sixth-form education in rural areas which, because of their sparse population, often meant uneconomic sixth forms, and the ever-increasing range of ability and aspirations of sixth formers. The Spens Committee (1938) considered and rejected the idea of sixth-form colleges as a solution to such probiems as 'a counsel of dispair'. Sixth forms were, in its view, the most valuable feature of grammar schools and on them depended all that was best in the grammar school tradition. Nevertheless, something had to be done to deal with the problems of their success. In the case of the small country grammar school, they argued strongly against 'beheading' and in favour of making sixth forms more attractive through the creation of general courses which, while not leading to university entrance, would enhance employment opportunities. Some members of the Spens Committee argued in favour of developing joint courses with neighbouring technical colleges to achieve this. An alternative arrangement for increasing the attractiveness of sixth-form courses and of keeping down costs was the creation of sixth-form consortia which could widen the choice of Higher School Certificate and other courses. This is what Circular 1112 in 1919 had described as 'mutual understandings', though the Spens Committee joined with the Directors of Education in opposing such 'drastic disturbance of pupils at the post-School certificate stage'.[5] By and large the Spens Committee favoured each grammar school grappling with its own sixth-form problems whenever possible without contact with other grammar or technical schools.

In contrast, by 1938 the Fisher alternative of mass part-time education for those over 14 was dead in practice, and had been abandoned by most educational theorists. Even while the Geddes axe was busily at work in 1922 cutting educational expenditure, the Labour Party had, under Tawney's insistence, come to see the Fisher scheme as 'a sorry makeshift' and 'an inferior substitute' for full-time education to 15 and further education therefter. His *Secondary Education for All* laid down Labour's policy of part-time further education as an extension of full-time secondary education to 15 and ultimately to 16, rather than an extension of elementary education beyond the age of 14. This position was accepted by Hadow, endorsed by Spens and gave Butler a chance to take a second bite at the cherry in 1944. Butler's task was made easier by the work of his war-time predecessor at the Board of Education, Herwald Ramsbotham, who had issued a green book on post-war educational reconstruction just before Butler arrived at the Board in the summer of 1941. This 'new testament of education' pointed to the inadequacies of leaving the education of young workers to the haphazard and ill-adapted system of evening classes, and of reliance upon the goodwill of employers to release them to attend technical schools. By 1939, however, there were as many being released voluntarily by employers for part-time attendance at technical colleges and schools in the daytime as there were students in full-time education in sixth forms, something in the region of 41,000. Ramsbotham, like Butler, wanted to put such further education on a sounder footing, and pinned his hopes upon continuation schools; Butler had an altogether grander vision, that of county colleges. In his Green Book, *Education After the War*,[6] Ramsbotham stated,

> The advent of Continuation Schools will of course go a considerable way to better the position. They will provide a measure of vocational training related to their employment or occupation for all young persons, and this may suffice for a large majority. In the case of those who should be encouraged to go further and proceed to more advanced forms of training, some relief will be given from the burden of study after the day's work, although some evening work will still be required.

But the day continuation school was to be more than a place providing one day's education a week. He argued that it was something different from Fisher's concept in that,

> It must be a real entity with its own corporate life, recognised as in some sense a Community Centre for Youth or a Young People's College. It should have all the facilities necessary to enable all kinds of activities, recreative and cultural, including school societies and clubs to be developed in and around it outside the actual hours of instruction. Workshops and other rooms should be kept open in the evenings for the benefit of pupils following technical or commercial courses and also for the prosecution of hobby activities in the form of various handicrafts. All this will mean that the school buildings will be fully occupied throughout the week, both in the daytime and in the evenings.

Butler developed this idea into a system of county colleges with the help of his permanent secretary, Maurice Holmes, who had done much of the spadework for the Green Book. Butler envisaged the county colleges scheme for further education providing for the majority of young people in the 15–18 age group; but like the Fisher scheme it suffered from the same fundamental problem of being separate from, and thus seen as inferior to, mainstream academic provision.

The Butler Act defined further education in terms largely accepted by Baker nearly half a century later. It encompassed not simply the more formal kinds of full- and part-time post-compulsory education but also the broader recreational and cultural activities. County colleges were to be the main providers of further education, particularly in terms of vocational training; local education authorities were to be legally obliged to set up such colleges and students to attend them, but only when the Minister considered it 'practicable to do so'. When this part of the Act came into operation, students would be required to attend county colleges for one day or two half-days a week for forty-four weeks a year. But other urgent priorities meant that these provisions never came into effect. The Crowther Report summed up the position in 1959 in its famous opening sentence: 'This report is about the education of English boys and girls aged from 15 to 18. Most of them are not being educated'.[7] The reorganisation of secondary education which the Butler Act achieved was not paralleled in further education. As Butler noted in his autobiography in 1971, much of the promise of his Act in this respect was unfulfilled. Day release was still voluntary not mandatory, and affected less than half of 18 year olds. The idea of the community college was born prematurely and was too weak to survive in the harsh, economic climate of the immediate post-war years. In 1959 Crowther was still trying to point the way towards the creation of county colleges; the time was not yet ripe for a systematic reorganisation that would bring together the various forms of post-compulsory education.

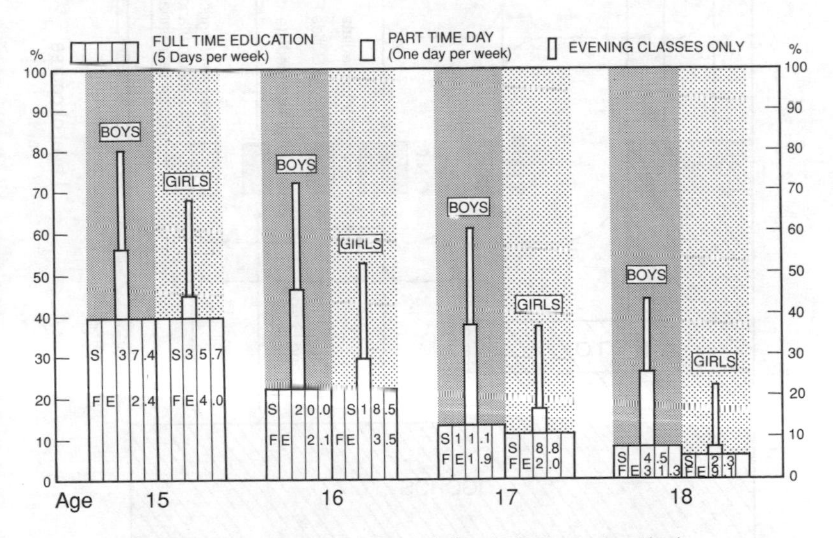

(S = Full-time at school; FE = full-time in further education)

Fig. 4.1 ***Proportion of age groups in different types of education 1957–58 (England and Wales)***

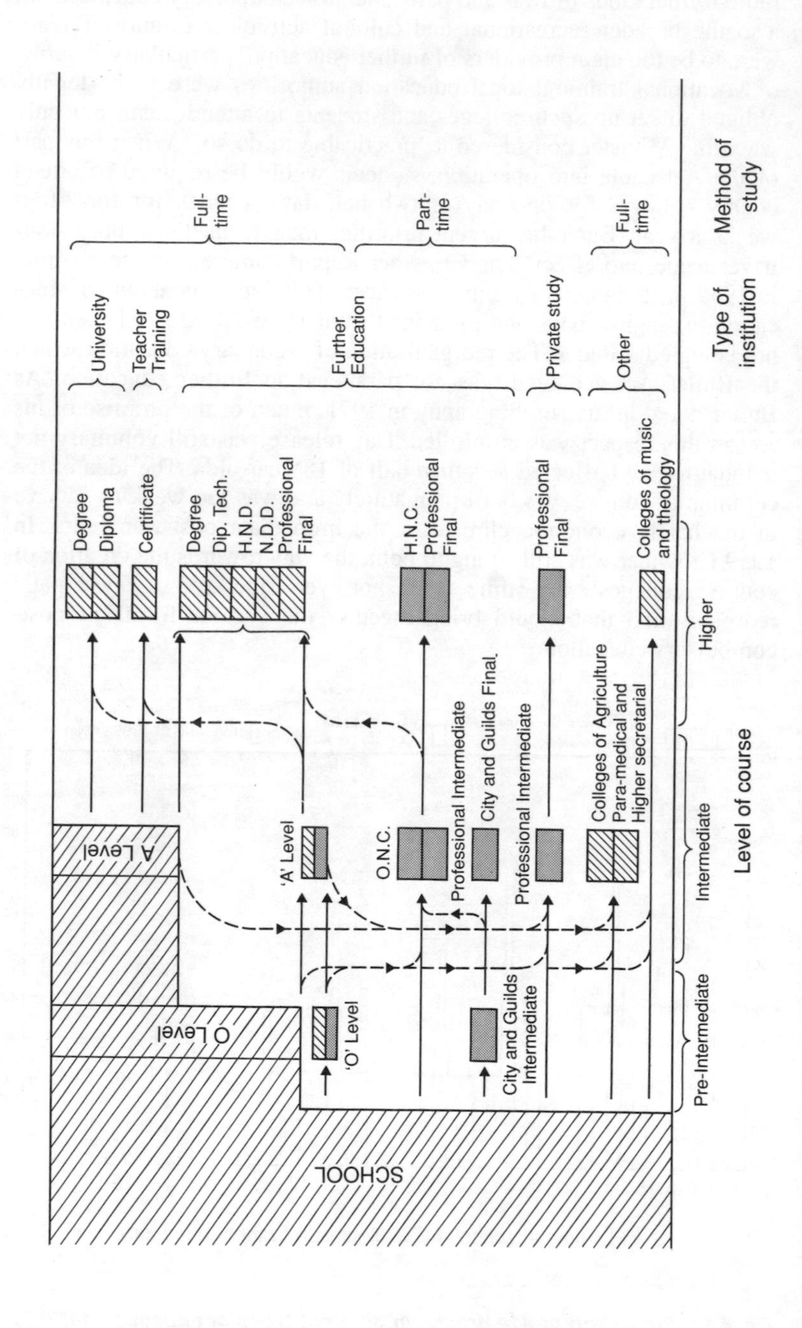

Fig. 4.2 ***Outline pattern of post-school education in England and Wales***

Neither a Second World War nor the post-war demand for a technologically skilled workforce had ended the British tradition of voluntary attendance, and piecemeal provision. Full-time and part-time further education attracted few 15–18 year olds compared with sixth-form education as the diagram for 1957/58 (Figure 4.1) shows.[8]

Much of the part-time education was provided in local technical colleges in technical, commercial, scientific subjects and GCE courses. The variety of post-15 education was summed up in the Robbins Report of 1963 (see Figure 4.2).[9]

Nowhere were national priorities better illustrated than in the contrast between the multi-volumed, elaborately researched, Robbins Report on higher education of over 2,000 pages, and the slim, 50-paged Henniker–Heaton Report of the following year on day release. The terms of the latter, which covered the vast majority of 15–18 year olds, were to report 'on what steps should be taken to bring about the maximum practicable increase in the grant of release from employment to enable young persons under the age of 18 to attend technical and other courses of further education'.[10] The Committee ruled out two approaches to the problem – the first out of necessity, the second out of choice. The first was compulsion. Although, in principle, a statutory right to day release was embodied in the 1918 and 1944 Education Acts, government pressure on the Committee ruled out this obvious means of increasing day release. A previous committee under J. A. R. Pimlott had pointed to the heavy recurring expenditure which a legal entitlement to day release would entail, and also to the strong, industrial opposition to such a measure. A different solution to the problem was favoured by the Government and by a majority of the Henniker–Heaton Committee: that was to increase the attractiveness of day release and expand it over a five-year period to provide accommodation for half a million day release students, thus doubling existing numbers by 1970. This was to be an essentially voluntarist development. What is important is that this was not to be achieved through the creation by government initiative of new and separate institutions on the lines of Butler's county colleges. Thus, the second approach that was ruled out was that of separate development. This separatist approach was seen as one of the reasons why Butler's scheme failed.

County colleges

The 1944 Education Act made provision for county colleges at which part time attendance was to be compulsory for young people under 18 who were not in full-time attendance elsewhere. Young people were to be obliged to attend for one whole day a week for 44 weeks in the year, or the equivalent. In view of other urgent priorities, the Government has not yet been able to bring these provisions into effect. Meanwhile, the 1944 concept of county colleges as something separate from the rest of further education has been modified, and the balance of educational opinion now probably takes the view that the local colleges of further education, whose work is centred on the needs of the younger age groups, form a natural focus for the development of county college work.[11]

The emphasis was to be on integrating day release students into the life of local colleges, and by devising relevant courses to attract students to such colleges and to persuade employers to support day release. The voluntarist principle meant that courses would mainly be directly relevant to employment, although the Committee was quick to point out that,

> Vocational education is often thought of as the acquisition of knowledge and skills directly applicable to the job; but in many posts what is required is not so much the acquisition of a skill as progressive development in the fields of human relations, of judgement, and of general educational standards. These are important over a wide range of ability and level of work.[12]

The term 'vocational' should not necessarily or always be defined in a narrow vocational sense.

The Committee recognised that the progress of day release had been slow despite the attention given to it by the White Paper of 1956 on technical education. They hoped that the compulsory raising of the school leaving age to 16, to be implemented in 1970/71, would lead to a greater demand for further education just as it would, they believed, for sixth-form study. What some on the Henniker–Heaton Committee wanted, but were prevented from recommending, was compulsory day release. Early on in the report, therefore, they urged that a further review of 'a right to day release' should be made before the first five-year target for increased voluntary attendance was achieved by 1970. The Committee remained adamant in its opposition to the creation of separate, *ad hoc* institutions for further education. Developments of a technical, vocational and general educational nature should take place within existing institutions of further education, especially as many of these already had close links with industry and commerce. The Advisory Committee on Further Education for Commerce pressed for faculties for business studies in line with those developed for technologists, supporting technicians, craftsmen and operatives – a demand which partly explained the reluctance of areas such as banking hitherto to support day release. The Henniker–Heaton Committee looked to the Industrial Training Act of 1964 to provide the administrative machinery, the industrial training boards, to coordinate and promote day release.

Few bodies or committees engaged in a comprehensive overview of the education and training of 16–19 year olds. Most, like the Henniker–Heaton Committee, were concerned with specific issues. For example the National Advisory Council on Education for Industry and Commerce set up a subcommittee in 1961 to examine sandwich courses. The United Kingdom Advisory Council on Education for Management pressed for the extensive development of education for business and management, pointing out in a series of reports how far behind Britain was compared with its industrial competitors. The Conservative Government in its White Paper *Better Opportunities in Technical Education* (1961) argued for more rigorous organisation of technical

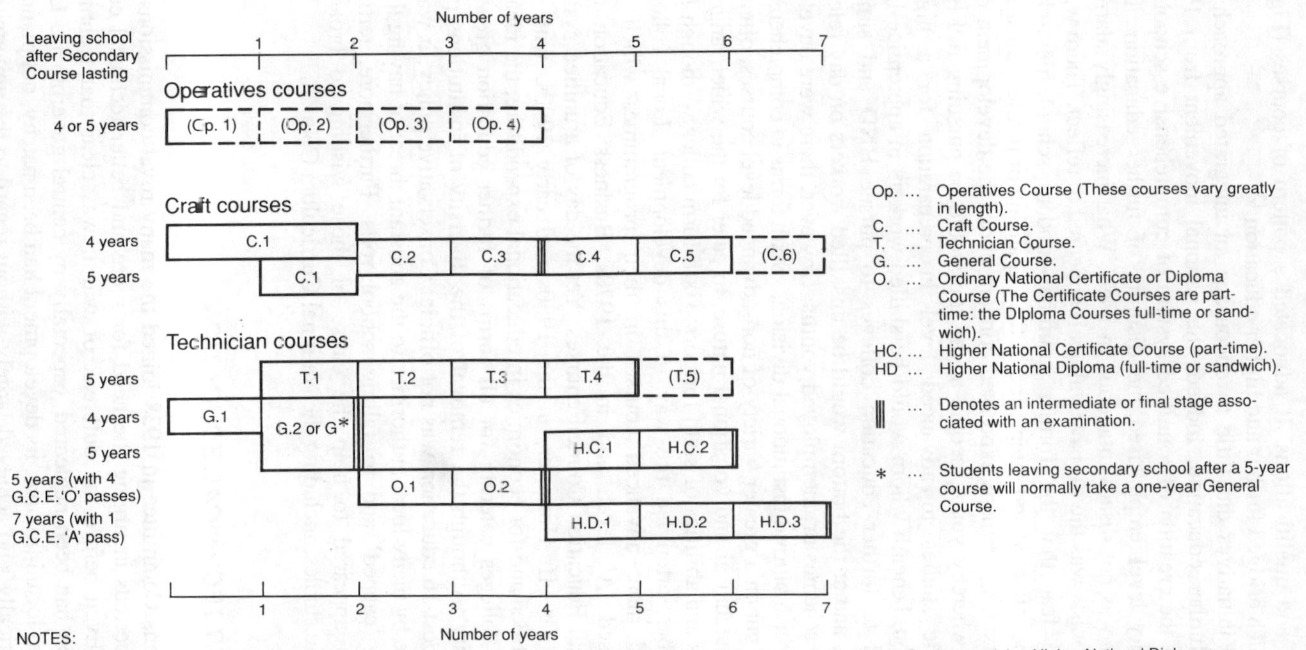

Fig. 4.3 ***Outline of the new pattern of courses***

courses and qualifications. It advocated a pattern of courses (Figure 4.3) which bridged further and higher education.[13]

Such initiatives did little to encourage an integrated approach towards further education. Indeed, the national movement from 1965 towards the creation of a unified system of comprehensive schools at secondary level emphasised the disunity of further education. This disunity was not disadvantageous in itself. What increasingly alarmed educationists was the divisive values it appeared to reflect. There was a growing fear that the former grammar–modern school hierarchies would be reflected and intensified in the expansion of further education. The Labour movement expressed concern about the development of a system whereby young people at the top would be pursuing full-time academic studies to advanced level in preparation for a higher education, beneath whom would be skilled workers in apprenticeships released to further education colleges to pursue HND and similar courses, and at the bottom would be unskilled workers on day release training schemes or unemployed youths. However, there were developments which blurred institutional divisions. Sixth forms in comprehensive schools put on a greater variety of non-advanced level courses, often of a quasi-technical and vocational nature, to cater for the wider range of interests and abilities of sixth formers; sixth-form colleges, though few in number, often led the way in this development. Local colleges included more advanced courses in their programmes which encompassed 'A' level, and in the 1970s, Business Education and Technical Education Council courses. Yet the day of a unified system seemed far off. However, in the 1980s and early 1990s, with the constant demand for economies in educational expenditure, the idea of tertiary colleges catering for all forms of further education grew in popularity. Although the removal of the diversity of institutions providing post-16 education was not official Conservative policy, it was a response by many local authorities to the constant threat of having their budgets 'capped' and to falling school rolls. Furthermore, tertiary colleges appeared to help the cause of those wishing to broaden academic studies, including the National Curriculum Council.

HIGHER TECHNICAL EDUCATION

The Spens Committee in 1938 joined the many royal commissions of earlier periods in urging the need for more and better technical education. Even before the outbreak of war it was clear that technical education had been neglected, especially by central government. Left largely to local initiative, its development had been patchy, not planned systematically, and achieved largely without regard to the universities. It was clear, even before the Second World War highlighted its shortcomings still further, that the whole system needed overhauling if British industry was to reverse its declining position in foreign markets.

Butler was not content simply to clarify the duties of local education authorities in respect of technical education in the 1944 Education Act. He set up a special committee under Lord Eustace Percy with terms of reference specific to higher technological education.

> Having regard to the requirements of Industry, to consider the needs of higher technological education in England and Wales and the respective contributions to be made thereto by Universities and Technical Colleges; and to make recommendations, among other things, as to the means for maintaining appropriate collaboration between Universities and Technical Colleges in this field.[14]

The Percy Committee emphasised that the problem was not simply the dearth of craftsmen and general technologists; it was one particularly of a shortage of 'scientists and technologists who can also administer and organise and can apply the results of research to development'.[15] Percy had long since recognised the root cause of the problem. In *Education at the Crossroads* (1930) he identified the dominant cultural tradition as a principal cause; the gentlemanly tradition, derived from the nineteenth century, led most able university students to enter non-industrial occupations. Yet the desperate economic situation demanded that the universities should help resolve the problem of the shortage of technologists. Of the five groups of personnel – senior administrators, engineering scientists (together with development engineers), engineering managers, technical assistants and draughtsmen, and craftsmen – the Percy Committee believed that the first three categories were the concern of the universities or of the universities and technical colleges jointly. It argued in favour of the development of new courses and new administrative machinery to increase transbinary collaboration. In the case of the former it advocated the establishment of full-time courses of a university standard but run by specially selected technical colleges for some 350 engineers each year. These courses would be concerned with the 'highest level of the teaching of the art of technology' – that is, the special application of general principles to particular problems of production and utilisation. The Committee rejected the suggestion of developing 'some new national technological university' to run these courses and award degrees (such as actually happened a few years later, in 1953, with the selection of the Imperial College of Science and Technology for special development) on the grounds that university affiliations and degree-granting machinery might be too cumbersome and inflexible to meet the needs of the new courses. In opting for special technical colleges the committee was anticipating the development of Colleges of Advanced Technology, so designated in 1956. In order to coordinate the development of higher technical education, the Committee recommended the creation of regional advisory councils with a national counterpart.

But new courses and administrative machinery would be of little value without an adequate supply of able students. The Committee addressed the problem of attracting such students. It recognised that the advent of secondary education for all would not necessarily ensure an adequate supply, given the prevailing cultural values. It advocated the wider dissemination of information to schools, the appointment by industry of apprentices who were likely to go on to higher education, and easing transfer between technical college and university; however, it gave no special attention to the encouragement of young women to take up a career in engineering.

Whereas the Percy Report was principally concerned with the development of special technical colleges, thus paving the way for colleges of advanced technology and polytechnics, the Barlow Report, published a year later, focused on the expansion of post-war science and technology in the universities. The Barlow Report helped to shape the first stage of an expansionist policy which led to the Robbins era. The Barlow Committee were anxious that more would not mean worse; that educational standards would not suffer as a result of a much needed expansion. Given the Committee's findings that less than 2 per cent of the population reached university, and that there were five times as many young people of equal intelligence who did not, there was an ample reserve of able people upon which universities could draw to increase their numbers and raise standards. While the universities could thus tap this vast reservoir of ability to promote science and technology, the Committee were adamant that this should not be done at the expense of the humanities and languages. It stressed the importance of a common culture, on the 'association of men and women which takes knowledge as its province and in which all branches of learning flourish in harmony'. The cloistering of specialists, whether they be technologists, scientists or arts specialists, should be discouraged.

One possible area of the country where post-war technological education at university level could be developed and yet balance could be achieved was North Staffordshire with its strong traditions of liberal adult education and technical education. Tawney, as a member of the University Grants Committee (UGC), urged the local branch of the WEA to raise the question of a university college in Stoke on Trent. He helped 'a group of persons representing educational and other interests in North Staffordshire' to formulate proposals to put before the UGC. The first meeting with the UGC to set up the first post-war university took place in March 1946 with Tawney assisting the UGC chairman, Sir Walter Moberly. At one point Tawney supported the idea of a new technological university growing out of Stoke Technical College. However, the University of North Staffordshire at Keele – which was established in 1949 under the principalship of Lindsay, Master of Balliol and close friend of Tawney – was a very different institution from an enlarged technical college, with its new, experimental broad curriculum.

The threat of Soviet technological dominance, emphasised in a speech by Sir Winston Churchill in 1955, kept the expansion of British higher technological education near the top of the educational agenda. The Percy Committee's idea for the development of special courses of advanced technology in selected technical colleges had already gained the backing of the National Advisory Council of Education for Industry and Commerce in its report in 1950 on *The Future of Higher Technological Education.* A Conservative government White Paper in 1956 on technical education put these ideas in a more concrete form with its proposals for extending full-time study through sandwich courses and by creating a new category of college, the College of Advanced Technology (CAT). The spur to action was stated clearly.

From the USA, Russia and Western Europe comes the challenge to look to our system of technical education to see whether it bears comparison with what is being done abroad. Such comparisons cannot be made accurately because standards and systems of education vary so much, but it is clear enough that all these countries are making an immense effort to train more scientific and technical manpower and that we are in danger of being left behind . . .

The intention of the White Paper was to provide a structure which went well beyond evening and part-time study for London external degrees. Hence it proposed a new award, the Diploma in Technology, particularly for study in new institutions and colleges of advanced technology. These colleges passed from local government control to direct-grant status in 1962, resulting in a four-tier system: Colleges of Advanced Technology, and regional, area and local colleges. The Robbins Committee in 1963 described the progress made in higher technological education since the Percy Report as 'rapid' but most education commentators agreed that much remained to be done. The resurgence of Japan and West Germany left some educationists very pessimistic about whether Britain could improve its international position, the Robbins survey of initial degrees confirming the extent to which the nation lagged behind (Table 4.1).[16]

Table 4.1 ***First degrees in technology in various countries as a percentage of first degrees in science and technology, 1959***

Country	*Percentage*
Great Britain	36
Canada	65
France	48
Germany (FR)	68
Netherlands	60
Sweden	54
Switzerland	59
USA	49

The emergency was seen as sufficiently serious to overcome objections to transferring the CATs to the university sector. The Robbins recommendation that they should become technological universities thus greatly assisted the upward movement of institutions which a decade before had been technical colleges. The Council for National Academic Awards was set up to provide degrees for students in non-academic institutions on the recommendation of the Robbins Committee.

The Robbins Report marked but one stage in the evolution of higher technical education. The Labour Government in 1966 expressed its concern about the proliferation of technical institutions undertaking higher levels of work and Crosland presented to Parliament in the May of that year a scheme for concentrating much of the higher technical education in polytechnics with 2,000 full-time students. His aim was to

Table 4.2 ***The variety of courses offered by polytechnics, 1970–1978***

Subject group	*1970*	*1972*	*1974*	*1976*	*1978*
Education	2,675 (2.1)	4,466 (3.1)	5,106 (3.5)	18,595 (9.6)	17,794 (8.6)
Medical health, welfare	3,613 (2.8)	5,404 (3.8)	5,913 (4.1)	7,462 (3.9)	7,455 (3.6)
Engineering and technology	43,628 (34.4)	42,488 (29.8)	37,744 (26.1)	40,885 (21.2)	43,593 (21.2)
Agriculture	18 (–)	– (–)	1 (–)	1 (–)	– (–)
Science	14,194 (11.2)	16,666 (11.7)	16,304 (11.3)	19,110 (9.9)	21,845 (10.6)
Social, administrative and business studies	42,326 (33.3)	48,959 (34.3)	54,882 (37.9)	64,673 (33.6)	68,557 (33.3)
Professional and vocational subjects*	10,531 (8.3)	11,480 (8.0)	11,863 (8.2)	12,733 (6.6)	14,098 (6.8)
Languages, literature and area studies	2,525 (1.8)	3,261 (2.3)	3,364 (2.3)	4,113 (2.1)	5,112 (2.5)
Arts (other than above)	1,427 (1.1)	1,877 (1.3)	1,202 (–)	1,103 (–)	4,692 (2.3)
Music, drama, art, design	5,498 (4.3)	7,237 (5.1)	8,095 (5.6)	9,471 (4.9)	10,557 (5.1)
GCE and CSE	655 (–)	892 (–)	169 (–)	298 (–)	310 (–)
Unclassified	– (–)	– (–)	– (–)	– (–)	– (–)

*Architecture, catering and institutional management, home economics, librarianship, nautical subjects, transport, wholesale and retail trades etc.

Source: DES, Statistics of Education, 1970–1978.

establish thirty polytechnics which would offer 'a wide variety of disciplines', concentrate 'expensive resources in fewer centres' while at the same time maintain high academic standards and a satisfactory corporate life. The variety of courses which they offered in the years immediately after their establishment is shown in Table 4.2.[17]

By the early 1980s the polytechnics, like so many of the institutions created in the 1960s, were beginning to gain an undeserved negative public reputation so much so that the *Times Higher Education Supplement* felt it necessary to spring to their defence. The crude criticisms of polytechnics were of two kinds: (a) they were strongholds of left-wing sedition; and (b) they had 'succumbed to the siren voices of academic drift, deserted their roots in vocational education and become second-rate universities rather than first-rate polytechnics.' Both charges were baseless but reflected how, even during the eighties when government policy placed such a high priority on regenerating industry, they failed to gain strong political backing. They were certainly not immune from the swingeing cuts of the 1980s. Such cuts did not, however, prevent the polytechnics from developing business education which, by the beginning of the 1990s, had become the most popular subject on offer.

UNIVERSITIES AND UNIVERSITY EDUCATION

Two very broad generic issues have dominated discussion about universities and university education this century. The first has provided a discussion point since the beginning of the century and earlier: restrictions on the access of certain groups of people to a university education. The second, the nature of university education and research, has emerged more recently, partly as a result of government insistence that universities should raise their funds more from private sources than from the state. By and large, most reformers early this century accepted the classic Newman position that universities should aim at disinterested scholarship; they were more concerned to spread the gold more widely, to provide wider access to a university education, than to question the nature of the currency.

A useful starting point for a consideration of the issue of restrictions on access is the Labour Party's memorandum on Scholarships and Free Places published in 1918 and referred to in Chapter 3. Tawney's analysis was concerned with working-class disadvantage. Of the 600,000 elementary school pupils who left school in 1910, only 566 reached university. The schools which educated over 90 per cent of the nation's children provided less than 1 per cent of university students. For some, the problem was even worse; the odds on going to university were even slimmer for those living outside the three counties of Lancashire, Yorkshire and London which accounted for over half of the 566 university places; counties such as Buckingham, Bedford,

Cornwall, Leicester, Oxford and Westmoreland sent no students at all to university.

Oxford and Cambridge, at the 'Harrods' end of the university market, raised the problems of access in their most acute form. As Jude in *Jude the Obscure* lay dying he heard that there were schemes afoot for making the university (Oxford) less exclusive. As there were in 1895 when Hardy wrote his indictment of Oxford élitism, so there still are in the 1990s. In 1850, a royal commission concluded that the university should open itself to 'a much larger and poorer class of the population'. At the end of the First World War yet another royal commission took another bite at that particular cherry. The evidence submitted to it in 1920 by the WEA, the body within the Labour movement with which Oxbridge had the closest links, reveals the generic issues and problems and their background. Set up like the public schools with whom they had close if not incestuous links, with endowments 'originally bestowed with special injunctions that they should be used to educate those who could not afford to educate themselves',[18] Oxford and Cambridge had dramatically changed their clientele. Contrary to the intentions of their founders they continued to recruit 'a surprisingly large proportion of their undergraduate members from schools of the well to do'. Undergraduates from state secondary schools were relatively few; those educated at elementary school were negligible in number. Greater representation at university of students from the largest social group, the working classes, was an obvious cause for educationists to champion, then as it is today. But it was not the only one, and was not looked at in isolation from other closely related issues, which are still with us. Again it would be worth returning briefly to the WEA evidence to identify these related issues. It pointed to three main areas of contemporary concern.

1. That owing mainly to the highest cost of residence in the Colleges of Oxford and Cambridge, the undergraduate population, to an even greater degree than in other Universities, is at present drawn from too narrow a circle and is not truly representative of the nation's talent, and that it is essential so to amend the present system as to enable boys of all classes, who possess the necessary intellectual qualifications, to enter the Colleges of Oxford and Cambridge freely and easily, irrespective of the income of their parents.
2. That the present position of women at Oxford and Cambridge is highly unsatisfactory.
3. That the provision made by Oxford and Cambridge for adult education, while it has increased in recent years, is not commensurate either with the importance of this department of education or with the resources and responsibilities of the Universities and Colleges, and should be largely increased in the near future.

These three, together with a fourth of a more general nature, provide a good focus for discussing the principal generic issues facing universities this century.

4. That the constitution and government of the Universities of Oxford and Cambridge do not adequately secure that they are kept in close touch with the changing educational needs and conditions of the community, and that they should be amended in such a way that while educational freedom is safeguarded the interests of the public shall be represented upon the governing bodies of both universities.

The WEA memorandum had much to say on the first of these issues, as one would expect from a body within the Labour movement. It looked closely at the scholarship examination which gave precedence to a knowledge of Latin and Greek, success in which did not even guarantee to cover all the costs of study. It thus operated in a socially selective, not just an educationally selective way. It admitted 'the well-to-do boy, even if he was idle and not very intelligent', and hampered 'the admission of the boy of small means, even if he is able and industrious'. Neither the Royal Commission's report of 1922 nor the statutes of 1926, which embodied several of its recommendations, provided the more fundamental financial remedies which the WEA advocated.

The increase in the number of secondary school places and pupils in the inter-war years and the advent of secondary education for all after 1944 made little immediate impact on the basic problem of working-class access as Table 4.3 shows. The table examines the opportunities for a university education of different social groups, for those born during four consecutive periods in the years 1913–52.[19]

Table 4.3 ***Attendance at university by birth cohort***

Father's social class	*1913–22* %	*1923–32* %	*1933–42* %	*1943–52* %
I, II	7.2	15.9	23.7	26.4
III, IV, V	1.9	4.0	4.1	8.0
VI, VII, VIII	0.9	1.2	2.3	3.1
All	1.8	3.4	5.4	8.5

Despite the size of the semi-skilled and unskilled manual groups (VI, VII and VIII) they remained abysmally under-represented at universities in the years following the Second World War. This was a fact which struck the Robbins Committee in its enquiry into higher education. It produced statistical evidence showing how relatively few university students came from the homes of manual, semi-skilled or unskilled workers. This under-representation helped to explain why there was such a relatively small percentage of 18–21 year olds at university compared with other countries, at the time of the Robbins enquiry only some 4 per cent. Among its recommendations, the Committee advocated greater flexibility in the selection processes, closer links between universities and their localities, more attractive and less intensive university courses and the establishment of six new universities by 1980/81. Even the establishment of the 'magnificent seven' new universities between 1961 and 1965 – Sussex, York, East Anglia, Essex, Lancaster, Kent and Warwick – did little to increase the percentage of students from semi- and unskilled backgrounds as the figures for the 1980s reveal (see p.42). The older universities made some efforts to revise their admissions policies, but while they still drew around 50 per cent of their students from the private sector, which educated less than 20 per cent of sixth formers, they were unlikely to provide much assistance in solving the problem. This was especially true from the 1980s onwards when it was clear that the relative size of the semi- and unskilled groups in society was declining from around 50 per cent at the time of Robbins to about 35 per cent in 1983. The system of student loans was likely to exacerbate the problem according to the Committee of Vice-Chancellors and Principals. Poorer students would be disadvantaged by being forced to borrow, whereas those from more affluent homes would not need loans, or would not need to borrow so much. Such a system might also discourage graduates from entering poorer paid occupations such as teaching and social work.

The second issue raised in the 1920 WEA memorandum, that of the under-representation of women, also had no easy solution. In its evidence to the Royal Commission the WEA recommended a first step of revising the proportion of women at Oxbridge to 25 per cent. This figure was in fact exceeded by universities in general. In 1922 when the Royal Commission's report was published it stood at just over 28 per cent, which increased to 30 per cent in 1926 but fell back a decade later to a little over 23 per cent. Family pressures, general expectations and the austere image of a male-dominated world all played their part in dissuading many woman from continuing their sixth-form education and entering university. Forty years later, in the so-called 'swinging sixties', the figure failed to swing markedly upward:

1959–60, 24.0%	1963–64, 26.7%	1967–68, 27.4%
1960–61, 24.5%	1964–65, 27.6%	1968–69, 27.7%
1961–62, 25.4%	1965–66, 26.4%	1969–70, 28.1%
1962–63, 26.3%	1966–67, 27.0%	1970–71, 28.9%
		1971–72, 29.7%

By the beginning of the 1980s, the percentage stood at 40 to rise to 44 by the end of the decade. But by then the principal issue was not the overall percentage of women at university but their distribution between the subject areas. The falling population mean that particular attention had to be paid to drawing women into those areas thought to be of immediate importance to the nation's economy, particularly science and technology. The extracts from the Universities Central Council for Admissions (UCCA) and UGC statistics (Table 4.4) show the difficulty of breaking traditional patterns of subject preference.

Table 4.4 ***Number of full-time university students (excluding postgraduates) 1922–88***

Year		*Arts inc. Educ.*	*Sciences*	*Dentistry/ Medicine*	*Technology Applied Sciences*	*Agriculture*	*Social Sciences*	*Business and Admin.*	*Languages**
1922–23	Women	7,999	2,129	2,368	78	101	–	–	–
	Total	18,231	7,763	11,866	5,567	1,192	–	–	–
1935–36	Women	7,885	2,019	1,747	88	140	–	–	–
	Total	23,684	8,602	12,923	4,432	888	–	–	–
1951–52	Women	12,349	3,304	2,933	181	325	–	–	–
	Total	25,936	17,053	13,930	10,215	20,419	–	–	–
1961–62	Women	15,132	6,433	3,541	413	234	2,827	–	–
	Total	36,156	28,676	11,756	17,222	2,050	12,461	–	–
1976–77	Women	10,614	5,320	2,471	498	483	7,097	–	6,459
	Total	17,443	17,816	5,958	9,600	1,414	18,470	–	9,926
1987–88	Women	6,367	9,021	4,363	1,541	674	13,724	5,936	9,778
	Total	12,203	27,063	9,244	14,274	2,147	27,952	13,741	14,275

Table 4.4 illustrates the more limited advances made in the traditionally male-dominated areas of sciences (excluding the biological sciences) and technology compared with the greater advances made in the arts and social sciences.

The third generic issue raised in the WEA evidence related to adult education both in the sense of extramural provision, which is dealt with later in this chapter, and of full-time university provision for mature students. It is only in fairly recent years that universities have seriously begun to tackle the problem of widening access to university for mature students without the standard higher school certificate or 'A' level qualifications. Most of the drive in the immediate post-Robbins era was towards increasing the number of 18 year olds at university as a post-script to secondary education for all. The Robbins Committee showed the disparity between the 27 per cent of overseas full-time under-graduates in 1961/62 aged 25 and over, and 3 per cent of home students who fell into this category. Robbins made no major proposals to improve this situation and it had to await two further developments before any substantial advances were made. The first of these was the founding of the Open University in 1969, which, although designed for part-time degree study, showed the existence of a large reservoir of adults who, despite lacking formal academic qualifications, were able to undertake degree studies successfully. The second and more important factor was the fear that the falling birthrate from the mid-1960s onwards would result in a decline in university applicants from schools. In fact, the reverse was the case by the 1990s with increased rather than lessened demand from schools; the effect of social class differences in the birthrate and changes in occupational structures led to an increase in the size of those groups who had traditionally made the greatest use of higher education. Nevertheless, in an age of uncertainties, universities hedged their bets by making a more concerted effort to widen access. But even by the beginning of the 1990s the percentage of undergraduates aged 25 and over still fell short of 10 per cent: in the thirty years since Robbins, the figure of 3 per cent had barely trebled.

The fourth issue raised in the WEA evidence was no less fundamental. In its recommendations concerning the constitution and government of the universities of Oxford and Cambridge, the WEA spoke of the relationship between universities and 'the changing educational needs and conditions of the community'. This, in a restricted constitutional way, pointed to the broader generic issue of the nature of a university education and research. The issue was not so hotly debated in the 1920s as it is today. Newman had argued the case in favour of disinterested pure scholarship so well in his book *The Idea of a University Defined and Illustrated* (1852) that even two world wars and a marked decline in Britain's economic position had not revived much support by the 1970s for the alternative view, of Locke, that 'money spent in defiance to all callings and business' is money wasted. However, the Newman–Locke debate was to take on a new and enforced urgency in the 1980s with the Government's insistence that universities should respond to what the WEA had termed 'changing educational needs and conditions of the community' by engaging in those kinds of applied research which would assist Britain's economic regeneration and attract funding from outside bodies. The UGC's strategy for the higher education in the 1990s[20] pointed the way by identifying more precisely alternative sources of income to the public purse.

Public function
UGC recurrent grant
Home student fees and research training support grants
Research grants from Research Councils
Computer Board grants

Other income
Endowments, donations and subscriptions
Services rendered: Overseas student fees
Research grants (other than from Research Councils) and contracts
Other items, including continuing education
Other sources

Professor John Ashworth in the Lockian tradition gave the 'market' cure for ailing campuses his full backing. Government, he argued,[21] should encourage businesses to purchase university expertise to the extent of subsidising small firms to do so. The fast-growing applied subjects would as a consequence attract a larger number of students to universities, including working-class students. He argued that industry would also invest in pure research. Mary Warnock,[22] while being no latter-day Newman, nevertheless condemned such reliance on a market-place philosophy. Universities, she argued, should not have to cater for the whim of the market, whether it be the student market or the industrial or commercial sponsor. It was unrealistic, she argued, to expect industry to fund the kind of pure research that did not offer an immediate return; government should undertake that task. Thus the more recent and continuing debate about the nature and purpose of education has taken on some of the urgency and strength of feeling of the earlier debate between Newman and Locke, especially with the introduction of the bidding system for students at the beginning of the 1990s. The further swing towards a marketplace philosophy, with universities being required by the University Funding Council (no longer a grants committee) to bid for the students they would like to take at a price at or below the guide price, marked another clear step away from the Newman ideal of a university.

THE SUPPLY, TRAINING AND EDUCATION OF TEACHERS

The issue of educational standards, brought to the centre of the political debate by Callaghan and kept there for a variety of reasons by his Conservative successors, was bound to highlight questions about the supply, training and education of teachers. But such questions were not new. They were as alive and as sensitive in the early years of this century, when teaching was being rescued from the ranks of a decaying trade and turned into a profession by such measures as the creation of the Burnham Committee in 1919 to negotiate nationwide salaries, as they are today in the post-Burnham era.[23] For example, the recent licensed teacher scheme, whereby certain categories of people without teaching qualifications could be taken on by a school and trained in-post, raises several issues which, around 1919, were discussed in the context of the pupil teacher system. But matters such as routes into the profession, types of training and the minimum academic attainment of entrants raise a whole variety of related questions. Should there be an all-graduate profession? What should be the balance between academic and professional studies in training courses? Should schools or training colleges be the principal bases of training? Are concurrent training courses to be preferred to consecutive? How long should training courses last? What should be the form and nature of in-service training and education?

The whole corpus of generic issues has had many access points. Baker's licensed-teacher scheme of the post-Burnham era was but one. He argued – contrary to the view of some of the larger teacher unions – that his proposals would raise standards rather than dilute them. To the teachers' unions, however, matters of entry into teaching had long been bound up with the question of professional status, so that even a scheme that could only scratch the surface of teacher shortage was likely to arouse opposition out of all proportion to its numerical significance. In 1922, G. S. M. Ellis of the NUT, writing in the early years of the Burnham era when teachers' salaries dominated the educational agenda, issued a cautionary note on the subject of teacher education and training. 'The problem which confronts teachers is not merely a problem of pay; it is one of status and it is bound up inseparably with the question of education and training.'[24] Teachers in conference around 1922 were demanding a full partnership with government over matters relating to education and training. The NUT, in particular, looked forward to 'a self-governing profession in which there is no room for the ill-qualified amateur'.

The teaching profession had three grades of teacher when Ellis wrote his memorandum on teacher education and training for the Labour Party. Table 4.5 shows these grades and their relative size.[25]

Table 4.5 ***Teachers employed at the end of March 1923***

	Number	*Percentage*
Certificated teachers	116,720	72.5
Uncertificated teachers	32,881	20.4
Supplementary teachers	11,448	7.1
Total	161,049	

Certificated teachers had passed the Board's final examination in training colleges or its alternative. Uncertificated teachers were originally assumed to be teachers in-post in the process of completing their studies for its alternative, the Certificate Examination for Acting Teachers, a predecessor of the Licensed Teacher scheme. But according to Ellis teachers were uncertificated for more than one reason. Some were uncertificated simply because they were content 'with their undignified status and their inferior pay'; others had attempted to enter training colleges but had failed to do so, often for lack of sufficient funds or of adequate accommodation; and yet others had studied, or were studying, assiduously in their spare time after a hard day's work in school and may have taken the Acting Teachers' examination but failed. The failure rate in this examination was 52.5 per cent, which may explain why it was to be phased out after 1926. The supplementary teachers were people who were recognised by the Board as 'suitable' but had no specific qualifications as teachers and whose own educational qualifications were often low. As a consequence they had no fixed salary and were often employed to save money on other grades of teacher. Ellis's memorandum is worth considering more fully for two reasons: it laid the foundation of Labour Party policy, and, more importantly for our present purpose, it identified many of the generic issues involved in teacher education and training.

The Ellis memorandum was timely in three ways. Firstly, it provided the Labour Party with an authoritative statement on an important area of education in which most members of its education advisory committee lacked expertise. Ellis had already written the sections on teacher education and training for Labour's 1922 election manifesto edited by Tawney, *Secondary Education for All*. In 1926, much of his memorandum was included verbatim in the Party's broad review of education policy. Secondly, it pointed to fundamental issues that were coming to the forefront of educational discussions when plans for reorganising the system into primary and secondary stages were being formulated. Teacher education and training had a clear relevance to the Hadow and Spens ideas about reorganisation. Thirdly, within a few months of Ellis drafting his memorandum, Wood, the President of the Board of Education, set up a departmental committee to look into teacher training in relation to elementary schools. The Ellis memorandum (see Table 4.6) helped the NUT and Labour to clarify their views in advance of the Committee's investigations and report.

The Report of the Departmental Committee on the Training of Teachers, published in 1925, accepted the idea of discontinuing the Certificate Examination for Acting Teachers and agreed that the ultimate objective should be the recognition by the Board of none but the certificated teacher. What the Departmental Committee ruled out of the region of practical politics was the notion of an all-graduate profession. It also related the generic issue of the all-graduate profession to that of the nature of the training course, believing that the latter would become too academic in pursuit of the former. The report had much to

Table 4.6 ***G. S. M . Ellis (NUT) 'The Education and Training of Teachers' (1922) A case study in the indentification of generic issues***

Generic issue	*1922 context*	*Viewpoint expressed by Ellis*	*His recommendation*
Special bursaries for certain categories of intending teacher.	For intending teachers to attend a secondary school under the 1902 and 1918 Acts.	'Young people, some of them of mediocre ability, are induced to become teachers when they cannot be expected to judge whether they wish to adopt that particular work!. (p.5)	Discontinue. Enhance pay and professional status to attract recruits and increase general opportunities for secondary education for all to 18. Provide adequate grants in training.
Preliminary test of aptitude for intending teachers.	For secondary school entrants to training college.	'... the secondary school course should be followed by a brief test of aptitude for the work of teaching (for) the student teacher year does not effect a satisfactory weeding out.' (p. 6)	Institute preliminary test.
Nature of training college course.	20 university training departments, 50 'voluntary' colleges and 22 LEA colleges require some kind of common approach.	'It is a mistake to imagine that the curriculum of a training college is framed merely with a view to providing the students with instructional material ... we must secure a real latitude in the range of cultural subjects to be studied.' (pp. 6–7)	Pending a complete revision of the training college system, a broad cultural course should be pursued.
Many training colleges separate from the rest of higher education.	Many colleges, expecially denominational colleges, segregate sexes under rigid discipline.	'The most forcible argument adduced against the (present) training college system is that ... it separates intending teachers (and) weakens their contact with the full current of life, and handicaps the development of broad, social interests. In too many cases we segregate young people of the same sex in barrack-like buildings ... in these respects the denominational colleges are the most unhappy.' (pp. 8–9)	To adopt the university model of which 'the free social life ... is the most valuable educational asset'. (p. 9)

Duration of initial training course	Two-year course,	'The two-year course will only permit a cursory survey of the arts and sciences ... the student is distracted at intervals to acquire a technical teaching efficiency ... the curriculum is overloaded; science teaching is too academic.'	'The higher education of the teacher should continue for three years and should normally lead on to a university degree.' (p. 10)
Concurrent or consecutive training.	Training colleges practised concurrent education and training.	'There is no reason why intending teachers should be expected to study for these fundamentally different things. That leads to a division of interest and to a diversion and waste of effort.' (p. 10)	'The training college system, even if extended and developed, together with the synchronised education and training (is) ... a second-rate compromise. 'The alternative - a new university faculty' with professional training following a degree course.
An all-graduate profession.	'The training college system is a survival from the times when there were only three universities in the country' (p.11).	University organisation is more economical and can offer 'an elasticity and variety of study which no training college could hope to approach' (p. 14) but intending teachers 'should enjoy perfect liberty to follow one of the existing (training college) courses if they so desire'.	Establish attractive university faculties and abolish pupil teacher system and pupil teacher centres. The existing system should *not* be abandoned at once with the alternative replacing it immediately.
The training course.	The two-year course included the principles and practice of teaching, hygiene, physical training and the study of one other subject area, taken from music, drawing, needlework, handwork, housecraft or gardening with 12 weeks' teaching practice.	The four-year university course should cover the professional subjects of the two-year course but the post-graduate component should 'be the subject of considerable experiment' avoiding a 'Prussian uniformity'; a University Training Department should be permitted to delegate the training of the students in the actual practice of teaching to the staff of an approved secondary school.	Concentration on professional studies with school teachers providing experience of 'school work and method unobtainable in any other way'. (p. 18)

say on the whole range of generic issues identified by Ellis three years earlier. It recommended the reform of existing training colleges in order that they 'become more professional'. Existing courses suffered from 'an undesirable distraction of aim', largely because of the bias towards academic work. Reforms were necessary in order to ensure that 'the essential function of training students to become effective teachers was ... their main consideration',[26] but such reforms involved no radically new departure. Professional work should be given more time and academic work lightened. Steps should be taken to reduce the overcrowded courses of many colleges. Included in the list of reforms suggested by the Departmental Committee were a number designed to bring the training colleges and universities into a closer relationship. To examine students of a training college or a group of training colleges, an examination board, including representatives of universities and the Governing Bodies of Training Colleges, should be created. Students undertaking third-year work for such courses as diploma courses should be encouraged to enter universities for this purpose and 'eminent university teachers' should be given the opportunity of delivering lectures at training colleges. University representation on the governing bodies of training colleges should be encouraged and conferences between university representatives and representatives from the training colleges and local education authorities should be fostered. These recommendations stopped far short of the proposals made by Tawney for the universities taking complete charge of teacher training. However, he could find some comfort in the note of dissent signed by Miss Conway of the NUT, and others, which argued in favour of 'places of professional training, content to leave academic studies to academic institutions and to devote themselves with a single eye to the important task of teaching recruits how to teach'.[27] In their view, a training college course which was 'strictly professional' should follow an academic education which should be 'completed ... to an increasing extent in universities'.

It is difficult to say whether or not the NUT scheme would have met with the general approval of teachers. Some, such as the person who wrote the following letter to *The Times Educational Supplement*, which expressed a view not uncommon today, would probably have disagreed with it.

Sir, As a trained certificated teacher of some considerable experience dating back to the 'eighties' and even somewhat earlier I should like to state some serious defects in the bureaucratic system under which the training of the rising generation suffers in England at the present time.

In the first place, under the present conditions governing our schools, the tendency is to train students instead of teachers, who when formally qualified are practically without any adequate experience necessary for controlling children or of adapting their academic knowledge to the capacities of their future charges. This grave defect is further emphasized by the importance attached by local authorities to the personal acquirements of the teacher rather than to his or her powers of maintaining discipline, and abilities for educating the crude and varied material which teachers of the young find to tax all their ingenuity, patience, and endurance. It is the first and last axiom in teaching that there is no possible connexion or relationship between personal knowledge and the power to impart it.

The development of thinking in the inter-war years about teacher education and training went hand in hand with the evolution of plans for the reorganisation of education into successive primary and secondary stages. The Hadow Report of 1926, *The Education of the Adolescent*, gave recognition to a special category of untrained teacher, namely 'the graduate who, without being trained in the formal sense, possesses special experience which might serve in lieu of training ... in some branch of social or industrial work', without apparently arousing the wrath of Miss Conway, the NUT representative on the committee. Even the loose qualification to their general statement that non-trained graduates should show some 'evidence of having devoted some study to the theory of teaching' aroused no response from union representatives. The second Hadow Report, *The Primary School*, issued in 1931, endorsed the movement to link training colleges to universities but coupled its support with the warning that a just balance between academic and professional studies should be maintained.[28] It also looked more closely than many other reports at another generic issue, the probationary year. It argued that the year should be an additional year of practical training but rarely was, as probationary teachers could rarely be regarded 'as supplementary to the ordinary staffing of the school'. The existing system was regarded as haphazard and said to result in a loss of efficiency and enthusiasm when newly qualified teachers were required to teach under difficult and depressing conditions. Rejecting the 'throw them in the deep end' philosophy it urged the careful utilisation of small rural schools to supplement college training under adequate supervision. Teaching loads and the nature of such supervision were not discussed.

By the time the Hadow Report, *The Primary School*, was published, some government action following the recommendations of the departmental committee's report had already taken place. The Certificate Examination for Acting Teachers had been abolished and eleven joint training college–university examining boards had been set up. Intending teachers, wherever practicable, were to follow a course of full-time education to the age of 18. The unfavourable economic climate of the 1930s with successive demands for the closure of some training colleges and cuts in student numbers did nothing to assist the development of teacher training and education. Even the Joint Boards made no great changes to examining techniques or standards. As in the case of most educational reform, it took a second world war to bring about a comprehensive review of the training system.

The Board of Education's Green Book *Education After the War* gave the general go-ahead to further discussion in June 1941; its report on

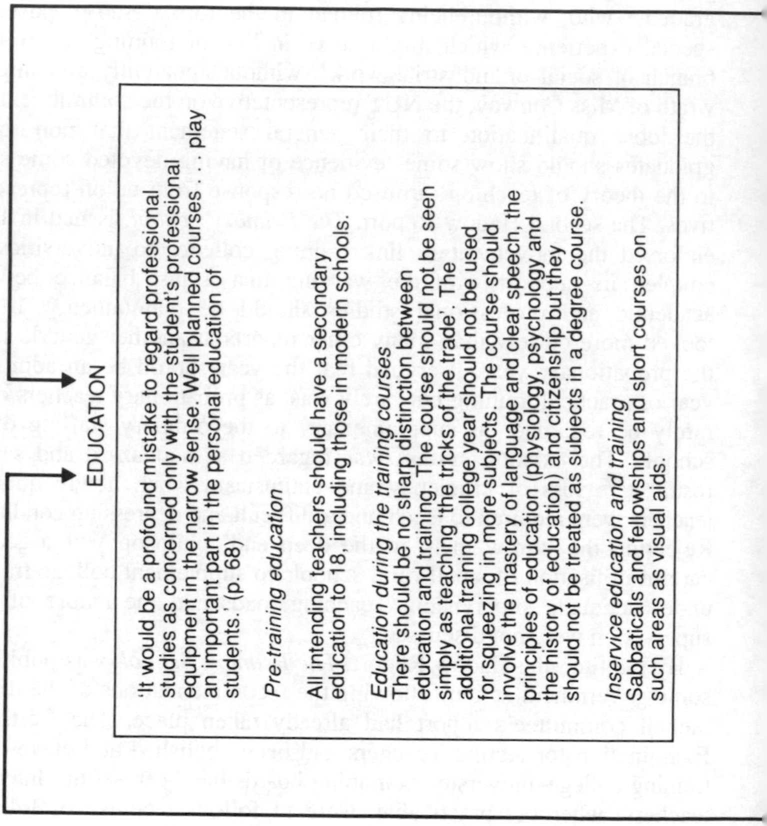

EDUCATION

'It would be a profound mistake to regard professional studies as concerned only with the student's professional equipment in the narrow sense. Well planned courses . . . play an important part in the personal education of students.' (p. 68)

Pre-training education

All intending teachers should have a secondary education to 18, including those in modern schools.

Education during the training courses
There should be no sharp distinction between education and training. The course should not be seen simply as teaching 'the tricks of the trade'. The additional training college year should not be used for squeezing in more subjects. The course should involve the mastery of language and clear speech, the principles of education (physiology, psychology and the history of education) and citizenship but they should not be treated as subjects in a degree course.

Inservice education and training
Sabbaticals and fellowships and short courses on such areas as visual aids.

Fig. 4.4 ***The McNair Report (1944) and generic issues in teacher education and training***

RECRUITMENT

'It would be foolish to rely upon missionary spirit. . .' (Report, p. 29)

Measures to assist recruitment and overcome teacher shortage

(a) Special allowances (without commitment for impecunious intending teachers at secondary school. Abolition of the 'pledge'.
(b) Widen field of recruitment to include mature people from industry, commerce and other professions. Special grants and shorter period of training.
(c) Married women not have to resign on marriage and to be encouraged to return part-time after having children. Equal pay not suggested.
(d) Better pay with general increases and wider distribution of special allowances
(e) Better conditions including teacher sabbaticals.
(f) Encouraging higher public regard for teaching. Not be seen seen as 'a race apart'.

TRAINING

'Centralisation of power and authority has potential dangers in every sphere of education and nowhere are those dangers so great and subtle as on the training of teachers.' (pp. 49/50)

Machinery: a central body to deal with 'unintegrated variety of existing institutions' to consist of 3-5 people and to coordinate local bodies (Central Training Council).
At local level *either* reconstituted joint boards *or* university schools of education (area training institutions in an area.

Course: Not an all-graduate profession. 'We are convinced that many good teachers would be lost to the professional if such a requirement were insisted upon.' (p. 51)
Either a three-year non-graduate course to replace existing two-year with longer contact with schools *or* one-year post-graduate course lasting from early September to late July with written tests and examinations cut to a minimum.

Probationary Year: 'For all including secondary teachers and to be regarded as an essential part of a teacher's preparation for his professional qualification'. (p. 65)

Special provision to be made for technical education.

Teacher Fellowships to encourage two way contacts with schools.

Teachers and Youth Leaders (the McNair Report) published in 1944, bore the fruit of much of the discussion. The former was no bland statement of areas for discussion. Its author, Maurice Holmes, gave his views on several generic issues, the first being that of the all-graduate profession: 'To require every teacher to take a university degree course would deprive the schools, and particularly the Infant and Junior Schools, of some of the persons best qualified by character and natural endowment to be teachers' (p. 45). He thus accepted the broad graduate /non-graduate division and extended it by adding a new category, Training Departments of Technical Colleges. In addition, he advocated a three-year training college course with at least six months of the second year being spent in schools; only in the third year would students decide whether or not to become teachers. Four-year UTD (University Training Department) courses should be abolished; only after graduation should intending teachers commit themselves. For qualified teachers there should be adequate in-service training.

The McNair Committee examined these and other issues in a major review of teacher education and training in the years 1942–44. Its report occupies an important place in the history of the development of generic issues in two ways. Firstly, it identified the full range of issues that had preoccupied educationists in the inter-war years and, secondly, its recommendations provided the basis for much discussion and action in the first two decades after the war, prior to the Robbins Report in 1963. Figure 4.4 summarises these issues and subsequent recommendations.

The two decades between the McNair and Robbins reports were dominated by three broad issues upon which the former had made several recommendations: teacher shortages, the administrative machinery for teacher training and education, and the three-year course. These in turn brought to the forefront of staffroom discussion a much larger number of connected matters such as the departures from standard training and entry qualification patterns that should be permitted to widen access to the profession. Were universities in general and University Departments of Education (UDEs) in particular fit bodies to play a leading role in new administrative structures? What should be the nature of a new three-year course and what should be the balance between academic and professional studies? What should be the nature and pattern of 'school experience', and 'teaching practice'?

The first of these issues, actual and impending teacher shortage, was evident to everyone at the dawn of the era of secondary education for all. Many of the first post-war generation of teachers were recruited from the armed forces under special schemes and provided the teaching profession with a much needed variety of experience until the 1980s. McNair had anticipated the need to widen the area of recruitment and its thinking was much in line with the Fleming scheme *Emergency Recruitment and Training of Teachers* of May 1944. With a pressing need to get members of the armed forces into the classroom after demobilisation, a one-year training course was established, followed by a further two years of teaching and part-time study prior to the award of a teacher's certificate and qualified teacher status. A shortened course did not mean an inferior course, for entrants were carefully selected and followed an intensive programme of personal and professional studies, assessed by innovative, informal methods. A pilot scheme run by Goldsmiths College training department set the pattern with lengthy teaching practice and other kinds of school experience. The colleges running the emergency training scheme remained in operation until 1951, training some 35,000 teachers. One of the basic flaws of the scheme – in line with much of past tradition and, one suspects, present practice – was the probationary period in schools, which was intended to allow for part-time study but rarely did. Little allowance was made in the teaching timetable and supervisory system for the kind of close guidance that was needed. Though the term 'emergency' was dropped from later training schemes designed to meet urgent shortage, there was the same tendency to rush recruits into the classroom without careful resourcing to provide adequately for the in-post training. Even those who had been trained under the more orthodox schemes often pointed to shortcomings in support in the probationary year.

A second and concurrent concern was the administrative structure of teacher education and training, and in particular the role of the universities within it. The McNair Committee was divided on the issue, with five member of the Committee favouring enlarged Joint Boards of equal partners, and four giving their backing to the idea of Schools of Education with ultimate control in the hands of universities. To the latter group, university control meant the maintenance of standards and the means by which universities with their tradition of independence could 'resist the encroachments of centralisation'. There were some who took an opposing view of the suitability of universities and UDEs for the task. These were summed up later by the Vice-Chancellor of Leeds University, Sir Charles Morris. They amounted to two strong reservations: (a), that 'universities have not been led by their own experience to be greatly interested in the art of teaching',[29] and (b), arising in part from this, that it was 'remarkable, and unfortunate, that, after so long a period of existence, these departments [UDEs] do not command more general confidence than in fact they do'. In practice, most, but not all, areas of the country rejected both of the McNair schemes and came up with the traditional British compromise of area training organisations (ATOs). ATOs retained the idea of a 'federation of approved training institutions', from which UDEs remained structurally separate; each federation or ATO was headed by a university and serviced by university staff in an Institute of Education based at a university. The university presence was thus dominant.

The third broad generic issue of the early post-war years was that of the duration of training college courses. McNair's recommendation for a three-year course met with general approval but raised the problem of

Table 4.7 ***The Robbins and James Committees on Teacher Education and Training***

Generic issue	*Subissue*	*Robbins observations and/or recommendations*	*James observations and/or recommendations*
Recruits and recruitment	Mature people	Needed especially to compensate for lack of science graduates. 4% of men came from the professions and 8% from industry compared with 6% of women coming from industry and the public services. 2/5 of men and one-quarter of women had a 'break' of at least one year before undertaking teacher training.	Be allowed to take up provisional appointments at once, with special course. (p. 30). The James Committee extended this aspect to include recruits from teaching to higher and other posts (e.g. educational psychologists).
	Re-entrants	Most important category was married women but no recommendations were made.	Married women should have a high claim on in-service training with part-time teaching and part-time re-training courses or full time secondment.
	Education of recruits	Number of 'O' and 'A' levels tabulated but no suggestions were made for raising entry qualifications. A progressive rise in the quality of entrants since 1958 was noted.	Generally under cycle one to Diploma in Higher Education standard or degree standard. Dip. HE courses would combine special and general studies and be taught in colleges of education.
Training colleges	Status	'... feel themselves to be only doubtfully recognised as part of ... higher education' (p.107). Should be renamed Colleges of Education.	'... since the Robbins Report ... the colleges have grown in status and confidence' (p. 49) and 'are now seen to be an integral part of higher education'.
	Size	126 of 146 below 500 students; not educationally efficient. 750 students should be the norm.	Small colleges are uneconomical. Much better for some of the smaller colleges to specialise, to become 'centres of excellence', with larger institutions developing 'a wide range of second cycle (initial training and probationary year) and third cycle (in-service) courses'
	Role	No departure suggested from training function.	The Committee regarded it as uneconomic for all colleges, irrespective of size, to attempt to do much the same thing. Such rationalisation was regarded as a matter for 'regional and national agencies:.

<table>
<tr><td>Courses of education and training
(a) Training Colleges</td><td>Concurrent or consecutive courses</td><td>Favours retention of concurrent pattern.</td><td>Concurrent courses were seen as suffering 'from a conflict and confusion of objectives'. Hence the James plan was based upon separate and - consecutive cycles. The concurrent model was regarded as 'creating conflicts between education and training'.</td></tr>
<tr><td></td><td>The all-graduate profession</td><td>Against the all-graduate profession but in favour of increasing opportunities to acquire a degree by transfer to university, four-year BEd. course of part-time study.</td><td>The Committee strongly favoured the all-graduate profession, with the award of BA (Ed) for successful completion of the second cycle and BEd. as an in-service award.</td></tr>
<tr><td></td><td>Course element and/or balance</td><td><table><tr><th>Appendix 2(B) p. 223 Type of training.</th><th>MS</th><th>CC</th><th>EC</th><th>TP</th><th>AW</th></tr><tr><td>Primary</td><td>38</td><td>31</td><td>17</td><td>14</td><td>100</td></tr><tr><td>Secondary</td><td>52</td><td>17</td><td>17</td><td>14</td><td>100</td></tr></table>MS = main subjects; CC = curricular courses; EC = educational courses; TP = teaching practice; AW= all work</td><td>The second cycle should concentrate on preparation for work appropriate to a teacher at the beginning of his career rather than on formal courses of 'educational theory'. Only the psychology, sociology (etc.) relevant to this task should be taught. There should be a variety of practical experience.</td></tr>
<tr><td>(b) University</td><td>Teaching practice</td><td>No recommendations were made for changing the pattern or system. Most students favoured existing pattern.10–13 week teaching practice with courses in the history and philosophy of education, psychology and teaching methods. No recommendations for change were made.</td><td>The Committee rejected the idea that UDEs should not be involved in the second cycle. They should become 'centres of excellence' in certain subjects or subject areas with the same aims as colleges of education, an immediately relevant course.</td></tr>
</table>

Table 4.7 ***Cont'd.***

Generic issue	*Subissue*	*Robbins observations and/or recommendations*	*James observations and/or recommendations*
The probationary year		Not within terms of reference.	James suggested a radical approach for the second year of cycle two, to replace a system where the 'probationary teacher ... leaves his college on the last day of term and never hears of or from it again'. The 'probationary year' should be seen as an essential part of the initial training course, with special school support schemes including a professional tutor, special professional centres and a special timetable. The teacher is a 'licensed teacher' when he or she begins this year, and a graduate BA (Ed.) when it is completed.
In-service training and education		University provision of short courses.	This is considered to be one of the Committee's most important areas of recommendation which went far beyond the Robbins 'short courses' and revived the McNair idea of teacher 'sabbaticals' (1 term in 7 years to start with, 1 term every 5 years later). In-service training was seen to include further degree work, refresher and up-dating courses, counselling courses, courses for teaching handicapped children (etc.), work in industry. The 'professional centres' would play an important role in in-service work.
Administrative machinery	General structure	Not in favour of Institutes of Education. Advocates Schools of Education.	Modification of existing ATO structure to achieve 'a more sensible grouping'. They should be replaced by Regional Councils under a National Council.
	Role of universities	To help and encourage the colleges, through 'a major responsibility for direct leadership'. Universities, hitherto had marginal role.	No special role suggested, except in relation to validating the Dip. HE. The colleges of education were thus 'to have an effective say'.
	UDEs	They were regarded as an essential element in Schools of Education, and should merge or become part of Schools of Education.	No special role was suggested except in relation to research.

reduced inflow into the profession. The announcement that the three-year programme would be introduced from September 1960 led to the intensification of discussion of several specific issues. What should be the relative priorities given to professional studies, especially the theory and practice of education and personal education? Should there be a common core of curriculum studies such as English and Mathematics? In the course of professional training, should the emphasis be more upon practice than theory? What should be the length and incidence of teaching practice and school experience? The Ministry's book, *The Training of Teachers* issued in 1957, saw the three-year course more as an opportunity for closing the academic gap between non-graduate and graduate teachers than as a mean of improving teaching expertise. The main subject courses were seen as a vehicle for achieving this. In practice, there was a variety of approaches throughout the country to the academic and professional curriculum. One of the principal advantages which many saw arising from the new course was that it brought the all-graduate profession one step closer through the attention that was given to raising the standard of main subject courses. Furthermore, many hoped that the three-year course would give teacher training and education increased standing and esteem in higher education.

This latter consideration was behind much of the thinking of the second and third of the trilogy of reports of the post-war years, the Robbins Report of 1963 and the James Report of 1972 (Table 4.7). Robbins was concerned to secure a stronger position for training colleges (146, of which 126 had fewer than 500 students) in higher education through strengthening their links with the universities, by renaming them Colleges of Education and by encouraging them to undertake degree work. James wanted to give them a broader role in both education and training, to raise their status from that of 'junior' partners. To do this the James Report put forward a radical three-cycle plan. The first encompassed higher education prior to training; the second, two-year cycle, included the training and 'probationary' years; and the third focused on in-service provision for the qualified teacher.

These generic issues remained at the forefront of discussions about teacher training and education in the 1980s and 1990s. (See pp. 34–41.)

ADULT EDUCATION

The Russell Report, *Adult Education: A Plan for Development* (1973), demonstrated one thing above all else, that the origins of formal adult education in the late nineteenth and early twentieth centuries had left a clear, indelible mark upon that sphere of education and, more importantly, upon the way in which educationists thought about it. The pioneers of adult education who were brought together during the First World War in the only other government-initiated, full-scale investigation of non-vocational education would have had little difficulty in recognising and commenting upon the four principal issues raised in the Russell Report: liberal and academic study, social and political education, trade union studies, and work with the educationally and socially deprived. They would have had little difficulty, but they would not have made any concrete divisions between these areas.

The composition and views of the 1917 to 1919 Committee on adult education tell us a great deal about the British tradition in adult education. It was chaired by A. L. Smith, Master of Balliol College, and included among its members, Ernest Bevin, Tawney and the founder of the WEA, Albert Mansbridge. It first met in the Master's Oxford College, the spiritual home of liberal, academic study, but established for itself a reputation as a radical body. Addison, who appointed it, found this out a little too late for he wrote a strongly worded letter to the Committee condemning the direction of its investigations after it had produced an interim report.

> Had the matters dealt with in the Interim Report been formally submitted to me I would have found it difficult to hold that a committee appointed to consider the possibilities of adult education were not travelling beyond their province in the first place to the limitation of these possibilities imposed by industrial conditions under which large numbers of adult working class members live.[30]

To have expected the Committee to have treated the subject otherwise, outside considerations of social class and the economic system, would have been to have expected it to fly in the face of history, for modern, mass adult education was conceived within such a context. Hence, from the outset, provision not directly made by the State veered away from technical education 'on the grounds that the advantages of economic efficiency which it promotes accrue mainly to employers of labour'.[31] It encompassed all the four areas identified by the Russell Committee over half a century later.

In between the two reports, that is, from 1919 to 1973, adult education seemed to stray a little from its traditional path and the Russell Committee attempted to re-establish some of its early priorities. Although the numbers following adult education courses increased in the inter-war years there were fears that the early missionary zeal was waning. In Tawney's view, 'Educational history was full of the ghosts of movements which began as crusades and ended as cliques of cultured persons.'[32] Some feared that bodies such as the WEA would lose both their vitality and academic standing by offering more and more classes to those who were most easily attracted. This market-led philosophy could well result in the splintering of courses into short courses, at best transmitting a 'conventional culture' and at worst more geared to entertainment than education. There were dangers that by attracting the leisured minority, adult education would change considerably in character. For people such as Tawney the way forward was that advocated later by the Russell Committee; 'we must go to them' as had been the practice of the early university tutorial classes. The strengthening of links with the trade union movement was also seen as a means of revitalising adult education; but there were significant differences throughout the country. The industrial north strongly supported adult education with a social and economic purpose, but in parts of southern England branches were not impressed by the more strident calls for working-class solidarity and favoured the further development of popular and not too demanding academic study. Thus, in some ways, the Russell Committee attempted to give priority to those activities that had been diluted over the years.

QUESTIONS

1. How does tertiary education seek to overcome traditional divisions and hierarchies in educational provision for 16–19 years olds?
2. What has higher technical educational sought to achieve since 1945 and what institutions have been developed to achieve these aims?
3. How far have recent developments in universities and university education further intensified generic discussions about the purpose and nature of such an education?
4. Identify the principal generic issues in teacher education and training today. Select one and examine its recent development.
5. Consider the historical arguments for and against the all-graduate teaching profession.
6. Discuss the relative merits of the models of teacher education and training found in the McNair, Robbins and James reports.
7. What are the relative merits and demerits of adopting a market-led philosophy in relation to the provision of adult education?

NOTES AND REFERENCES

1. *Guide to the Education Reform Act 1988*, The National Association of Head Teachers in Association with Longman, 1989, Sections 6/3 and 6/29.
2. 'The Organisation of Education After 11+', *The Papers and Correspondence of Sir P. Nunn 1907–1918*, London Institute of Education.
3. *Will Continued Education Ruin the Cotton Industry*?
4. Maclure, op.cit., p. 172.
5. Spens Report, p. 337.
6. *Education After the War*, p. 22.
7. The Crowther Report, p. 3.
8. Adapted from the Crowther Report, p. 7.
9. *Higher Education*, Appendix Two (B), p. 122.
10. *Day Release*, HMSO, 1964, p.6.
11. Ibid., p. 11.

12. Ibid., pp. 7–8.
13. *Better Opportunities in Technical Education*, HMSO, 1961, p. 24.
14. *Higher Technological Education*, HMSO, 1945, p. 3.
15. Ibid., p. 4.
16. Robbins Report, p. 127.
17. DES Statistics 1970–1978; reprinted in P. Gosden, *The Education System Since 1944*, Martin Robertson, 1983, p. 182.
18. WEA Memorandum for the Royal Commission in the Universities of Oxford and Cambridge.
19. Halsey *et al.*, op.cit., p. 188.
20. *A Strategy for Higher Education into the 1990s*, The UGC Advice, September 1984, HMSO, p. 34.
21. 'The market cure for our ailing campuses', *The Sunday Times*, 12 November 1989.
22. *Universities: Knowing our Minds*, 1989.
23. The Burnham Committee for negotiating teachers' salaries was suspended in 1987 and later replaced.
24. *The Training of Teachers*, a memorandum edited for the Labour Party in 1922, p. 1.
25. From a Labour Party Memorandum, 1926, on the Recognition of the Unqualified Teachers.
26. Report of the Departmental Committee on the Training of Teachers for Public Elementary Schools, p. 78.
27. Ibid., p. 175.
28. *The Primary School*, 1931, HMSO, p. 87.
29. *The Universities and the Teaching Profession*. N.U.T. Pamphlet p. 6.
30. Letter to the subcommittee dated 8 August 1918.
31. Interim Report of the Committee on Adult Education: *Industrial and Social Conditions in Relation to Adult Education 1918*, p. 6.
32. Presidential Address to the WEA, 1932.

CHAPTER 5

Understanding the 1990s

It has been a basic axiom of this book that all discussion should be informed discussion. Part One aims to help readers to clarify current issues in education by relating them to their immediate historical context. Callaghan's speech appeared to introduce something new. The unprecedented intervention in education by a prime minister in 1976 to deliver an educational-state-of-the-nation speech to inaugurate a planned national debate, followed by an equally unprecedented rush of legislation and initiatives in the 1980s, left the feeling in staffroom and common room alike that something new and strange was happening in the world of education. Together, they represented an intensity of interest and legislation more associated with the crises of world war than with the years of peace. What gave the impression that the old order had gone, and gone for good, was the new language of change. Since 1944 teachers had grown used to the talk of 'brand new initiatives', of 'fresh starts' and of 'new directions'. But the political rhetoric of the consumer and marketplace ideology was largely unfamiliar in the staffroom until the 1980s. Terms such as 'learning contracts', 'negotiated learning' and 'the delivery of curricula' rapidly made the old 1970s jargon of 'options', 'syllabuses' and 'courses' seem outmoded. The educational world had scarcely stood still long enough for the 'objectives model' and its accompanying concepts and terminology to be assimilated before their context was entirely transformed.

But does a change in terminology mean new and radical changes from past ideas and practices? Part Two of this book, in focusing on generic issues, aims to relate current issues to their more distant history in order to provide broader insights into their nature, and into the nature of educational change. It is their evolution as part of cultural, political, social and economic developments within Britain from the beginning of this century and earlier which give contemporary issues in education their meaning. This is often immediately obvious to those who have discussed such issues with teachers, students and informed lay people from overseas. What at first appear to be identical or similar issues and problems appear on closer inspection to be markedly different because of their historical and cultural conditioning.

This final chapter of the book is aimed at helping the reader to understand the evolution of educational issues in the 1990s. It adopts a tripartite strategy to achieve this. Firstly, it outlines, from the limited viewpoint of the early 1990s, what appear to be the main issues that will dominate the decade. Readers will thus have a comparative baseline for the period. Secondly, it provides a model of enquiry, derived from the previous chapters, which can be used to analyse the issues and thus achieve a fuller understanding of those issues. Does the new language of tomorrow's educational world mask issues that have long been with us? Thirdly, to assist group discussion and the clarification of the model, it provides exemplar materials.

THE AGENDA FOR THE 1990s

Many of the (re)training manuals for practising teachers project the image of the 1990s as a brave new world in education in which there is little room for historical considerations. The dramatic changes which they outline for the decade make the schools of the Callaghan era appear almost antediluvian and those of the Butler period and earlier, almost prehistoric. Training courses for new recruits to the profession have rightly rejected formal courses in the history of education, but unfortunately, in concentrating on the most recent and immediate developments, leave the impression that the historian has little or nothing to contribute to teacher training compared with the educational administrator, psychologist or sociologist. Manuals and training courses, in banishing the historian to the most remote parts, have left the educational kingdom all the poorer. Once the error of the clean slate philosophy and the myopia of the immediate are exposed, then the contribution of the historian towards understanding the 1990s can be appreciated. What, perhaps, the historian can do best is to act as a corrective to the instant snapshot approach by demonstrating that all initiatives and reforms of the 1990s can only be fully understood as part of a rolling historical film.

Change in the 1990s will be evolutionary within the context of a variety of British traditions. The instant snapshot approach looks only at single frames, and often implies brand new starts. The schools of the year 2000 will be as recognisable to teachers, parents and governors of the early nineties as the schools of the early nineties were to the educationists who took part in Callaghan's 'Great Debate' of the late seventies. That is not to say that change will not *appear* to be greater or the speed of change, swifter. What then are likely to be the areas and directions of change?

Reintroducing a national curriculum

When the details of the National Curriculum appeared in 1988, they seemed immutable, enshrined as they were in an Act of Parliament. In a similar way, the first national curriculum, embodied in the Revised Code of 1862, appeared to contemporaries to be set in tablets of stone, but after subsequent revisions the yearly assessments (as part of teacher appraisal and pay) were dropped in 1895 and control of the curriculum was abandoned in 1926.

Even during the first steps towards implementation in the early 1990s, the contours of the Baker 1988 curriculum began to soften. It may be that just as the history of the first curriculum points to the possible dangers of too detailed an intervention in school syllabuses, so governments in the nineties may beat a more hasty retreat from the door of detailed prescription. No doubt the curricular landscape will continue to change throughout the nineties; in the early stages of implementation, there was the danger that foundation subjects would be dropped for older pupils as the problems of accommodating the core subjects and the full range of foundation subjects within the school timetable became apparent; this negated somewhat the original aims of the reform. The curriculum of young children and its assessment were radically altered as the early problems of implementation became apparent, an adjustment not too dissimilar to that made to the first national curriculum when much of the prescriptive detail was removed. Whether the initial phase of reducing prescriptive detail will be followed by a second and longer phase of curricular devolution, which, when complete, will leave most curricular decisions in the hands of schools and their governing bodies, is not yet certain. The first national curriculum proved to be an increasingly troublesome child and one which became increasingly costly to maintain; it finally found good foster parents with the teaching profession, school governors and local authorities. It seems unlikely, at the very least, that the curricular forces of the nineties will remain unidirectional, from government to schools. School governors, head teachers, parents and the more enlightened industrial interests may insist on the maintenance of a broader curriculum than the National Curriculum will allow. Having established a working partnership in school resource-management, it would seem a natural growth point of the 1990s for government to give more local control of the curriculum to governing bodies within broadly prescribed limits through a quiet transfer of authority. This, in many ways, would be to follow similar lines of development to the first national curriculum after 1926.

The primary school curriculum will probably change less. Its eclectic nature, described in Chapter 2, has led it to maintain a central position for two of the three core subject areas since early this century. Its major shortcoming has been the comparative neglect of science and technology which may well provide one of the main thrusts of in-service provision in the 1990s.

Returning some of the powers to schools

Curricular devolution will take some time, but managerial devolution in relation to school resources is with us now. One of the major trends of the 1990s will be the restoration to headmasters and governing bodies of some of the powers they had at the birth of the State secondary system at the beginning of the century. Though such schools charged fees, their head teachers and governing bodies often had to manage tight budgets; headmasters had to take careful note of the requirements of their market and engage in publicity work. Reduced intakes meant reduced fees and the threat of sacking staff to meet budgetary requirements. The head teachers of the nineties will need to develop the powers of the businessperson, those of communication, publicity and persuasion, thus continuing the trend, already apparent in the 1980s, of head teachers having less time for classroom teaching.

Head teachers and governors may well appear more as a board of directors with more pronounced professional relationships, and more concerned with marketing and management than at present. However, as an earlier generation of head teachers discovered, change in education takes longer to implement and is more difficult to manage than change in the commercial sphere. The values of the marketplace are often short term and precise, whereas those of education, as previous chapters have shown, are more diverse, often in conflict and are concerned with longer term aims. Neither good management nor pleasing the whims of the market will, by itself, serve the long-term interests of students. Parents may well recognise, as happened after 1926, that the teaching profession is the best guardian of the curriculum and students' long-term interests.

The revival of the direct-grant list

The 1988 Education Act reintroduced the direct payment of grants to schools in which the majority of parents had voted to opt out of local authority control. Such grant-maintained schools differ from the old direct-grant schools in that they are prohibited under the Act from charging fees, but like the direct-grant schools they replaced they may become an influential group in the 1990s. It is probable that they, like their predecessors, will remain in a minority but they could well be a growing minority in the 1990s for several reasons. Firstly, as schools grow in experience and expertise in handling most of their budgets under Local Management of Schools (LMS) they may well wish to manage that part of the budget retained under normal arrangements by the local authority. Opting out of local authority control and receiving a larger grant from central government could thus prove to be an increasingly attractive option. Secondly, the 1988 Act allows grant-maintained schools with the approval of the Education Secretary to make a significant change in character five years after opting out. Perhaps indicative for trends in the nineties is the first example given in the act of such a change, 'the reintroduction of selection on the basis of ability or aptitude in the case of a comprehensive school'. Other examples include introducing or ending single-sex education, and a change in the age range of a school. It could thus be the case that the unsuccessful attempts to revive grammar schools in the two years after the passing of the Act were the result of undue haste rather than ministerial opposition to the idea of ending comprehensive education. Whether Labour will stand by its 1990 policy statement and return grant-maintained schools to LEA control if returned to office will be an important factor in any attempted revival of selective schools.

The continuing debate over educational values

One of the factors which influenced Percy's decision to drop the first national curriculum was the way in which it conflicted with a full technical and vocation education. The first national curriculum could have fostered the development of the kind of education advocated by the Royal Commission on Technical Education towards the end of the nineteenth century. What emerged by 1926 was predominantly a national curriculum based upon a practical liberal education. The 1990s will see the intensification of the debate over the curriculum, and the place of technical and vocational education within it. Both of the leading parties were agreed on the paramount importance of the latter at the beginning of the 1990s, but the traditional academic liberal values, which Percy argued stood in the way of economic regeneration, could come to dominate the National Curriculum, despite the intentions of education secretaries. There may be a growing number of educationists who deny that there is a conflict between traditional liberal values and those of technical and vocational education. The historical identification of a liberal education with a number of particular subjects or with a given body of knowledge may end in the 1990s with the more widespread realisation that technical and vocational education can be liberal in its goals and in its approach.

Bac. to the future?

The 1990s will see further attempts by advanced level review committees to broaden the pattern of 'sixth form' study. The closer integration of Britain within Europe could lead to a closer consideration of the model of the International Baccalaureate, although this is by no means certain for scant regard has been given to the well-tried, broader framework nearer home, north of the English border. One of the chief objections to structural reform has been the dilution of standards which any move away from the existing 'A' level pattern will represent. However, the 'A' level pattern is already changing with the introduction in 1988 of a two-tier 'A/AS' system and the steps to reform 'A' levels to remove the mismatch between 'A' level and GCSE. It may well be that the reform of 'A' levels will have to proceed a little further with reductions in content and a broadening of the range of skills (almost Higginson's streamlined 'A' levels by the back door) before the system is itself reformed. Such developments at subject level will make 'the standards argument' less tenable if the yardstick by which they are measured has changed. The streamlining of subjects may ease the movement towards a modified 'N/F' structure with the possible introduction of common core skills or other technical and vocational elements. The growing number of places of tertiary education in the 1990s should assist the broader pattern of study for 16–19 year olds, enabling students not only to pursue 'A' levels or their equivalents with more vocationally orientated studies, but also to combine part-time with full-time study.

Independent schools: a return to Labour's traditional policies?

The Crosland crusading zeal is nowhere apparent in the policy statement, *Looking to the Future*, issued by the Labour Party in 1990. The ending of state subsidies (through the assisted places scheme) and tighter tests for charitable status are policies well in line with traditional, moderate thinking, and the proposal to extend the National Curriculum to fee-paying schools amounts to little more than the Chuter Ede Committee, set up by the second Labour Government in 1930, sought to achieve (see pp. 136–139). The 1990s seem ripe for the revival of the voluntarist argument that measures such as the National Curriculum, together with market forces operating within the state sector, will raise the quality of state education to such an extent that many parents will forsake the private sector. But as the history of independent education has shown, 'the public school problem' is not simply an educational one. Labour's unwillingness in its 1990 manifesto to recognise the existence of 'the social argument' for intervention indicates that the independent sector in the 1990s will be left to enjoy its privileges, which has been Labour's traditional approach to the public schools for most of this century.

Reinstating the pupil teacher?

The increasing emphasis in initial training in the 1980s was upon lengthening the period spent in schools, so that in its most extreme form – for example, those transferring to teaching from other occupations under the licensed teacher scheme – virtually all of the training will be in-post. It is likely that the trend towards more in-school training will continue for those on PGCE and other courses, as links between schools and training institutions are strengthened. Collaboration on courses on the National Curriculum for serving teachers and on the placement of lecturers, who are required to up-date their classroom skills, will serve to blur the distinction between training institutions and schools. The close regulation of initial training courses, and of the lecturers who participate in them, will probably be a continuing feature of the nineties. Special measures, including enhanced salaries, to deal with teacher shortages, especially in certain subject areas and geographical regions, will be required to overcome what had become a major problem in education by the early 1990s.

Further and higher education

A long-standing problem that will prove equally difficult to overcome in the 1990s is the reluctance of students to stay in full-time education after the age of 16. A survey at the beginning of the nineties showed that boys were less inclined to remain than girls, and students in the north of England more reluctant than those in the south-east and Wales. Such reluctance, rooted in cultural values, will prove difficult to overcome, although the growing diversity of full- and part-time courses and the development of tertiary colleges may assist in overcoming this resistance. However, by 1994 there will be half a million fewer 16–18 year olds than there were in 1988.

One of the major issues in higher education will be that of widening access to universities and polytechnics for mature students without standard qualification. The growth in access courses with a terminal qualification will be one of the measures to secure a broader clientele. It could well be, however, that the socio-economic background of conventional students in the 18–21 group will be more restricted as the system of loans takes effect, though Labour has promised 'a fairer system of student grants' if returned to office.

Market forces will create the greatest changes in higher education as bidding systems are developed and universities and polytechnics are driven more and more to find their own funding from commercial and other ventures.

THE MODEL OF ENQUIRY

The previous section has indicated some of the items that may appear on the educational agenda of the nineties. This section suggests a six-stage model of enquiry by which these and other issues can be analysed.

Stage 1 Identification
Identify the current issue(s) of interest (e.g. the technical curriculum, teacher training) and the broad generic category to which each belongs. *Refer to the headings in Chapters 1 to 4* for the latter.

Stage 2 Clarification
Clarify what each issue is about through discussion and by reference to current educational journals and newspapers. Summarise its chief features in a short paragraph.

Stage 3 Consultation (*Consult Chapter 1*)
Outline the development of each issue since 1976, noting any relevant documents, changes in emphasis etc. Consult other books for clarification.

Stage 4 Consultation (*consult Chapters 2 to 4*)
Trace the generic origins and development of each issue, noting which particular aspects were regarded as important and why at different times.

Stage 5 Comparison
Compare the development of the issue(s) in the 1990s with earlier developments, noting any major similarities and differences in attitudes, actions or reactions.

Stage 6 Evaluation
In the light of your findings, discuss the nature of the historical development of each issue. (Did it involve radically new departures, the full or partial restoration of discarded practices, small modifications, a discernible and continuous move in one direction (etc.)?)

Taking the historical development of all the generic issues together, state what is revealed about the nature of historical change and/or development.

EXEMPLAR STUDIES

The reports given below can act as a means of clarifying the method of enquiry. This extract appeared in *The Sunday Telegraph*, 10 June 1990:

CALL TO SCRAP VARSITY TEACHER TRAINING
by Sarah Johnson

Teacher training departments in universities should be disbanded and teachers should be trained on the job, according to a pamphlet to be published tomorrow by the Centre for Policy Studies, a Right-wing think tank.

Dr. Sheila Lawlor, one of the Centre's new young campaigners against the allegedly 'Leftish' education establishment, argues in 'Teachers mistaught' that too much time in teacher training courses is devoted to the theory of education instead of to training students to teach their subject.

Dr. Lawlor has also supported the 'traditionalist' history lobby fighting the national curriculum.

She proposes that the staff of university education departments, who produce the bulk of postgraduate teachers, should be offered early retirement, jobs in academic departments (if they are academically distinguished) or in schools. The funds saved would pay for 'school-based mentors' to supervise graduates learning to teach.

Dr. Lawlor proposed abolishing the Bachelor of Education qualification and replacing it with a two-year course in a range of subjects to roughly first-year degree standard or A-level as preliminary to primary teaching, followed by a year's on-the-job training. This Certificate of Advanced Study, she argues, would also be useful to non-teachers.

She argues that good graduates are put off teaching by the emphasis on theory in colleges, and points out that in France, Germany and New Jersey teachers are trained in the classroom. The Government's reforms, such as introducing the licensed teachers programme, should be taken further to cut out the influence of teacher trainers, says Dr. Lawlor.

The following are extracts from the Labour Party Manifesto, *Looking to the Future*, 1990:

(a) *Education and training for young people*
Everyone knows that Britain gives its young people less education and training than the industrial countries with whom we compete. Fewer 16 year olds stay on in education than in South Korea or Taiwan.

Many young people do not see training as important, since they have been badly disillusioned with the education and training they have already received. Sixty per cent of those on the present Youth Training Scheme leave without a proper qualification. Girls on YTS are too often left only to train for traditional and lower paid jobs.

Every 16 year old must have the opportunity to go on learning and the right to get a qualification. As we explain later, we will raise standards in schools, and reform the A level system in England and Wales, to overcome the problem of too early specialisation.

(b) *Better schools*
We want more opportunities in education. We also want to ensure that we get more from the resources we invest. There are wide and unnecessary differences in the performance of otherwise similar schools in similar areas. Labour's commitment to comprehensive education will help to ensure that we raise the educational standards of all our children. The standards of education would be transformed if schools were improved simply within the current range of performance.

Labour will mount a major programme to make schools more effective. Nationally, an Education Standards Council will be established. It will co-ordinate the work of the Inspectors, set fair but rigorous systems for measuring schools performance, and agree targets with local education authorities for raising the proportions of 16–19 year olds in education. The Schools Examination and Assessment Council and the National Curriculum Council will be merged.

We will also create a National Schools Award – similar to the Queen's Award to industry – to recognise those schools which have demonstrated their effectiveness.

(c) *The National Curriculum*
The national curriculum must also apply to *every* pupil, including those at fee-paying schools. It must encourage girls to take up opportunities in all subjects. It must be free of cultural bias so that, for instance, students can choose a European or Asian language as their second modern language.

Above all, the national curriculum must put the student at its centre. Each student should be entitled to an annual curriculum review with parents and teachers.

The schemes for opting out and City Technology Colleges have been expensive, divisive failures. Grant maintained schools and CTCs will be brought within the local authority sector.

At a time of great pressure on resources, and spare places in maintained schools, public funding of private schools cannot be justified. The assisted places scheme will be phased out, without affecting existing pupils. Private schools will have tighter tests for charitable status.

THE LANGUAGE OF CHANGE

The preceding exemplar studies illustrate a key point raised earlier in this chapter, the need to look critically and carefully at the language of change. It will become increasingly important to ask the question in the nineties whether a change in educational terminology signifies a fundamental change in direction. Experienced teachers have long adopted a critical attitude to the educational jargon of the moment and look behind it to ask whether it signifies any real change in attitude, outlook or direction. New recruits to the profession in the nineties are and will continue to be confronted by a barrage of new terminology as no previous generation has. This is largely because the eighties saw an unprecedented rush of initiatives and legislation which are being implemented or emasculated in the 1990s alongside other changes. The newly qualified teacher will not be allowed the relative tranquillity and fairly lengthy period for reflection that previous generations had to understand the nature and direction of change. Thus from the outset of their careers, students in training can usefully look back over the generic issues of the past to acquire a perspective on the present, to see whether the issues and problems that confront them as practitioners have reached a new stage in their historical evolution or whether all that has changed is the language with which they are described. As was emphasised in the opening chapter, a carefully directed study of the history of education is more not less relevant to the initial and in-service training of teachers in the nineties, when directed not towards a simple chronology of dates and digest of reports but towards an analysis of key generic issues.

BIBLIOGRAPHY

Barnard, H.C. 1947. *A History of English Education since 1760*, University of London Press.

Blyth, W.A.L. 1975. *English Primary Education*, vol. 2, Routledge.

Cox, C.B. and Dyson, A.E. 1971. *The Black Papers in Education*, Davis Poynter.

Gosden, P. 1983. *The Education System since 1944*, Martin Robertson.

Lawton, D. 1989. *Education, Culture and the National Curriculum*, Hodder and Stoughton.

Lawton, D. 1986. *The Politics of the School Curriculum*, Routledge.

Lowe, R. 1987. *Education in the Post-war Years: A Social History 1945–1964*, Routledge.

Maclure, J.S. 1979. *Educational Documents: England and Wales 1816 to the present day*, Methuen.

Morris, M. and Griggs, C. 1988. *Education the Wasted Years 1973–1986?*, Falmer Press.

Rae, J. 1981. *The Public School Revolution, Britain's Independent Schools 1964–1979*, Faber.

Rae, J. 1989. *Too Little, Too Late*, Collins.

Rubinstein, D. and Simon, B. *The Evolution of the Comprehensive School 1926–1966*, Routledge.

Simon, B. 1965. *Education and the Labour Movement 1870–1920*, Lawrence and Wishart.

Simon, B. 1974. *The Politics of Educational Reform 1920–1940*, Lawrence and Wishart.

Simon, B. 1975. *The Victorian Public School*, Gill and Macmillan.

Tawney, R.H. 1989. *Secondary Education for All* (1922); reprinted Hambledon Press.

INDEX